D1565165

# Vocabulary Building:

## A Process Approach

# Vocabulary Building:
## A Process Approach

Edgar Dale
Joseph O'Rourke

under the editorial direction of
**Walter B. Barbe**

**Zaner-Bloser, Inc.**
Columbus, Ohio

ISBN No. 0-88309-122-4
Reorder No. 280199

# Contents

*We would like to dedicate this book to the memory of Dr. Edgar Dale. His extensive work in the field of vocabulary, as well as that of Dr. Joseph O'Rourke, forms the basis of this book. Dr. Dale was an outstanding educator, an exacting researcher, and a good friend.*

# Chapter One

# Techniques of Teaching Vocabulary

The purpose of this book is to help you as a teacher improve the rate of your students' vocabulary acquisition. We use the phrase "improve the rate" because a person's vocabulary increases every day through interactions with people and exposure to the various media of our times. But this is a sort of "unconscious" vocabulary acquisition.

While listening to a news broadcast you may hear something about commodities trading, but you don't know what that means. Later, if you see a film clip of a trading floor and a graph showing the prices of items such as wheat, corn, silver, gold, bonds, and treasury bills, you suspect (and correctly) that commodities are agricultural and mining products, and financial futures.

Note that you did not listen to the newscast for the purpose of learning new words, but from that activity you became acquainted with a word you did not know. You learned it from an experience. The more experiences you have, the more likely you are to come across new words.

This experiential method of vocabulary acquisition operates continuously, but slowly. You learn words from your experiences, but you usually do not learn them very fast. Experiential vocabulary acquisition results in what we might term incremental acquisition—a relatively small, gradual increase in the number of words in your vocabulary.

Teachers should be aware that in the experiential method of learning new words there is no predictable pattern to the words learned, no structure for learning and remembering. For example, although a student might have learned *commodities* from a newscast, he or she is not likely to learn that the word is from Latin *com-*, meaning "with," + *modus*, meaning "measure," and is related to *commodious, accommodate,* and *modal.*

Sometimes experiential acquisition of vocabulary slips into a temporary pattern of sorts. When astronauts first began orbital flights, the news was filled with space terms: *capsule, module, pad, thrust, orbit, perigee, apogee, retrorocket, re-entry, splashdown.* As a result, many children and adults used these words with ease. When astronauts landed on the moon, many people knew the acronym LEM (lunar excursion module). But LEM is no longer a household word.

As space travel has become somewhat more commonplace, space terms have diminished in general popularity. Instead, other topics produce a different set of words that gain prominence. For example, the news today includes *embargo, junta, cartel, glut, hostage, terrorist, reprisal, jihad* —words that reflect more closely the tenor of our times.

Teachers know there is a close relationship between vocabulary and comprehension,[1] so they should encourage students to note and learn words they run across. But learning words incidentally from experience is not enough. Teachers also need a plan to accelerate the rate at which experience-based words can be better understood and new words added to the student's vocabulary.

## The Process Approach to Vocabulary Instruction

In this book you will be introduced to a strategy for teaching vocabulary, a strategy that is both pedagogically sound and enjoyable. We propose a process approach to vocabulary instruction. This efficient, tested method supplements the usual "accidental learning" by which much of a student's vocabulary is often acquired. It also eliminates notoriously ineffective rote memorization—the bane of students and teachers alike. Most important to you and your students, the process approach is based on the regular, systematic application of learning methods and activities with which you are really already familiar.

What is the process approach to teaching vocabulary? It is based on three tenets:

1. Effective vocabulary development depends on how skillfully and how thoroughly the teacher introduces students to the structure and content of language. The meaning of a word can be derived not only from external context clues (sentential, syntactical clues) but also from internal context clues (meanings of word parts within the word itself). Vocabulary study should also involve the origin of words, the semantic changes of words, the connotation of words used as figures of speech, the synonyms and antonyms of words.

In a process approach, students are both encouraged and given the opportunity to practice deriving the meanings of unfamiliar words by using structural word clues and the general context of the words.[2] Students learn the flexibility and variability of language in various uses.

2. Vocabulary improvement should be related to all school endeavors. It should cut across the curriculum, encouraging students to develop a "vocabulary consciousness"—a critical awareness of the importance of vocabulary in their lives. We must help students develop an awareness of words so that they use words correctly, appropriately, and effectively in their studies and in out-of-school activities as well. Current research

---

[1] Isabel Beck and Margaret McKeown, "Learning Words Well: A Program to Enhance Vocabulary and Comprehension," *The Reading Teacher*, vol. 36 (March 1983), pp. 622-625.

[2] Richard Anderson and Peter Freebody, "Vocabulary Knowledge," In H. Singer and R. Ruddell (Eds.), *Theoretical Models and Processes of Reading*, Newark, DE: International Reading Association, 1985, pp. 343-371.

shows that students who extend their study and discussion of words outside the classroom become versatile in verbal processing skills.[3]

3. Vocabulary improvement should be enjoyable. The concept of pleasure in language is a significant aspect of vocabulary development. Children need an atmosphere that encourages them to play with and create words. Infants babble for the fun of it, using a kind of sound play.[4] Young children like to play with sounds. They imitate our speech sounds. As Wordsworth points out, the child is involved in "endless imitation."

Older children also experiment with the sounds of words. They repeat words that sound interesting, from the *zing, zoom,* and *shazam* of the comic strips to catchy slang words such as *zilch, zap,* and *zonk.* At every age students can be made sensitive to the sounds of language, can learn to notice onomatopoetic words such as *murmur, whisper, screech, scratch,* and *clang.* Children and adults like to use reduplicative, or echoic, words such as *willy-nilly, shilly-shally,* and *razzle-dazzle.* In short, we like to play with language. We all enjoy a pun, a riddle, a word puzzle or game.

## What The Process Approach is Not

The process approach stands in sharp contrast to the rote memorization of word lists. Memorizing lists of words results in very brief improvement in vocabulary growth, barely lasting beyond the test for which the students were preparing. Moreover, rote memorization engenders a distaste for vocabulary study, even among more able students who have a natural curiosity about language.

Words are not meant to be learned for a test. Vocabulary improvement should be permanent, with options for further improvement. It should affect the student's life, having a lasting effect on reading, writing, speaking, and thinking skills. The process approach to vocabulary acquisition integrates language skills.

Once students develop vocabulary consciousness, they profit more directly from vocabulary instruction, making significant gains in word knowledge. Through the process approach, exemplified in Zaner-Bloser's vocabulary series designed for students, they learn more than words; they learn to use key principles about vocabulary that apply to general language skills. Furthermore, the process approach is contagious. Students often catch vocabulary consciousness from one another. It's an epidemic we should promote. But can we say the same for the word-list approach?

## Teaching and Learning Vocabulary

As we mentioned earlier, the process approach to teaching vocabulary is not necessarily new; some knowledgeable teachers have been practicing

---

[3] Beck and McKeown, "Learning Words Well;" Margaret McKeown, Isabel Beck, Richard C. Omanson, and Martha T. Pople, "Some Effects of the Nature and Frequency of Vocabulary Instruction on the Knowledge and Use of Words," *Reading Research Quarterly,* vol. 20 No. 5 (Fall 1985), pp. 522-534.

[4] Eric Lenneberg, *Biological Foundations of Language,* New York: John Wiley and Sons, Inc., 1967.

its principles for years. But for the process approach to be most effective, teachers must have a love of language, a romance with words. They must like to work with words and play with words. They must feel comfortable with words, know something about word histories, derivations, and meanings, and they must strive to integrate vocabulary improvement with every part of the curriculum.[5]

Of course, teachers may use word lists and periodic tests as measurement tools, but they must recognize that these tools do not themselves foster vocabulary improvement. Mere memorization of words and meanings does not improve language competence. It does not zero in on the speaking, reading, writing, and recognition vocabularies of students or allow for individual differences in their learning styles.

## Students' Learning Styles

The process approach allows teachers to be more sensitive to the individual learning styles of students in their classrooms. It is now a well-established belief that students vary with respect to the modality through which they learn best. Some students learn most efficiently through seeing (visual), others through hearing and speaking (auditory), and others through moving and touching (kinesthetic). This means that, while everyone uses all three modalities for learning, most individuals will rely on one or two in times of great concentration or stress.

According to recent research, approximately 30 per cent of the students in a typical classroom are visual, 25 per cent are auditory, 15 per cent are kinesthetic, and 30 per cent exhibit strengths that combine two or more modalities.[6] Of course, teachers who are aware of these differences will adapt their instructional techniques in vocabulary to take advantage of the modality strengths of their students.

Adapting instruction may be as simple as encouraging visual students to highlight or underline and write notes about new words they come across; allowing auditory students to subvocalize, use tapes, or discuss vocabulary concepts; and providing opportunities for kinesthetic students to write on the chalkboard (for large muscle involvement) or to write on and manipulate index cards for lessons such as roots, affixes, and synonyms. Another example of how a teacher using the process approach can capitalize on students' modality strengths follows.

The word *boycott* appears in a reading selection, but many of the students don't know what it means. The teacher explains that a boycott is a form of protest in which those participating refuse to deal with a certain person or organization.

To help visual students, the teacher describes a boycott now taking place somewhere in the world. He or she then asks these students to look in newspapers or magazines for articles and photos about boycotts.

---

[5] Richard Hodges, "Vocabulary," Urbana, IL: ERIC Clearinghouse on Reading and Communication Skills, 1984.

[6] Walter Barbe and Raymond Swassing, *Teaching Through Modality Strengths: Concepts and Practices,* Columbus, OH: Zaner-Bloser, Inc., 1979.

To assist the auditory students, the teacher encourages them to recall what the boycotting people have said or to present arguments that the boycotters might use to justify their actions.

The teacher also involves the kinesthetic students by asking them to dramatize the issue. They might enact a scene in which they demonstrate the problems of both sides of the question, thus illustrating the importance of expression and gesture in communicating ideas.

Finally, the teacher might discuss the origin of the word, which came from the name of Captain Charles Boycott, a land agent in County Mayo, Ireland, who was ostracized because he refused to lower rents. The teacher can also point out that other words for *ostracize* are *banish* and *shun.*

At first glance this may seem like a great deal of effort to teach a single word, but it is not. It does not take long to carry out the entire process. Besides, you are teaching more than a single word; you are helping develop an attitude about learning. As a teacher you are modeling thought processes for the student, presenting strategies for learning how to learn words.[7]

The students will get a sense of your excitement about vocabulary as they encounter words used in a variety of contexts and imaginative ways. They will soon realize that they are not only studying words, but also learning interesting things about words, and about the history of words, which includes much of the history of mankind.

## Discovering and Uncovering Meanings

The process approach is heuristic; that is, students are encouraged to discover and investigate new words and their meanings. Using the process method, the teacher reveals the existence of what we might call a word-web, a natural and logical relationship existing among many words.[8] Once students are initiated into the process, they also discover that one word leads to another, that knowing one word often makes it easier to learn or remember another.

In the case of the word *ostracize,* the teacher can illustrate this semantic web of relationship between words by pointing out that when the Irish people ostracized Captain Boycott, they were doing something that the ancient Greeks did to an unwanted person in Athens. The Greeks would use a tile or *ostrakon* to vote whether or not the person should be exiled.

The process may stop here; or it can go on. For example, the teacher might also ask interested students to trace the root of *ostracize* (related to hard tile) back to another hard substance, *osteon,* the Greek word for *bone.* Of course, the combining form *osteo* produces many medical terms

[7] Margaret McKeown, "The Acquisition of Word Meaning from Context by Children of High and Low Ability," *Reading Research Quarterly,* vol. 20, No. 4 (Summer 1985), pp. 482-494; David Pearson, "Changing the Face of Reading Comprehension Instruction," *The Reading Teacher,* vol. 38 (April 1985), pp. 724-738.

[8] Joseph O'Rourke, *Toward a Science of Vocabulary Development,* Alantic Highlands, NJ: Mouton, 1974; Jerry Zutell, *Developmental and Cognitive Aspects of Learning to Spell,* Newark, DE: International Reading Association, 1980.

dealing with bones and bone diseases, some of which we hear about today, such as *osteoporosis.*

The process approach works best in an atmosphere of discovery and spontaneity in which one word or situation brings another to mind. The teacher as a vocabulary expert (much expertise will come from using this book) acts as a model and a guide, encouraging freedom of expression and a curiosity about words. But the structure within which the teacher works and the key elements he or she employs are well defined and pedagogically sound. We describe these elements in the following pages. They can be classified under two main headings: those pertaining to the word itself and those relating to how the word is used.

## Teaching Vocabulary from the Structure of a Word

One of the key techniques offered in this book and indeed in studying words in general is to analyze word structure: word parts, word origin, spelling, and pronunciation. Learning how to use these internal clues enables students to more readily understand new words as they appear in a contextual setting. These elements also provide a structure for classifying and discriminating between words through recognition of common roots and affixes and through analysis of spelling patterns and pronunciation.

### Word Parts: Roots, Prefixes, and Suffixes

Every teacher knows that knowledge of word parts can be used to derive the meaning of a word. This is perhaps the most important element of the process approach to teaching vocabulary. Students who can break a word into its constituent parts and determine the meaning of each part can make a more intelligent guess about the word's meaning based on the context in which it is used.[9] This ability to distinguish word parts is often the chief factor differentiating average students from verbally superior students.

The parts of a word determining its meaning are the root, the prefix, and the suffix. The root of the word contributes most of its meaning, but the prefix can significantly alter the meaning implied by the root. For example, the root *flam* implies something that can be burned, but the addition of the prefix *non-* reverses this meaning. Nonflammable material is unburnable.

This process is apparent in many other words. The root *act,* meaning "do," gives us the word *active.* The prefix *in-,* not, changes the word to *inactive,* a word with the opposite meaning of the original word. The teacher will call to mind many similar examples.

The salient factor in the process approach is the students' understanding that component parts of words carry meaning in themselves. In the word *propel, pel* means "push" and *pro-* means "forward." In the word *repel,*

---

[9] William Nagy and Richard Anderson, "How Many Words Are There in Printed School English?" *Reading Research Quarterly,* vol. 19, No. 3 (Spring 1984), pp. 304-330.

*re-* means "backward." The opposite meanings of the words *propel* and *repel* are dependent on the meaning of the prefix in each word. In teaching prefixes and roots by the process approach, emphasis is placed on having the student associate word parts with meaning.

The suffix of a word generally has less bearing on meaning than either the prefix or the root, but it does tell us something about how the word is used, perhaps indicating its part of speech. Teachers know that the suffix *-er,* for example, may be added to the adjective *tall* to change it from the positive to the comparative degree *taller.* The suffix *-er* added to a noun can also describe a person performing an action (as in *teacher*). The suffix *-less* (without) changes the meaning of many words: *hatless, coatless, beardless, heartless.*

Using the process approach means learning and applying the principles involved in vocabulary development. It means making sure that students learn to determine the meaning of a word not only through context but also by using transferable word-structure skills.[10]

## Word Origins

Teachers who practice the process method in vocabulary instruction discover that word origins are probably the most interesting aspect of word study and that students find word histories quite fascinating, at times even surprising. Further, teachers find that word-origin activities help promote word consciousness and provide excellent memory devices for recalling many word meanings.[11] We all remember an experience, a person, or a word that is connected with an anecdote. We generally remember words encountered in an interesting story, because the words appear in a context and we remember them best in that setting.

Providing experiences with picturesque word origins is probably the best way to develop in students an interest in words and a love of words. Students who are athletes, who have perhaps felt the pain or agony associated with a long run or a wrestling match, will not likely forget that our word *agony* is derived from the Greek word *agonia,* meaning "athletic contest" or "struggle for a prize." Students will probably not need to know the names of various bones in the body, but there is one they will not forget after they learn the origin of the phrase "funny bone." "Funny bone" is, in fact, a pun on the name of the bone that runs from the shoulder to the elbow — the *humerus!*[12]

## Pronunciation and Spelling

Just as a knowledge of roots, prefixes, and suffixes can make it easier to derive the meaning of a word, so too can the correct spelling and pronunciation. When spelling or pronunciation is incorrect, the meaning of a word can be obscured. The difficult word *fiduciary* (holding in trust)

---

[10] Nagy and Anderson, "How Many Words Are There?"

[11] Richard Hodges, "Improving Spelling and Vocabulary in the Secondary School. Theory and Research into Practice (TRIP)," Urbana, IL: ERIC Clearinghouse on Reading and Communication Skills, 1982.

[12] William Morris and Mary Morris, *Morris Dictionary of Word and Phrase Origins,* New York: Harper & Row, Publishers, Inc., 1977, p. 232.

can be more easily defined in context if you know that the root *fid* means "faith" or "trust." But the meaning of the word is impossible to derive if you mispronounce it and spell it *feduciary* and then wrongly associate it with words such as *federal, federation,* and *confederate.*

*Capitol* and *capital* confuse a great number of children and adults, because these words are so similar in spelling and pronunciation. *Affect* and *effect* are another bothersome pair. A significant component of the process approach is helping students learn correct pronunciation and spelling. But we should be careful not to do this by rote learning. There are many more efficient ways to achieve this goal. An easily learned spelling clue often suffices to instill the meanings and spellings of troublesome words. In the phrase "You need *capital* to build a *capitol*" the student remembers to write the first word with the vowel that is first alphabetically. The imaginative teacher can think of others, such as "A *capitol* usually has a *dome.*" The student remembers that *capitol,* like *dome,* contains an *o.* In short, the teacher using the process approach is likely to become proficient in the use of such spelling strategies.

## Teaching Vocabulary from Word Use

We do not learn most of our words by looking them up in the dictionary. Rather, we learn them through context (spoken and written), and we often approach a new word with partial knowledge of it. While internal analysis is an important part of vocabulary development, the study of word use (e.g. context, semantics, synonyms, and antonyms) encourages conceptualization and critical, imaginative language ability.

### Context Clues

The process approach to vocabulary development encourages the student to be on the lookout for a variety of clues to word meaning. The teacher must regularly point out that besides deriving the meanings of words from their constituent parts, the student should also learn to infer the meanings of unfamiliar words from the context in which they appear.[13]

An essential ingredient of the process method, therefore, is making the student keenly aware that context clues appear in a variety of forms. With the teacher's guidance the student will learn about useful syntactical clues like appositives, comparisons, and contrasts. The student will also be on the lookout for other contextual aids (such as synonyms) that provide clues to the meanings of unfamiliar words.

### Figures of Speech

A significant goal of the process approach is to help students extend the range of their vocabularies. This means taking them beyond the literal definitions of words to the use of words in a figurative sense. Understanding figures of speech is crucial to comprehension and

---

[13] William Nagy, Patricia Herman, and Richard Anderson, "Learning Words from Context," *Reading Research Quarterly,* vol. 20, no. 2 (Winter 1985), pp. 233-253.

enjoyment of literature.[14] Figures of speech also add interest to the language. They are used in all areas of life, ranging from poetry to politics. Milton uses personification to describe the swift passage of the years when he calls time "the subtle thief of youth." The person in the street uses a more direct figure—"Time flies."

Students who recognize imagery and appreciate the use of figurative language get more enjoyment and understanding from their reading. Such students not only develop more extensive vocabularies, they also develop creativity in their speaking and writing skills.

## Synonyms, Antonyms, and Homophones

The richness of our vocabulary is nowhere more evident than in our use of synonyms, antonyms, and homophones. The process approach encourages students to generalize about words, first to classify according to broad meaning and later to learn specific definitions and discriminate among shades of meaning.[15] This classification theory of vocabulary development applies to both synonyms and antonyms.

The theory of opposition suggests that when we know the opposite of a word, we generally know more about the word and its various relationships. This is true because opposition implies relationship, a latent relationship between words.[16] We know *dark* better because we know *light*. We know *heat* because we have experienced *cold*. Antonyms can also be used as part of word analysis activities involving prefixes and suffixes: *able, unable, active, inactive, bearded, beardless.*

Homophones can be used to sharpen semantic and spelling skills. Students learn to discriminate between the meanings of these words that sound alike. Also, the confusion and ambiguity caused by homophones can be turned to advantage by involving the students in word play. Homophones are the basis for puns and riddles, and students can have fun while learning to discriminate between words such as *bizarre* and *bazaar, weight* and *wait, bridle* and *bridal.*

## Semantics

In the process approach the teacher helps to stimulate students' interest in words by involving them in semantics, the study of meanings. Students can learn that, although words have certain meanings, people often change or extend those meanings to suit their purposes. Thus the word *point* has taken on several meanings, such as pen *point; point* out the landmark; do you get the *point?*

It is important that students understand the semantic characteristics of denotation and connotation, the difference between the literal meaning and the figurative meaning of a word. For example, the teacher may point

---

[14] David Pearson, "The Function of Metaphor in Children's Recall of Expository Passages," *Journal of Reading Behavior,* vol. 13 (Fall 1981), pp. 249-261; Wanda Rogers, "Teaching for Poetic Thought," *The Reading Teacher,* vol. 39 (December 1985), pp. 296-300.

[15] O'Rourke, *Science of Vocabulary Development;* Shane Templeton, "Young Children Invent Words: Developing Concepts of Word-ness," *The Reading Teacher,* vol. 33 (January 1980), pp. 454-459.

[16] C.K. Ogden, *Opposition,* London: Kegan Paul, French, Trubner and Co., Ltd., 1932.

out that a simple word such as *blue* can have at least two distinct meanings, the literal, denotative meaning referring to a color, the other connoting a mood.

It can also be very interesting for students to look at historical changes in word meanings and to see how shifts in meaning affect our choice of words in speaking and writing. As students discuss word meaning they will be stimulated to see likenesses and differences, to think critically about how and why we use words in certain ways, and to interpret and apply words in their own work.

## Reading and Vocabulary

Vital to efficient, forward-moving vocabulary instruction is exposure to good literature. As a student becomes more involved with good literature, vocabulary skills improve. In turn, as a student's vocabulary increases through selective reading, the challenge of understanding complex literature is more easily met. In short, the literature-vocabulary relationship is undoubtedly a mutual one.

Reading good literature promotes vocabulary development in two main ways. First, the student is exposed to new words. Active readers may attempt to derive the meanings of new words from their constituent parts or their context or may turn to the dictionary as a last resort.[17] Even passive readers who are not motivated to expand their vocabulary skills may stumble upon the meaning of a word solely from the context in which it is found. Thus the *act* of reading, at whatever level, is crucial to the vocabulary-building process.

Second, literature promotes vocabulary development by extending a student's interests and activities. Sharks were relatively low on everyone's popularity list until *Jaws* hit the bookstores. After the publication of this bestseller, sharks and books about sharks were very popular with adolescents. As a result, many students picked up a vocabulary dealing with sharks, their habits, where they are generally found, and how they are caught or photographed.

Actually, literature promotes vocabulary growth through a kind of incidental learning. But such learning needn't be haphazard. Teachers can provide structured reading activities that include books likely to stretch the students' minds and introduce them to a wide variety of new and useful words. Students' vocabularies may be enriched by books and articles that range from descriptions of ancient Egyptian structures to the recent restoration of the Statue of Liberty, from Charles Dickens's tales of London to Studs Terkel's oral histories. Whatever students read, at least a small percentage of the material should challenge them and add new words to their vocabularies.

## Using the Dictionary

Unlike the incidental method of learning words from wide reading, using the dictionary is a direct route. But knowing how to get the most out of a

---

[17] Nagy and Anderson, "How Many Words Are There?"

dictionary is critical, and teaching this skill is an integral part of the process approach. Students who are well acquainted with a good dictionary, who know how to use it, have more extensive vocabularies than students with poor dictionary skills.

Too many students are unaware of the many ways in which the dictionary can help them with language skills. Students should know that besides helping the reader with spellings, meanings, and pronunciation, a good dictionary provides helpful hints on grammar, appropriate word usage, word origins, figurative language, and the use of idioms.

## Using Word Games

Another significant component of vocabulary growth involves the occasional and effective use of word games. Learning proceeds rapidly when it occurs in a recreational form. Most students enjoy well-devised word games and participate in them with enthusiasm. Whether word games are printed products, board games, or computer programs, they help build vocabulary skills. Even unstructured games involving personal interaction (such as those using puns and riddles) are useful vocabulary activities.[18]

Vocabulary games stimulate *creativity,* an important aspect of the process approach. In activities of this kind students are encouraged to experiment and have fun with words, to *notice* words, their structures and their idiosyncrasies. For example, in dealing with anagrams, students learn to manipulate letters to form different words. In the process, students learn the importance of putting a letter in the right place. Thus students develop not only a word consciousness but also a spelling consciousness.

Keep in mind that we are not prescribing regular class periods devoted only to word games, although this might happen occasionally. Rather, we suggest that the teacher introduce word-game activities at appropriate times. Encouraging students to have fun with words in class can lead to word games and play with family and friends outside the classroom environment. In using word games our aim is to make students word conscious, to help them experience some of the joy of language.[19]

## Testing as Teaching

An often-overlooked aspect of vocabulary instruction is the use of tests as a means of teaching. Traditionally, testing has been viewed as an assessment tool for measuring student progress. In the process approach, however, testing is an important *instructional* tool, especially when the student benefits directly from the activity of correcting the test.

When used as a teaching technique, testing loses much of its anxiety-provoking character and becomes an accepted and expected part of the

---

[18] Eleanor Tyson and Lee Mountain, "A Riddle or Pun Makes Learning Words Fun," *The Reading Teacher,* vol. 36 (November 1982), pp. 170-173; Linda Geller, "Riddling: A Playful Way to Explore Language," *Language Arts,* vol. 58 (September 1981), pp. 669-674.

[19] Karen Swisher, "Increasing Word Power Through Spelling Activities," *The Reading Teacher,* vol. 37 (April 1984), pp. 706-710.

instructional process. Working in the right classroom atmosphere, students look forward to the challenge of a test and approach it with a more positive outlook. As a result, their performance is optimal rather than minimal. They acquire a self-checking attitude and a helpful habit of self-evaluation. The frequent and imaginative use of brief vocabulary tests whose outcome is openly discussed in class in a learning situation can be a valuable experience.

## A Final Word

The aim of all instruction is to develop concept formation. Vocabulary development is concept development. Building an extensive and discriminating vocabulary enhances cognitive growth. The process approach to vocabulary study helps students make connections between concepts and helps them make important generalizations about language that are useful in all their studies.

In this first chapter we introduced the process approach to teaching vocabulary. In the following chapters, we discuss each aspect of word structure and context more fully. We also present relevant examples and actual teaching techniques, including the theories, processes, and principles involved in effective, systematic vocabulary instruction.

These examples and teaching suggestions are enough to get you started with the process approach, but we hope you will expand upon them and make them better, fitting them to your particular needs. One of the most important ingredients in vocabulary improvement is the teacher. We are well aware that the best implementation of the process approach to teaching vocabulary will take place only through the efforts of enthusiastic teachers. We hope this book helps you convey this enthusiasm to your students.

# Chapter Two

# Word Parts: Roots

A teacher said to a colleague, "My students don't need instruction in vocabulary. What they need is to learn to speak, read, and write better." Actually this *is* the purpose of all vocabulary study. This teacher assumed that vocabulary instruction meant the dull, uninviting, repetitious task of memorizing words out of context. He said further, "We teach words when they come up in class." But this approach contains a fallacy. New words come up not just in class, and words that are taught come up outside the classroom. Students need a system for receiving, storing, and retrieving words at any time.

Many people have had the experience of looking up an unknown word and finding it popping up again in their reading or listening. An eleventh-grade pupil complained to her father that she had to learn the "silly word" *vertigo.* "I'll never use it," she said. But that very night she saw it on television as the title of a movie. "Why should I learn the word *acrophobia*?" asked a high school student. He saw it the next day in a magazine article on why some people are afraid of heights.

But in this book we do not recommend teaching single words out of context or without relating them to cognates (words formed from the same root). For example, we might suggest the teacher structure a lesson on the meanings of roots such as *sol, aster, luna,* and *naut.* We show that they appear in words like *solar* and *solarium, aster* and *asteroid, lunar,* and *nautical.* Indeed, we suggest that students might coin some of their own words. Given the example of *astronaut,* a sailor of the stars, students are asked to think about *lunarnaut* and *solarnaut* and then to make up their own space words.

## Words and Word Parts

Word parts have meanings of their own. A word part by itself may be a symbol for an object, an idea, or a concept. Two or more word parts may combine to give us a combination of ideas. For example, in the word *contradict* the root *dict* means "say" or "speak," and the prefix *contra-* means "against." Thus *contra + dict = contradict,* a combination of two ideas that results in a new concept: to voice an opposite point of view, to deny, to declare untrue—in short, to "speak against."

Students with knowledge of word elements have little difficulty unlocking the meanings of long words. Students of medicine, biology, and botany who know word parts easily transform polysyllabic terms into simple phrases indicated by the various parts of the word to be defined. For example, *multiflorous* (*multi-*, many, + *flor*, flower) merely means "many-flowered." A grasshopper places eggs in the ground with its *ovipositor* (*ov*, egg, + *pos*, put, place).

We feel that mastering the meanings of words through a systematic study of word parts is as necessary for elementary and secondary students as it is for college students. Students adequately instructed in the process of dividing words will quickly learn how words are formed and will acquire the habit of automatically analyzing unfamiliar words whose meanings can often be inferred from the sum of their parts.

## Word Families

Students should understand that words derived from the same root belong to a word family. If students know the meaning of a word, they can figure out the meanings of other words in the same family.

The following illustrates one kind of exercise that helps students generalize word meanings and word families. Students are given multiple-choice answers to complete sentences.

1. If active means "moving," then activate must mean ___?___.
   a. to make something move       b. to make something stop
   c. to make something appear
2. If capture means "to take by force," then a captive is a ___?___.
   a. hat      b. sailor      c. prisoner
3. If fury means "great anger," then someone who is furious is ___?___.
   a. sorry      b. very angry      c. upset

A more advanced form of selecting words to complete sentences requires students to discriminate between similar words, choosing the word in the same family as the underlined words.

1. Construction is the act of building, so ( distraction   destruction ) must be the act of tearing down.
2. An origin is a beginning or starting place, so when you invent or start something, you ( originate   organize ) it.
3. A book you refer to for information is a ( refinery   reference ) book.

## Forming Words from Roots

Learning the meanings of roots will give students clues to word meanings. Teachers will want to point out that roots often occur at the beginning of a word, but they also occur in the middle and at the end. Students should be cautioned that the spellings of roots within words often vary.

A lesson that starts by giving roots and their meanings can proceed in a number of ways. The following will help students notice roots in words.

**gram** means "written" or "letter"
**hos(p)** means "host" or "one who grants"
**migr** means "move"
**cap** means "head" or "most important"

Students are to choose the word that completes each sentence and then underline the root.
1. Dan was the host and offered fine ___?___ .
   a. monogram   b. hospitality   c. immigrant
2. The governor lives in the ___?___ of our state.
   a. hospitality   b. telegram   c. capital
3. My aunt, Marge Reynolds, has her ___?___ , MR, on her letter paper.
   a. captain   b. monogram   c. migration
4. When we went birdwatching, we watched the ___?___ swallows.
   a. capital   b. hospice   c. migrating

Another activity can guide students to generalize root meanings among different words containing those roots.

**duc** means "lead"
**fort** means "strong"
**crea** means "create or make"

Students match a phrase to the word it describes.
1. fortify        a. to lead or guide
2. conduct        b. one who makes
3. creator        c. to make strong

Students choose a word to complete each sentence and underline the words in which there is a spelling change in the root.

| forcefully   introduce   creativity |

1. Mrs. Lucas spoke ___?___ to the barking dog.
2. Carla's design for the stage set showed much ___?___ .
3. Let me ___?___ you to my sister.

A more open-ended activity would be to give students roots, their meanings, and words derived from those roots. After determining the meanings of the words, students write sentences using them. Teachers should remind students to recall what they already know about prefixes and suffixes when determining the meanings of the following words. Students should be encouraged to use a dictionary before writing their sentences if they need help.

**script** or **scrib** means "write"      **dic(t)** means "say" or "tell"
**vers** or **vert** means "turn"          **terra** means "earth"
**spect** means "look at" or "see"

predictable    convert    aspect    description    terrain

# Discovering Roots in Words

Students can discover the meaning of a given root by analyzing a series of words derived from that root. In the following exercise students are given a group of words. They match each word to its word family and determine the meaning of the root from which the word family comes.

| migrate | minute | multiply |
|---|---|---|

1. diminish, minor, minus, _____
   The root **min** means __?__.    a. fast    b. less    c. smooth
2. multitude, multiple, multiplication, _____
   The root **multi** means __?__.    a. less    b. high    c. many
3. immigrate, migration, migratory, _____
   The root **migr** means __?__.    a. choose    b. move    c. send

Another pattern is to ask students to determine which word in a group does not belong in the word family.

| settler | settlement | sterling | resettle |
|---|---|---|---|
| computer | compare | comparison | comparable |
| manufacture | many | manipulate | manual |

# Roots as Words and Parts of Words

Some roots form complete words (*break*); others seldom do (*fract*). Teachers may point out that roots such as *fract* are used with a prefix or suffix or both. For example, *infraction* means "the act or result of breaking." The following exercises demonstrate several ways of teaching vocabulary and word building with roots and affixes.

Students add endings to the root *vis,* to see, to make words. They write the word that fits best in each sentence.

### root + ending
vis    -itor
       -ible
       -it

1. I plan to __?__ my aunt in Kansas next month.
2. The mountains are __?__ from our kitchen window.
3. Who is the __?__ staying at Sharon's house?

Students read the meanings of the word parts. They choose the correct word to complete each sentence.

1. **pend** means "hang"    **-ant** means "condition of"
   A <u>pendant</u> could be __?__ .
   a. a pension    b. a locket    c. a cliff
2. **facil** means "easy"    **-ate** means "to make"
   If John <u>facilitates</u> this for me it will become __?__ .
   a. dangerous    b. easier    c. more fun
3. **mal** means "bad"    **funct** means "perform"    **-ion** means "state of"
   When the car <u>malfunctions</u> it is __?__ .
   a. not running well    b. overheating    c. out of gas

24

Students study the word parts and the words that contain them. They write the word that best completes each sentence.

| Word Parts | | Words |
|---|---|---|
| **omni** means "all" | **sciens** means "knowing" | omniscient |
| **bene** means "good" | **fic** means "do" | beneficial |
| **inter-** means "between" | **sect** means "cut" | intersection |
| **com-** means "with" | **pan** means "bread" | companion |

1. One road cuts across another at an __?__ .
2. Someone who eats bread with you is your friend. A friend is a __?__ .
3. A person who knows all things is __?__ .
4. When something good is done for you, it is __?__ .

## Finer Discriminations between Roots

Students may experience some difficulty when using roots to determine word meaning. Some words may look as if they have the same root when they actually do not. Such words are called false cognates, words mistakenly assumed to come from the same root. For example, students may complete a lesson that includes the words *conserve, reserve,* and *preserve,* which come from the root *serv* from Latin *servāre*, meaning "to save" or "to keep." If a student then comes across the word *deserve*, it would be easy for him or her to group it with the words just learned. However, *deserve* comes from the Latin word *servīre*, meaning "to serve." Other words from *servīre* include *servant, service,* and *serving.*

Students should know that when they use roots to form words or to determine meaning, they should use the dictionary for help if the result does not make sense. By looking for the derivation at the end of the word entry, students will find the information that will help them identify the root and discriminate between words. Teachers may refer to the List of Common Roots included in the Appendix of this book for roots that may be confused. Such roots will appear next to or near each other because of their similarity in spelling.

Another problem students may have with roots in word analysis is that the root of a word, like the root of a plant, is often unseen. The following items may be used to illustrate this point. The list merely provides some examples of words whose roots are not always apparent; teachers may prefer to use their own examples.

1. When we make a *decision* about a problem we cut off further argument—from *cisus* (form of *caedere,* to cut) as in *incision, excision, concise, incisor* (tooth), *scissor.*

2. A *corner* has a sharp edge or point somewhat like a horn—from *cornu* (horn) as in *cornet, unicorn, cornucopia* (horn of plenty), *cornea* (transparent or hornlike substance coating the eyeball).

3. A *rebel* wants to fight again (make war again)—from *bellum* (war) as in *belligerent, bellicose, ante-bellum, post-bellum.*

4. A *terrier* catches animals that burrow in the earth—from *terra* (earth; land) as in *territory, terrain, subterranean* (underground), *terra cotta, terra firma, Terre Haute* (high land), *Mediterranean* (sea in the middle of the land), *pied-à-terre* (temporary lodging, literally "a foot on the ground").

5. Merchants *advertise* a product to turn the customer's attention to it—from *vert* (turn) as in *divert, revert, invert, convert, vertigo* (dizziness).

6. The *albumen* of an egg is the white part—from *alb* (white) as in *albino, alb, albescent, album.*

7. An *anachronism* (*ana*, not, + *chron*, time) is the placing of an event or action in time where it doesn't belong. For example, the clock in Shakespeare's Julius Caesar is an anachronism: clocks hadn't been invented when Caesar lived. Note also *chronicle, chronic, chronology, synchronize, synchroflash.*

8. Would you guess that the word *cosmetics* comes from a word meaning universe? *Cosmetic* comes from *kosmos,* the Greek word for order, arrangement, or universe; the opposite of *chaos,* no order. *Cosmetics,* dealing with arranging, adorning, beautifying, comes from the Greek *kosmetikos* (skilled in arranging). Other words from the root *cosm* include *cosmic, cosmography* (description of the cosmos), *cosmonaut* ("sailor" of the cosmos), and *microcosm.* A *cosmopolitan* person feels at home in any city of the world (from *polis,* city).

9. The *pendulum* on a clock hangs from a fixed point and swings freely (from *pend,* hang). Some other *pend* words are *impending* (hanging over threateningly), *pendant* (hanging ornament, for example, a locket), *appendage* (something attached, hung on), *appendix, pendulous, suspend, perpendicular.*

10. *Amphibious* animals live both in water and on land (from *bio,* life, and *amphi-,* both). *Bio* also gives us *biography, autobiography, biology, biochemistry, microbiology, macrobiotic* ("long-lived," from *macro,* long or large), *biometry* (the measuring of life expectancy), and *biopsy* (the removing of tissue from a living body to examine it).

11. In early times a *coroner* represented the king or queen, investigating untimely deaths in the name of the crown—from *coron* (crown) as in *coronet* (small crown), *coronation* (crowning ceremony), *coroniform* (crown-shaped), *corona* (crown or halo of the sun), *coronagraph* (instrument used to observe the sun's corona).

12. The North and South Poles are *antipodes:* two places on directly opposite sides of the earth (from *anti-,* against, + *pod,* foot). The region around Australia and New Zealand has been called the *Antipodes* because it is almost directly opposite England. Note also *bipod, tripod, chiropodist, apod* (an animal without feet), *gastropod* (a shellfish that uses its stomach like feet to move from place to place).

26

# Roots and the Words They Generate

A sampling of roots and words derived from them is presented below. The roots might be discussed in terms of their original meanings and extended meanings within other words. This list is a small part of a more extensive list that has been included for the teacher's use at various levels. (See List of Common Roots and Derived Words in the Appendix.) From this the teacher can not only teach key words but also emphasize the principle of generalization: filing, classifying, and making associations between words formed from common generative roots.

## Roots and Words

| form (shape) | fac (make, do) | multi (many) | dict (say) |
|---|---|---|---|
| uniform | fact | multiply | contradict |
| reform | factory | multiplicand | verdict |
| formation | manufacture | multimillionaire | prediction |
| deform | faction | multitude | dictate |
| transform | facsimile | multiple | abdicate |

| vis (see) | cap (head) | meter (measure) | mov (move) |
|---|---|---|---|
| television | captain | diameter | move |
| vision | cape (headland) | barometer | movement |
| visual | capital | perimeter | remove |
| visa | capitol | centimeter | movable |
| visage | decapitate | metronome | immovable |

| gram (letter) | color (color) | duc (lead) | min (less) |
|---|---|---|---|
| telegram | discolor | conduct | minus |
| diagram | colorful | educate | minor |
| grammar | colorless | abduct | minimize |
| monogram | Colorado | aqueduct | minuscule |
| pictogram | coloration | induce | minority |

| div (separate) | phon (sound) | man (hand) | cycl (ring; circle) |
|---|---|---|---|
| divide | earphone | manual | bicycle |
| division | microphone | manuscript | tricycle |
| indivisible | saxophone | manipulate | cycle |
| divisional | symphony | manufacture | cyclone |
| divisor | phonics | manacle | cyclist |

| equ (equal) | graph (write) | circ (ring) | fer (bring; bear) |
|---|---|---|---|
| equality | phonograph | circle | transfer |
| equator | autograph | circus | fertile |
| equation | biography | circular | refer |
| equilateral | paragraph | circuitous | infer |
| equivocal | graphic | circumspect | confer |

27

| civ (citizen) | mob (move) | mare (sea) | dent (tooth) |
|---|---|---|---|
| civic | automobile | marine | dentist |
| civil | mobile | submarine | dental |
| civilization | mobility | mariner | indent |
| civilized | mobilize | maritime | trident |
| civics | immobilize | aquamarine | dentifrice |

| face (face; form) | micro (small) | cur (run) | mod (manner; measure) |
|---|---|---|---|
| face | microphone | current | mode |
| surface | microfilm | currency | model |
| facial | micrometer | occur | modern |
| deface | microbe | excursion | moderate |
| efface | micron | curriculum | modulate |

# Chapter Three

# Word Parts:
# Prefixes and Suffixes

Most students understand the importance of context—they know that words have meaning in relation to other words in a sentence. But not so many understand that words also derive meaning from their component parts. Two Greek elements are an example: *a-*, not, + *tom*, cut, = *atom*, the smallest unit of matter, which scientists once thought could not be cut.

Students who know the component parts of a word possess a potential for transfer. They can use their knowledge of the prefix *a-*, *an-*, meaning "not" or "without," to help them analyze other words such as *amoral*, *anonymous*, and *atheist*.

Prefixes and suffixes are word parts added at the beginning and end of base words to make new words. Students can be taught that prefixes and suffixes have meaning and that their meaning is constant from one word to another. Knowing the meaning of a base word and the meaning of a prefix or suffix can help students figure out the meaning of a new word.

This chapter provides examples and practice in the use of key prefixes and suffixes. Once students are familiar with a number of affixes, teachers can provide exercises that combine known root words, prefixes, and suffixes. Suggestions of such exercises are included in the List of Vocabulary Testing Methods in Chapter 13.

## Prefixes

The following common prefixes are covered below: *un-; in-; re-; dis-; pre-; ex-; anti-; ante-; sub-; super-; com-; mid-; trans-; ad-; de-; pro-; mis-;* and number prefixes. A master list of prefixes and derived words is included in the Appendix.

During work on prefixes teachers may want to discuss or review the following spelling hints with their students.

When the final letter of a prefix and the first letter of a basc word or root are the same, both letters must be written. For example:

un- + necessary = unnecessary
dis- + similar = dissimilar
mid- + day = midday

When the final letter of a prefix and the first letter of a root word are the same vowel, it is usually preferable to separate the two parts with a hyphen, although there are exceptions to the rule. For example: *re-entry, re-examine, de-escalate,* and *co-opt,* but *coordinate* and *cooperate.*

## The Prefix *un-*

The prefix *un-* means "not."

unhappy          A person who is not happy is _____ .
untied           A shoelace that is not tied is _____ .
unlocked         A door that is not locked is _____ .

Students may add *un-* to base words selected by the teacher for the appropriate grade level. Other words that might be included are *uneven, unfamiliar, unfavorable, unfinished, unfriendly, unfortunate, unbroken, unbalanced, undesirable, unaffected, unconstitutional.*

## The Prefix *in-*

The prefix *in-* can mean "not" (as in *infrequent*). The prefix *in-* can also mean "in or into" (as in *investigate*).

inconsiderate    A person who is not considerate is _____ .
incorrect        If the answer is not correct it is _____ .
inexpensive      Another way to say "not expensive" is _____ .
indoors          When you are in your house you are _____ .
inhale           When you take air in you _____ .
include          To put into a group or to have as a part of is to _____ .

The prefix *in-* is usually spelled *im-, il-,* or *ir-* before root words beginning with *m* or *p, l,* or *r* respectively. This process is called *assimilation*—changing a sound (such as the final consonant of a prefix) to make it identical to or similar to a nearby sound (such as the first consonant of a root) for easier pronunciation.

The following exercise illustrates one way of teaching a prefix that has more than one meaning. Students circle the meaning of the prefix as used within a sentence.

not        Shakespeare's plays are considered by some to be immortal. (not   in)
not        The message on the bulletin board was illegible. (not   in)
in         Did the police imprison the criminal? (not   in)
not        It was impossible for Linc to arrive on time. (not   in)
not        The smell of popcorn was irresistible. (not   in)
not; in    She became impatient with the delay at the immigration office. (not   in) (not   in)

Teachers may wish to point out that the prefix *in-* can be used as an intensifier, which makes a word stronger. The word *invaluable,* for example, means "extremely valuable or important."

## The Prefix *re-*

The prefix *re-* means "again."

reuse      When you use something again you _____ it.
reread     When you read a story again you _____ it.
rebuild    Another way to say "build again" is _____ .

*Re-* can also mean "back."

| | |
|---|---|
| remove | To move back or move away is to _____ . |
| receive | To take back is, in a sense, to _____ . |
| repair | To put back in order is to _____ . |
| remain | To stay back in place is to _____ . |

## The Prefix *dis-*

The prefix *dis-* can mean "not." It can also mean "away," "apart," or reversal of the base word meaning.

| | |
|---|---|
| disagree | If you and I do not agree, then we _____ . |
| dismiss | To send away or allow to leave is to _____ . |
| disband | To break apart a group is to _____ it. |
| dislocate | To _____ something is the reverse of being in the usual location. |

## The Prefix *pre-*

The prefix *pre-* means "before" in time or position.

| | |
|---|---|
| prepare | To make ready ahead of time is to _____ . |
| prevent | To _____ something, you keep it from happening by taking some action first. |
| preschool | School before regular schooling begins is called _____ . |

## The Prefix *ex-*

The prefix *ex-* means "out."

| | |
|---|---|
| exclaim | Another way to say "call out" is _____ . |
| exhale | To breathe out is to _____ . |
| exception | Something that is taken out of general rules or principles is an _____ . |
| export | Something that is carried or sent out of a country is an _____ . |

## The Prefix *anti-*

The prefix *anti-* means "against."

| | |
|---|---|
| antibiotic | A substance that fights against bacteria is an _____ . |
| antiseptic | Something that works against germs is an _____ . |
| antifreeze | A liquid that protects against freezing is _____ . |

Some teachers may wish to point out to students a similar prefix, *ante-*, that may cause some confusion. The prefix *ante-* means "before."

| | |
|---|---|
| antecedent | Something that comes before is an _____ . |
| anteroom | A room that comes before or is in front of another is an _____ . |
| antedate | To come before in time is to _____ . |

## The Prefix *sub-*

The prefix *sub-* means "under" or "below."

| | |
|---|---|
| subway | A train that runs underground is a _____ . |
| subtitle | A title that appears below a main title is a _____ . |
| subsoil | The layer of earth just under the topsoil is the _____ . |

31

Teachers may want to explain that the prefix *sub-* can change its spelling to match certain root words through the process of assimilation.

| | |
|---|---|
| suffix | A word part fixed beneath or after the root is a _____ . |
| suffer | To bear up from under pain or sadness is to _____ . |
| support | To carry or hold up from below is to _____ . |

## The Prefix *super-*

The prefix *super-* means "over," "above," "more than usual."

| | |
|---|---|
| superfluous | Something that is over or more than what is needed is _____ . |
| superstructure | The part of a building that is above the foundation is the _____ . |
| supersonic | A jet that can travel faster than the speed of sound is called _____ . |

## The Prefix *com-*

The prefix *com-* means "together" or "with."

| | |
|---|---|
| committee | A group of people working together for a purpose can be called a _____ . |
| compact | Something put together in a small space can be described as _____ . |
| compete | To strive together with others for a prize is to _____ . |

The prefix *com-* may be spelled *co-, col-, con-* or *cor-*, depending on the first letter of the base word. Note the following examples:
coincide, coexist, coordinate, cosign, coworker;
collect, collapse, collate, collide;
connect, congregate, contract, connote, contact;
correspond, correlate, corroborate.

## The Prefix *mid-*

The prefix *mid-* means "in the middle."

| | |
|---|---|
| midstream | A person in the middle of a stream is in _____ . |
| midsummer | Another way to say "in the middle of the summer" is _____ . |
| midday | The middle of the day is called noon or _____ . |

## The Prefix *trans-*

The prefix *trans-* means "over" or "across."

| | |
|---|---|
| translate | To _____ literally means "to carry from one language across to another." |
| transmit | When I send a message over a distance I _____ it. |
| transatlantic | A ship going across the Atlantic is making a _____ voyage. |

32

## The Prefix *ad-*

The prefix *ad-* means "to" or "near to."

| | |
|---|---|
| adjacent | Two buildings that are near to each other are _____ . |
| adhere | If you want one thing to stick to another you want it to _____ . |
| adapt | When you change to fit to a situation you _____ . |

Through the process of assimilation, the prefix *ad-* can also be spelled *a-, ac-, af-, ag-, al-, an-, ap-, ar-, as-, at-*. Some examples are as follows:

amuse, amass, ascribe, aspect;
accept, accident, access, acquire;
affect, affair, affirm, affix;
aggression, aggravate, aggregate;
allocate, allude, alliteration;
annex, annul, announce, annotate;
appear, approve, applaud, apply;
arrest, arraign, arrive;
assist, assign, assess, assert;
attain, attempt, attest, attract.

## The Prefix *de-*

The prefix *de-* means "down" or "away."

| | |
|---|---|
| deduct | Another way to say "take away from" is _____ . |
| dejected | A person who is down in spirits is _____ . |
| descend | To go down is to _____ . |

## The Prefix *pro-*

The prefix *pro-* means "forward," as in *proclaim*. It can also mean "support for," as in *prorevolutionary*.

| | |
|---|---|
| proceed | To go forward is to _____ . |
| propel | To cause to move forward is to _____ . |
| promontory | A piece of land that juts out into the water is called a _____ . |

## The Prefix *mis-*

The prefix *mis-* means "wrong" or "wrongly."

| | |
|---|---|
| misunderstand | To understand incorrectly is to _____ . |
| misbehave | If you _____ , you behave wrongly. |
| mislead | If you lead someone in the wrong direction, you _____ him or her. |
| misinform | To give the wrong information is to _____ . |

## Number Prefixes

When a student learns that words can be put into logical groupings based on roots, prefixes, and suffixes, he or she is on the road to building an effective vocabulary. One such logical grouping is that of number.

Some key number prefixes are *mono-, mon-,* and *uni-* (one); *bi, bin-,* and *di-* (two); *twi-* (two; half); *tri-* (three); *deca-, dec-, deka-* (ten); *centi-, cent-* (hundred).

| | |
|---|---|
| monorail | A train that runs on one rail is a _____ . |
| unicorn | A mythical animal with one horn is a _____ . |
| bicycle | A cycle with two wheels is a _____ . |
| digraph | Two letters that represent a single sound make a _____ . |
| twilight | The time of day that is half day and half night is called _____ . |
| tripod | A camera stand which rests on three feet is a _____ . |
| decathlon | An athletic contest with ten events is a _____ . |
| centimeter | A measurement equal to 1/100 of a meter is a _____ . |

A teacher might write the following prefixes on the chalkboard: *uni-* (one), *bi-* (two), *tri-* (three), *quadri-, quadr-* (four), *penta-, pent-* (five), *sex-* or *hexa-* (six), *septi-* or *hepta-* (seven), *octo-, oct-* (eight), *nona-* (nine), and *dec-* (ten). The teacher then asks the students to form as many words as they can using these prefixes.

Another approach is to select base words or roots and alternate number prefixes to change their meanings. For example: *unicycle, bicycle, tricycle; pentagon, hexagon, heptagon, octagon.*

Students may be challenged to write a paragraph using as many words with number prefixes as they can. They may use them in any order they like, or they may try to use them in numerical order.

## Suffixes

Students need to know that a suffix can change the function or the meaning of a word. Once students know the meaning of a particular suffix, they can transfer that meaning from one word to another. For example, the student who knows the word *fearless* can transfer the suffix *-less* from *fearless* to other words of negation: *careless, thoughtless, homeless.*

A number of spelling hints are included within appropriate sections below. A list of general spelling hints relating to affixes can be found at the end of the chapter.

### The Suffix -s or -es

The suffix *-s* or *-es* is added to nouns to form plurals. The teacher should point out that when a word ends in *s, ss, sh, ch, x,* or *z,* the ending *-es* is added to make the word mean more than one.

| | |
|---|---|
| pillow — pillows | bunch — bunches |
| pencil — pencils | bush — bushes |
| riddle — riddles | fox — foxes |
| balloon — balloons | bus — buses |
| blanket — blankets | glass — glasses |
| Mr. Brown — the Browns | Mrs. Davis — the Davises |
| one Sarah — two Sarahs | one Mitch — two Mitches |

The teacher will need to point out special plural forms and spelling changes such as the following:

leaf — leaves        mouse — mice
wolf — wolves        man — men
child — children     goose — geese

For nouns ending in *y* preceded by a consonant, the *y* is changed to *i* and -*es* is added. For nouns ending in *y* preceded by a vowel, *s* is added.

army — armies        monkey — monkeys
city — cities        turkey — turkeys
berry — berries      play — plays
lobby — lobbies      valley — valleys

## The Suffixes -*s*, -*ing*, -*ed*

The endings -*s*, -*ing*, and -*ed* are added to verbs to indicate tense: present, present participle, and past tense.

look — looks — looking — looked
walk — walks — walking — walked

The teacher will want to point out spelling changes that occur with certain groups of words. When a word has only one vowel and ends in a single consonant, the consonant is doubled before a suffix beginning with a vowel is added.

chop — chops — chopping — chopped
drag — drags — dragging — dragged
pin — pins — pinning — pinned

When a base word ends in *e*, the *e* is dropped before a suffix beginning with a vowel is added.

live — lives — living — lived
move — moves — moving — moved
raise — raises — raising — raised

## The Suffixes -*er*, -*est*

The suffixes -*er* and -*est* are added to base words to make comparisons. Students should understand that -*er* is added to a word to form the comparative for two persons or things and that -*est* is added to a word to form the superlative for three or more persons or things.

long        My arm is longer than my baby sister's. My father's arm is the longest of all three.

warm        Spring is warmer than fall. But summer is the warmest season of all.

pretty      I think violets are prettier than daisies. But roses are the prettiest of all.

## The Suffixes -*er*, -*or*

The suffixes -*er* and -*or* indicate "person who." The teacher may point out that the base word is the clue to what the person does.

builder     A _____ is someone who builds.
farmer      The _____ is planting the crops.
writer      The _____ is working on a new book.

Teachers should remind students to drop the *e* before adding *-er* to base words such as *write, bake,* and *race.*

## The Suffix *-ly*

The suffix *-ly* indicates how something is done or how something happens. Usually, the suffix *-ly* is added to adjectives to form adverbs, which modify verbs, adjectives, and other adverbs (greeted *warmly, unusually* strong, *highly* unlikely). But *-ly* can also be added to some nouns to form adjectives (*cowardly* lion, *daily* occurrence).

| | |
|---|---|
| slowly | Turtles walk _____ . |
| brightly | The sun shines _____ . |
| quietly | Whisper a secret _____ . |
| nicely | The class sang the song _____ . |

## The Suffix *-ful*

The suffix *-ful* means "full of" and turns base words into adjectives.

| | |
|---|---|
| careful | You must be _____ when you cross the street. |
| useful | A can opener is a _____ tool in the kitchen. |
| cheerful | A _____ person is full of cheer. |

The suffix *-ful* can also be added to base words to mean "enough to fill." In this sense, such words are used as nouns.

| | |
|---|---|
| armful | He carried an _____ of books. |
| handful | You may have a _____ of peanuts. |
| houseful | We had a _____ of guests. |

## The Suffix *-less*

The suffix *-less* means "without."

| | |
|---|---|
| useless | This broken toy is _____ . |
| helpless | I felt _____ when I could not do the work. |
| powerless | We were _____ to change the weather. |
| spotless | She put on her _____ uniform to go to work. |

## The Suffix *-ous*

The suffix *-ous* means "full of" or "having the qualities of."

| | |
|---|---|
| famous | Another word for "having much fame" is _____ . |
| dangerous | The job of lion tamer can be a _____ one. |
| humorous | We laughed at the _____ story. |

The teacher might point out that the ending *-y* sometimes means "full of," as in *salty, bumpy, cloudy, windy,* and *dirty.*

## The Suffixes *-ist, -ian*

Both *-ist* and *-ian* are used to refer to people. The suffix *-ist* indicates "one who is skilled or trained in." The suffix *-ian* indicates "a specialist in or follower of."

| | |
|---|---|
| botanist | A person who is trained in or studies botany is a _____ . |
| cyclist | A person who is skilled in riding bicycles or motorcycles is a _____ . |

| dramatist | A person skilled in writing plays is a _____ . |
|---|---|
| magician | The tricks performed by the _____ amazed us. |
| grammarian | A person who specializes in grammar is a _____ . |
| vegetarian | My friend does not eat meat; she is a _____ . |

## The Suffix *-ness*

The suffix *-ness* means "state of being."

| sickness | Jean's _____ kept her home from school. |
|---|---|
| awareness | Tim's _____ of the problem helped him to be careful. |
| Happiness | _____ is the feeling we get when we've done something good. |

Teachers should remind students that in some base words ending in *y*, the *y* changes to *i* before *-ness* is added: *happiness, weariness, dizziness.* Some words do not change *y* to *i*: *dryness, slyness, shyness.*

## The Suffix *-fy* or *-ify*

The suffix *-fy* or *-ify* means "to make into something" or "to become."

| purify | To _____ something means to make it pure. |
|---|---|
| beautify | To _____ something means to make it beautiful. |
| terrified (terrify) | We were _____ by the ghost story. |

## The Suffix *-en*

The suffix *-en* means "to make" or "to cause to be." As with *-fy*, adding *-en* turns nouns and adjectives into verbs.

| lengthen | To make longer is to _____ . |
|---|---|
| moisten | To _____ a paintbrush, dip it in water. |
| fasten | Would you please _____ this sign to the bulletin board so it won't fall down? |

Teachers may wish to point out that the suffix *-en* is also used with some verbs to form past participles, for example: *bitten, broken, fallen, frozen, taken, written.*

## The Suffix *-able*

The suffix *-able* means "can be," "able to be," or "deserving of."

| lovable | A _____ person is deserving of love. |
|---|---|
| reliable | A person you are able to rely on is said to be _____ . |
| admirable | An action deserving to be admired is _____ . |
| detachable | The hood on my jacket can be taken off. It is _____ . |

Teachers may want to explain that the suffix *-able* can also be spelled *-ible,* as in *legible, edible, audible, possible, visible.*

## The Suffix *-ion* or *-tion*

The suffix *-ion* or *-tion* indicates an action, process, or the outcome thereof.

| construction | My little sister loves building with her new _____ set. |
|---|---|
| rebellion | An act of defiance against a ruling party can be a _____ . |

| fraction | A small piece or fragment of something is a _____ . |
| introduction | The first chapter in the book is an _____ to computer programming. |

## The Suffix -logy

The suffix -logy indicates "the study of." Words ending in -logy may at first look more difficult to the student than they really are. Once the student learns the meaning of the suffix, he or she can then concentrate on the base word. Thus etymology means the study of word origin. Biology is the study of life; zoology is the study of animals. Many names of the sciences end in -logy. Teachers may wish to list roots and their meanings for students, pointing out that -logy can be added to each of them to form the name of a science.

| | |
|---|---|
| astro (star; planet) | meteoro (high atmosphere) |
| anthropo (man) | ornitho (bird) |
| entomo (insect) | pharmaco (drug) |
| geo (earth) | psycho (soul; mind) |
| archaeo (ancient; primitive) | neuro (nerve) |

## The Suffixes -et and -ette

The suffixes -et and -ette indicate "small."

| kitchenette | A small kitchen is called a _____ . |
| coronet | A small crown is called a _____ . |
| diskette | A small disk used in a computer is a _____ . |

The suffixes -let and -ling can also mean "small," as in booklet, droplet, starlet, and duckling, gosling, seedling, and yearling.

## The Suffix -ish

The suffix -ish means "like" or "somewhat."

| foolish | It was _____ of him to skate on that thin ice. |
| waspish | A _____ person makes sharp, stinging remarks. |
| childish | Her _____ behavior annoyed her parents. |

The suffix -ish can also indicate nationality, as in Swedish and Spanish. Teachers may want to discuss other suffixes that show nationality, such as -an (Mexican), -ian (Norwegian), -ch (French), and -ese (Japanese).

## The Suffix -ward

The suffix -ward means "toward" or "in the direction of."

| upward | A balloon going _____ is rising in the air. |
| homeward | After the long trip Mike was glad to be heading _____ . |
| westward | The pioneers traveled _____ in their wagons. |

The suffix -ways also indicates direction or manner as in sideways and crossways.

## The Suffix -ship

The suffix -ship means "skill," "occupation of," or "condition of being."

| horsemanship | Luke's fine _____ has earned him many blue ribbons in riding contests. |

| governorship | Do you know who is running for the _____ of our state? |
| citizenship | Manuela is studying to earn her American _____ . |
| partnership | We formed a _____ to sell our invention. |

## The Suffix *-ment*

The suffix *-ment* means "action, process, or state of."

| government | The process of governing is called _____ . |
| achievement | It was quite an _____ for our class to win the award. |
| arrangement | The _____ of desks was quite neat. |

Spelling errors may occur when *-ment* is added to words ending in *e*. Teachers may remind students that generally a final *e* is retained before *-ment* (or any other suffix that begins with a consonant) is added. Examples include *pavement, movement, requirement, statement, advertisement.* Exceptions to the rule are the words *judgment* and *acknowledgment,* which can be spelled either without or with the *e*.

Some words that end in *y* preceded by a vowel add *-ment* without changing their spelling: *payment, enjoyment, employment.* Words ending in *y* preceded by a consonant change the *y* to *i* before adding *-ment: merriment, embodiment, accompaniment.*

## The Suffix *-hood*

The suffix *-hood* means "condition of" or "state of."

| childhood | The state of being a child is called _____ . |
| neighborhood | Most of the houses in my _____ have two stories. |
| brotherhood | The fraternity emphasized the _____ of all its members across the country. |

## The Suffix *-ry* or *-ery*

The suffix *-ry* or *-ery* can mean "the product of an action" or "the place where."

| poetry | The product of a poet is _____ . |
| injury | The product of injuring someone is an _____ . |
| pottery | The potter explained her work and showed us some of her _____ . |
| bakery | The place where the baker works is the _____ . |
| hatchery | A place where eggs are hatched is called a _____ . |
| cannery | A place where foods are canned is a _____ . |

## The Suffix *-ary*

The suffix *-ary* can mean "that which" or "place where."

| contrary | That which is against is _____ . |
| sanctuary | A _____ is a place of refuge. |
| Unitary | _____ means "that which pertains to a unit." |

## The Suffix *-arium* or *-orium*

The suffix *-arium* or *-orium* means "place for" or "thing used for."

| auditorium | A room or building for meetings and performances is an _____ . |

| | |
|---|---|
| planetarium | A room or building used for viewing images of planets and the solar system is a _____ . |
| terrarium | A closed container with earth for small plants or animals is a _____ . |

### The Suffix -ize

The suffix -ize means "to make or make into" or "to cause to be."

| | |
|---|---|
| apologize | To make an apology is to _____ . |
| legalize | To make something legal is to _____ it. |
| dramatize | Our class wants to _____ a story from one of our books. |

### The Suffix -ism

The suffix -ism means "action or practice of."

| | |
|---|---|
| heroism | The fire chief was cited for _____ . |
| vandalism | The act of damaging property is _____ . |
| favoritism | A good teacher does not show _____ toward students. |

### The Suffix -ine

The suffix -ine means "like" or "relating to."

| | |
|---|---|
| marine | The _____ exhibit displayed things relating to the ocean. |
| feline | Her _____ movements were like those of a cat stalking a mouse. |
| elephantine | The heavy footsteps plodding down the hallway sounded almost _____ . |

## Spelling Rules

Spelling rules are possible only because there is predictable structure in words. In prefixes such as *pre-, pro-, eu-, dys-,* and many others, the letter patterns are stable and can therefore be easily retained once they are observed.

In the same way, roots have regular letter patterns that help the speller who is aware of them. It is easy for students to recognize the spelling of recurring roots, such as *vis* in *vision, television, visionary,* and *visor,* if they are alerted to them.

A student who knows the root *labor,* work, is less likely to misspell the word *laboratory* as *labratory.* A student who knows the root *rupt,* break, and the prefix *inter-,* between, is less likely to misspell *interrupt* as *interupt.*

At the appropriate time the teacher may wish to review some of the following rules and spelling hints. We include here only a few examples to illustrate each principle; students might be encouraged to gather additional illustrative examples and discuss them in class.

### Spelling Hints

1. When the final letter of a prefix and the first letter of a base word or root are the same, both letters must be written (*unnoticed, underrate, dissimilar*).

2. When the final letter of a prefix and the first letter of a root word are the same vowel, it is usually preferable to separate the two parts with a hyphen, although there are exceptions to the rule (*re-enter, de-escalate,* but *cooperative*).

3. When adding certain prefixes to base words, change the final consonant of the prefix to make it identical or similar to the first consonant of the root for easier pronunciation. This process of assimilation applies to prefixes such as *in-* (spelled *im-, il-,* or *ir-*), *com-* (spelled *co-, col-, con-, cor-*) and *ad-* (spelled *a-, ac-, af-, ag-, al-, an-, ar-, ap-, as-, at-*). See List of Prefixes and Example Words in the Appendix for other prefixes and examples of words.

4. Make most singular words plural by adding *-s* (*book, books; magazine, magazines; puzzle, puzzles*).

5. Make singular words that end in *s, ss, sh, ch, x,* and *z* plural by adding *-es* (*bus, buses; glass, glasses; wish, wishes; church, churches; box, boxes; topaz, topazes*).

6. Note words which do not follow rules; make internal changes to indicate plural (*man, men; child, children; mouse, mice; tooth, teeth*). Also note that some plurals are the same as the singular (*deer; sheep*).

7. Add only *-s* or *-es* (not *'s*) to make names plural (*Mary,* two *Marys;* Mr. and Mrs. *Brown,* the *Browns;* Mr. and Mrs. *Jones,* the *Joneses*).

8. For nouns that end in *y* preceded by a consonant, change the *y* to *i* and add *-es* (*city, cities; berry, berries*).

9. For nouns that end in *y* preceded by a vowel, add *-s* (*monkey, monkeys; play, plays; valley, valleys*).

10. In general, add *-s* to the main word of a hyphenated compound (*brothers*-in-law; *attorneys*-at-law; *passers*-by).

11. In general, drop the final *e* of a base word before adding a suffix beginning with a vowel (*love, loving; range, ranger; confide, confidence; pure, purify; admire, admirable*).

   If the word ends in *ce* or *ge,* keep the final *e* to retain the soft sound of *c* or *g* (*peace, peaceable; replace, replaceable; advantage, advantageous*).

12. In general, keep the final *e* of the base word when adding a suffix that begins with a consonant (*care, careless; arrange, arrangement; spite, spiteful*).

   Words that end in two vowels (a vowel + final *e*) retain the final vowel when a suffix is added (*shoe, shoeing; canoe, canoeing; foresee, foreseeable*).

13. In general, when a word ends with a consonant preceded by a single vowel double the final consonant when adding a suffix that begins with a vowel (*skip, skipping; scan, scanner*).

14. When a word of more than one syllable ends in a single consonant preceded by a single vowel and has its accent on the final syllable, double the consonant before adding a suffix that begins with a vowel (*begin, beginning; compel, compelled; forgot, forgotten; commit, committed*). If the accent is not on the final syllable, do not double the consonant (*benefit, benefited; counsel, counseled; travel, traveling*).

15. Check the dictionary for nouns ending in *o* before adding *-es* for the plural. There are about a dozen common words ending in *-o* whose plurals end in *es* (*vetoes, mosquitoes, potatoes, tomatoes, heroes, echoes, torpedoes, embargoes, volcanoes, buffaloes*); however, it is acceptable to add only *-s* to form some of those (*mosquitos, volcanos, buffalos*). Words ending in *-o* that add only *-s* are *silo, cameo, radio, dynamo*.

16. Form the plurals of numbers, signs, letters, and words used as words by adding *'s* (*a's; 9's; &'s; p's* and *q's;* You used too many *said's*).

17. One use of the apostrophe is to show ownership. In general, add *'s* to singular nouns (*girl, girl's*). If a singular noun ends in *s* or an *s* sound, add *'s* (*Tess's* book, *Illinois's* population), except when followed by a word beginning with *s* (your *conscience'* sake). To plural nouns ending in *s*, add just an apostrophe (*girls'* bikes). To plural nouns not ending in *s* add *'s* (*men's* lockers).

18. Check the dictionary when forming the plural of loan words from Greek and Latin. Either the Greek and Latin plurals or the English plurals can be acceptable.

| Greek or Latin Singular | Greek or Latin Plural | English Plural |
|---|---|---|
| alumna | alumnae | |
| alumnus | alumni | |
| medium | media | mediums |
| datum | data | |
| radius | radii | radiuses |
| spectrum | spectra | spectrums |
| fungus | fungi | funguses |
| phenomenon | phenomena | phenomenons |
| locus | loci | |
| crisis | crises | |
| oasis | oases | |
| thesis | theses | |
| formula | formulae | formulas |
| index | indices | indexes |
| memorandum | memoranda | memorandums |

# Chapter Four

# Word Origins

Why should students study word origin? There are three main reasons: (1) the study of word history can promote word consciousness; (2) it can help the student develop an interest in word study; and (3) it can function as a memory device by providing additional information.

Visualizing a given word in a certain setting helps us remember the word. The student may more readily remember the word *fauna* (animal life in a certain period of time or a certain part of the world) if the teacher also discusses *flora* (plant life) and points out that in mythology, *Fauna* was the sister of *Faunus,* god of animal life, and *Flora* was the goddess of flowers and plants: thus the phrase "flora and fauna."

The concept of association, seeing existing relationships between words, is central to effective vocabulary study. In learning the prefix *tri-,* three, students may encounter *trident,* a three-pronged fork. However, *trident* will have greater meaning for them when they read a description or see a picture of Neptune, the god of the sea, holding a three-pronged spear in his hand.

## Proper Names

Words come out of a need to communicate. Words, like persons, have histories, and each person's name has a history. Thus the teacher might introduce the study of word origins by calling students' attention to the origins of their own names.

The teacher might make a list of common first names and their original meanings and point out that names have come from flowers, birds, legend, mythology, and ancient history. Some names come from the Bible; *Abraham,* for example, means "father" or "leader" in Hebrew.

In early American times parents often gave their children names they hoped their offspring would live up to: *Faith, Hope, Charity, Purity, Patience, Christian, Justus.* Native Americans have given their children names that describe or suggest something in nature, such as "Yellow-Wings-Flying" or "Swift-Waters-Running." We often find famous surnames as given names: *Washington, Jefferson, Lincoln, Franklin.*

Some words are the basis for many different names for both girls and boys. The teacher might point out that the names *John, Jane, Jean, Hans, Janet, Joan, Juan, Juanita, Sean, Jeanette, Jack,* and others all come from a Hebrew word that means "God's Gift" or "God is gracious."

The teacher might find the following list helpful.

## Some Common First Names

| Boys | Girls |
|------|-------|
| Adam: red earth | Abigail: my father is joy |
| Alan: harmony, peace; fair, handsome | Alice: noble |
| | Amanda: worthy of love |
| Albert: noble; bright | Andrea: strong; courageous |
| Alexander: protector of men | Amy: beloved |
| Andrew: manly | Angela: angelic |
| Anthony: worthy of praise | Ann: gracious |
| Benjamin: son of my right hand | Barbara: stranger |
| Brian: strong | Bonnie: good; pretty |
| Charles: strong | Carol: joyful song |
| Christopher: Christ-bearer | Caroline: strong |
| Daniel: God is my judge | Deborah: a bee |
| David: beloved | Diana: divine |
| Donald: proud chief | Donna: lady |
| Edward: happy guardian | Dorothy: gift of God |
| Eric: honorable ruler | Elizabeth: God's oath |
| Francis: free | Emily: ambitious; industrious |
| George: farmer | Eve: life |
| Gregory: vigilant, watchful | Gabrielle: God is my strength |
| Henry: home lord | Gwen: white |
| James: held by the heel | Hannah: gracious; merciful |
| Jason: healer | Heather: a heath |
| Jeffrey: God's peace | Helen: light |
| John: God is gracious | Jane: gracious; merciful |
| Jonathan: God has given | Jennifer: friend of peace |
| Joseph: God will increase | Jessica: riches or God's grace |
| Joshua: God is my salvation | Jill: girl |
| Justin: just | Julie: soft-haired |
| Kenneth: handsome | Karen: Danish form of Katherine |
| Kevin: handsome | Katherine: pure |
| Lawrence: a laurel, a crown | Kelly: variant of Kelt, Celt |
| Louis: famous in battle | Laura: laurel |
| Mark: warlike | Linda: beautiful |
| Matthew: gift of God | Margaret: pearl |
| Michael: Who is like God? | Mary: bitterness; sorrow |
| Nathan: He gave | Megan: Welsh form of Margaret |
| Patrick: noble | Melanie: dark in appearance |
| Paul: little | Melissa: a bee; honey |
| Peter: rock | Michelle: Who is like God? |
| Philip: person who loves horses | Nancy: gracious |
| Richard: bold fighter | Rachel: lamb |
| Robert: bright fame | Rebecca: to tie; bind |
| Roger: famous warrior | Rita: brave; honest |
| Ronald: old and wise | Rosa: rose |
| Roy: king | Ruth: companion; friendship |

| | |
|---|---|
| Scott: a Scot | Sara: princess; noble |
| Steven: a crown | Stephanie: a crown |
| Thomas: a twin or sun god | Susan: lily |
| Timothy: to honor God | Theresa: to reap |
| Todd: fox | Tracy: brave |
| William: resolute protector | Wendy: fair |

Surnames (last names) came into use to differentiate between two or more people with the same first name. Surnames have sometimes come from the name of a town or description of a place in which the earliest members of the family lived. The name *Douglas* comes from a section of Scotland near the Douglas River. *Burton,* which means "hill town," is the name of a town in England.

A last name may be the result of a physical trait of a family: *Brown* (dark hair or complexion); *White* (light hair, fair complexion); *Black* (black or dark); and *Gray* (old, gray). Some names are not so obvious. *Boyd* means "yellow-haired"; *Russell* means "red-haired"; *Lloyd* means "gray" or "dark ."

Many surnames are derived from occupations. Two of the most common surnames are *Smith* and *Wright,* both meaning "maker." These names appear alone and combined with more specific terms: *Cartwright* and *Arrowsmith,* for example. Surnames can relate to the actual work done (*Baker, Carpenter, Tanner, Taylor, Fowler*) or to the tools or products of the work (*Naylor,* a nail maker; *Saltzman,* a seller of salt; *Sawyer,* a carpenter).

Some surnames indicate family relationships: *Johnson, Davidson,* and *Robertson* for example. The French word for *son* is *fils.* With a slight change in spelling we have English names such as *Fitzgerald* (son of Gerald) and *Fitzwilliam* (son of William). The prefixes *Mac-* and *Mc-* indicate the same thing in Scottish and Irish names like *MacDonald, MacArthur,* and *McCarroll.*

While we have derived names from other words, we have also derived common words from proper names. Some objects have been named for the people who invented, discovered, or first used them. Some have been named for the places where they were first found or used. The following list is not meant to provide students with words to memorize, but for their use in noting how apparent and how interesting word derivation can be. Teachers can develop activities for students such as matching names and objects or completing sentences using the words. Teachers may select as few or as many words as may interest the students. These words may also provide a starting point for special projects involving the words, the objects they name, or the people for whom they are named.

| | |
|---|---|
| Ferris Wheel | G.W. Gale Ferris |
| saxophone | Adolphe Sax |
| bloomers | Amelia Bloomer |
| cardigan | Earl of Cardigan |
| leotard | Jules Leotard |

| | |
|---|---|
| calico | Calicut, India |
| limerick | Limerick, Ireland |
| denim | de (from) Nimes, France |
| guppy | R.J.L. Guppy |
| sandwich | Earl of Sandwich |
| hamburger | Hamburg, Germany |
| frankfurter | Frankfurt, Germany |
| tangerine | Tangier, Morocco |
| Roquefort cheese | Roquefort, France |
| melba toast | Dame Nellie Melba |
| ohm | George Ohm |
| ampere | Andre Ampere |
| watt | James Watt |
| volt | Allesandro Volta |
| curie | Marie Curie |
| galvanize | Luigi Galvani |
| derrick | Thomas Derrick |
| mesmerize | Franz Mesmer |
| pasteurize | Louis Pasteur |
| boycott | Capt. Charles Boycott |
| braille | Louis Braille |
| silhouette | Etienne de Silhouette |
| maverick | Samuel Maverick |
| diesel | Rudolf Diesel |
| Fahrenheit | Gabriel Fahrenheit |
| Cincinnati | Cincinnatus |
| Victorian | Queen Victoria |
| begonia | Michel Begon |
| poinsettia | Joel Poinsett |
| gardenia | Alexander Garden |
| hyacinth | Hyacinth (a Spartan youth) |
| iris | Iris (goddess of the rainbow) |
| loganberry | J.H. Logan |
| magnolia | Pierre Magnol |
| forsythia | William Forsyth |
| Bunsen burner | Robert Bunsen |
| cologne | Cologne, Germany |
| guillotine | Joseph Guillotin |
| lynch | Charles Lynch |
| laconic | Laconia (whose inhabitants were reputed to be terse) |
| maudlin | Mary Magdalene |
| mackintosh | Charles Macintosh |
| Morse code | Samuel Morse |
| odyssey | Odysseus |
| panama hat | Panama |
| panic | Pan, Greek forest god |

| | |
|---|---|
| praline | Count du Plessis-Praslin |
| pullman | George M. Pullman |
| lavaliere | Duchess de La Valliere |
| rhinestone | Rhine River |
| shanghai | Shanghai, China |
| zeppelin | Count Ferdinand von Zeppelin |

## Names of the Months

The teacher may wish to discuss with the class the origins of the names of the months. Some months are named for Roman rulers or gods. Others are named for months of the Roman calendar.

| | |
|---|---|
| January | Janus, the two-faced god |
| February | *Februa,* a Roman feast |
| March | Mars, the god of war |
| April | Latin *aprilis,* opening of the buds |
| May | Maia, a goddess |
| June | Juno, Roman goddess of marriage |
| July | Julius Caesar |
| August | Augustus Caesar |
| September | Latin *septem,* seventh month of Roman calendar |
| October | Latin *octo,* eighth month of Roman calendar |
| November | Latin *novem,* ninth month of Roman calendar |
| December | Latin *decem,* tenth month of Roman calendar |
| month | Anglo-Saxon *mona,* moon |

## Days of the Week

| | |
|---|---|
| Sunday | day of the sun |
| Monday | day of the moon |
| Tuesday | day of Tiu (Teutonic god of war) |
| Wednesday | day of Woden (Teutonic god) |
| Thursday | day of Thor (Norse god) |
| Friday | day of Fria (Woden's wife) |
| Saturday | day of Saturn (Roman god) |

# Greek and Latin Word Origins

History has given us some interesting words. The word *candidate* has its roots in ancient Rome, where a politician running for office wore a white toga as a sign of pure and noble intentions. The Latin word for *white* is *candidus,* and the office-seeker was called *candidatus.* A candidate, then, is someone with pure (purely) political intentions.

The Latin word for "old man" was *senex.* On the whole, older men filled the Roman *senate.* Although the U.S. Senate has younger men, most of the members are older and, in the Roman sense, are rightly called *senators* (old ones).

No matter how we use words today it is difficult to escape the fact that many had their beginnings in ancient Greece or Rome. For example,

47

would you believe there is a connection between dogs and canaries? There is. Roman sailors who stopped at a group of islands off the west coast of Africa found large dogs on the islands. Since the Latin word for *dog* is *canis* as in *canine,* the Romans called the islands the *Canarias.* Later on, birds from the Canary Islands were called *canaries.*

Greek is the basis for thousands of words we use today, and there is good reason. The Greek language had over 92,000 words, all pure Greek, not borrowings from other languages. Many of the words used in city affairs today are derived from Greek. From Greek *polis,* city, we get the words *politics, police, cosmopolitan. Metropolis* comes from *mētēr,* mother, + *polis,* and thus means "mother city."

Some of the words in our language come from names of characters in Greek and Roman mythology. Some examples follow.

| Name | Examples of Derived Words |
|------|---------------------------|
| Vulcan, Roman god of fire | volcano |
| Helios, Greek god of the sun | helium |
| Hygeia, Greek goddess of health | hygiene |
| Hypnos, Greek god of sleep | hypnotic, hypnotize |
| Mars, Roman god of war | martial, Martian |
| Fata, three Fates who were in charge of life and death | fatal, fatalistic |
| Morta, Roman Fate who caused death | mortal, mortician |
| Clotho, Greek Fate who spun the threads of life | clothing |
| Ceres, Roman goddess of grain | cereal |
| Nox, Roman goddess of the night | nocturnal |
| Terra, Roman goddess of earth | terrestrial |
| Iris, Greek goddess of the rainbow | iridescent |
| Muses, Greek goddesses of the arts | museum |

Astronomers have usually been sensitive to the mythology concerning the stars, and as they have mapped the heavens, they have taken into account many of the legends of the ancient peoples. Thus, as they discovered new planets and other heavenly bodies, they gave them names according to their relative position or appearance in the sky. The beautiful and brilliant planet Venus was named after the Roman goddess of love and beauty. *Phosphorus* (Greek for "lightbearer") was another name for the planet Venus, the morning star seen in the east; and from this name we get the noun *phosphorus* and the adjective *phosphorescent.*

Astrologers and astronomers noticed that one planet whirled around the sun faster than the other planets did. They named this planet *Mercury,* after the messenger of the gods, who was known for his speed. From Mercury we get the adjective *mercurial.* Astrologers also thought that persons born under *Saturn,* a slow-moving planet, were gloomy or grave (the opposite of mercurial). Gloomy persons are sometimes described as *saturnine.* Persons born under the planet Jupiter, another name for the god *Jove,* were supposedly cheerful, or *jovial.*

When the Russian moon rocket Lunik II and the United States lunar probe Ranger IV hit the moon, the Latin language, which had spread over much of the earth, had also gone to the moon. *Lunik* comes from the Latin word for "moon," *luna.* Printed on Ranger IV were the words *United States,* from the Latin *unus,* one, + *sta,* stand, that is, "we stand as one." The phrase *lunar probe* comes from the language of the Romans, Latin *probo* meaning "prove; test; or inspect."

The names of American rockets, spaceships, and satellites are often deeply rooted in the mythology of the Greeks and Romans. When astronaut John Glenn orbited the earth in 1962, he did it in a Mercury capsule. *Capsula* is Latin for "little box." Like the planet, the Mercury capsule was named for the swift messenger of the gods.

American astronauts have orbited the moon in an Apollo Command Module, which gets its name from Apollo, the Greek god of the sun and the ideal of youthful manliness. The word *module* comes from the Latin *modulus,* a diminutive of *modus* (a measure), and in space terminology a module is "a small measure of," or a single part of, a spaceship from which it can be separated for a lunar landing.

In 1960, the United States launched a "passive" satellite that reflects, or echoes, signals back to earth. This satellite was called *Echo I.* The name *Echo* also stems from Greek mythology: Echo was a mythical character who would not stop talking. The goddess Hera took away her ability to speak, except for the power to repeat the last word anyone said to her. The first American meteorological satellites were called *Tiros,* from Latin *tiro,* a novice. And a satellite used to detect the number of meteoroids in space is named *Pegasus,* from the mythological flying horse named *Pegasus,* which also gave its name to a constellation.

The more scientists probe into the future, the more they seem to reach back into the past for words. As space scientists look out from our planet, they are first aware of the air that surrounds the earth, or the *atmosphere,* from Greek *atmos,* vapor, + *sphaira,* sphere. The space between planets is called *interplanetary space,* from Latin *inter-,* between; among, + *planetary,* which comes from a Greek word meaning "to wander" (the planets seem to wander in their courses through the heavens). Beyond interplanetary space is *interstellar space,* from Latin *stella,* star.

Future space explorers who travel to the moon or the planets will naturally depend on navigation. Space navigation is called *astrogation,* navigation carried on by means of sighting the stars. *Astrogation* is formed from *astro-* + *navigation* from the Greek *astro-,* star, + Latin *navigāre,* to sail. The word *astronaut* itself is a name coined from *astro-* + *nauta,* sailor. Astronauts are literally "sailors among the stars." In Russia they are sailors in the universe: *cosmonauts.*

## Borrowed Words

Many words we use today have been borrowed from other languages, some unchanged in spelling, others with different spellings but the same meanings. Teachers might develop student interest in word origin by structuring a lesson on food names and sources. Words and descriptions could be presented for a matching activity, or clues could be provided and students could fill in the blanks.

| | |
|---|---|
| ketchup | *ke-tsiap,* Chinese, meaning "brine of fish" |
| chowder | *chaudière,* French, meaning "stew pot" |
| tangerine | fruit originally from Tangier, Morocco |
| zucchini | *zucca,* Italian, meaning "gourd" |
| coleslaw | *koolsla,* Dutch for "cabbage salad" |
| frankfurter | a sausage named for Frankfurt, Germany |
| hamburger | a meat patty named for Hamburg, Germany |
| broccoli | *brocco,* Italian, meaning "little spike" |
| succotash | *msickquatash,* a Native American name for a dish of corn and lima beans |
| squash | a vegetable called *askootasquash* by Native Americans |
| tortilla | *torta,* Spanish for "cake" |
| chili | Spanish word for a spicy dish |
| banana | Portuguese and Spanish name for a yellow-skinned fruit |
| waffle | *wafel,* Dutch word for a light batter cake |
| cookie | *koekje,* Dutch, meaning "little cake" |
| pretzel | German name for a salted biscuit often shaped in a loose knot |
| noodle | *nudel,* German word for a food made of flour and eggs |
| pizza | Italian name for a type of pie with sauce, cheese, and other trimmings |

A sampling of other borrowed words might include *garage, chef, menu,* and *ballet* (French); *studio, piano,* and *violin* (Italian); *patio, cargo, rodeo,* and *corral* (Spanish); *gumbo* (African); *khaki* (Urdu); *geyser* (Icelandic); *ski* (Norwegian); *ukulele* (Hawaiian).

## Native American Words

Many words we use come from the Native American languages of North and South America. Explorers and traders coming to the New World learned these words and added them to their own vocabularies. Some of the examples listed below are probably familiar to students as Indian words. The origin of some as Native American may be a surprise.

Objects: *canoe, moccasin, wigwam, mackinaw, totem, caucus, hogan, igloo*

Animals: *moose, raccoon, skunk, caribou*

Food: *pecan, squash, persimmon, hominy*

# Coining New Words

Even when people coin words they often rely on known words or word elements. Lewis Carroll, the mathematician who wrote *Alice in Wonderland* for amusement, coined the word *chortle,* a combination of *chuckle* and *snort.* Words formed by blending parts of other words together are called portmanteau words. *Motel* is another example; it is formed from *motor* and *hotel.* Newspaper writers often coin words to keep stories or headlines concise. For example, sportswriters use the term *twinight double-header* to describe a double-header, or set of two baseball games, that starts at twilight and goes on into the night.

The name of the *Spanish Armada,* which Philip II of Spain sent against England in 1588, was coined by the Spanish from the Latin word *armata,* armed. Spanish explorers in America used another derivative of the Latin word *arma,* arms or weapons, in naming an animal with a bony shell resembling an armored plate. They called the animal an *armadillo.*

Many of our words have long and varied histories. By digging up the past we often discover hidden curiosities that can make certain words come alive for us. Teachers might ask the students if they realize that the words *curfew* and *fire* are related. *Curfew* comes from the French *couvrir,* cover, + *feu,* fire. In olden days the curfew bell meant "cover up (put out) the fire and go to bed."

How many students know why Philadelphia is called the "City of Brotherly Love"? The name *Philadelphia* comes from two Greek words, *philo,* love, + *adelphos,* brother. In the same word family is *philosopher,* a lover of wisdom (sophos). A *philanthropist* is a lover of mankind. A *philatelist* loves stamps. People who like harmony or good music may listen to a *philharmonic* orchestra. A certain plant that seems to like the shade is called a *philodendron* (from Greek *dendron,* tree).

Knowing word origins can give students a sense of the historic continuity of language and an understanding of association and classification in word study. Word history is necessary to the study of word families, which makes up a significant part of the mental filing system that gives vocabulary a boost.

# Chapter Five

# Pronunciation and Spelling

Pronunciation and spelling are important in vocabulary development because they involve discrimination between sounds and between letters that combine to form words and concepts. Thus, students must be aware of the sounds of words such as *wear* and *where, ever* and *every, while* and *wile*. Likewise, students must learn to make discriminations in spelling, as in *stake* and *steak, pain* and *pane, flew* and *flu*.

The chief reason for discriminating between sounds is to communicate clearly. There are other reasons. For example, the relationship between the pronunciation of words and social approval is important. We refer here to accepted standards of schools, professions, business, and industry, where correct pronunciation may be of prime concern; where it is important, for example, not to pronounce *our* like *are,* or *for* like *fur,* especially if mispronunciation not only is unacceptable but leads to misunderstanding as well.

Pronunciation and spelling are means by which we send and receive words and exchange ideas. Students need to be reminded that poor enunciation, mispronunciation, and incorrect spelling distract the listener or the reader and cause static in the communication system.

## Practicing Pronunciation

We sometimes mispronounce words because we spell them incorrectly, though more often the reverse is true. Students are nevertheless embarrassed when they mispronounce words that others know well. Obviously, then, it is best to create a situation in which students' pronunciation can be corrected in the spirit of constructive criticism.

Students should be encouraged to take note of mispronunciations they hear and discuss them in class. Common mispronunciations might include *ast* for *asked, chimley* for *chimney, excape* for *escape*. Such words can be spelled aloud or written on the chalkboard. Members of the class can repeat each one to themselves until the correct pronunciation is firmly implanted. For an auditory learner, the teacher might prepare tapes that spell out problem words, allow intervals for the student's pronunciation of each one, and present the accepted pronunciation in each case.

# Variety in Pronunciation

Few words are limited to one pronunciation. Words that change the accented syllable when they change from noun to verb or adjective are common. We "_refuse_ to be laughed at" but we "empty the wastebasket into the _refuse_ container." Other words, while not changing their general meaning, shift from one part of speech to another:

a. The newspaper editor decided to _reprint_ the award-winning story.
b. I sent away for a _reprint_ of the article.

Some words are pronounced more than one way though their meaning or part of speech does not change. You may say "advertizement" and the television announcer may say "advertisment." The word is the same, and both pronunciations are acceptable. Actually, our pronunciation is influenced by where we live, what we have been taught, and how our friends and family pronounce words.

In dealing with pronunciation, differences in regional dialects must be considered. Therefore, we do not suggest a preference for one pronunciation over another. As previously suggested, the main reason for "careful" pronunciation is clear communication. The teacher should not stress an exclusive pronunciation of a word, since family background, regional tradition, experience, and travel all influence the pronunciation of words and the changing of pronunciations.

# The Role of Accent in Words

The development of oral and written language skills requires extensive practice in auditory discrimination. As pointed out above, the part of speech and/or meaning of certain words depends on which syllable is accented.

The student needs to know that the way he or she pronounces a word or accents a syllable often gives a certain meaning to the word or influences the listener's comprehension of the meaning intended. A verb may become a noun or vice versa; a noun may become an adjective.

The following list may be used to illustrate that words spelled alike are not necessarily pronounced alike, and that accent often changes the meaning or use of a word.

| | | | |
|---|---|---|---|
| absent | absent | conduct | conduct |
| abstract | abstract | conflict | conflict |
| address | address | conserve | conserve |
| ally | ally | console | console |
| collect | collect | content | content |
| compact | compact | contest | contest |
| compound | compound | converse | converse |
| compress | compress | convict | convict |
| concert | concert | defense | defense |
| concrete | concrete | digest | digest |

54

| | | | |
|---|---|---|---|
| essay | essay | project | project |
| export | export | protest | protest |
| extract | extract | recess | recess |
| frequent | frequent | record | record |
| import | import | refuse | refuse |
| impress | impress | reject | reject |
| incense | incense | relapse | relapse |
| incline | incline | relay | relay |
| increase | increase | reprint | reprint |
| insert | insert | rerun | rerun |
| insult | insult | reset | reset |
| intern | intern | retake | retake |
| invalid | invalid | subject | subject |
| object | object | survey | survey |
| offset | offset | suspect | suspect |
| permit | permit | transfer | transfer |
| proceeds | proceeds | transplant | transplant |
| progress | progress | transport | transport |

## Pronunciation Demons

Many students hesitate to use words they know simply because they are unsure of how to pronounce them. The words listed below (many of which are hard to spell) are often mispronounced. Careful attention to many of them should help the average upper-grade student. Note that some words may be pronounced two ways:

abdomen (ăb'də-mən, ăb-dō'mən)
abstemious (ăb-stē'mē-əs)
affluence (ăf'lōō-əns)
alias (ā'lē-əs, āl'yəs)
anathema (ə-năth'ə-mə)
apropos (ăp'rə-pō')
archetype (är'kə-tīp')
bade (băd, bād)
comparable (kŏm'pər-ə-bəl)
condolence (kən-dō'ləns)
covert (kŭv'ərt, kō'vərt')
crevasse (krə-văs')
dais (dā'ĭs, dās)
decadent (dĭ-kā'dənt, děk'ə-dənt)
despicable (děs'pĭ-kə-bəl, dĭ-spĭk'-)
desultory (děs'əl-tôr'ē)
devotee (děv'ə-tē', děv'ə-tā')
disheveled (dĭ-shěv'-əld)
dour (dŏŏr, dour)
efficacy (ef'ə-kə-sē)

ephemeral (ĭ-fěm'ər-əl)
exacerbate (ěg-zăs'ər-bāt')
exquisite (ěks'kwĭ-zĭt)
facade (fə-säd')
formidable (fôr'mə-də-bəl)
forte (fôrt, fōrt) (person's strong point)
forte (fôr'tā) (in music, loudly)
genuine (jěn'yōō-ĭn)
halcyon (hăl'sē-ən)
haphazard (hăp-hăz'ərd)
harbinger (här'bən-jər)
height (hīt)
heinous (hā'nəs)
hospitable (hŏs'pə-tə-bəl, hŏs-pĭt'ə-bəl)
incognito (ĭn-kŏg'nə-tō', ĭn-kŏg'nē'tō)
incongruous (ĭn-kŏng'grōō-əs)
indict (ĭn-dīt')

55

indigent (ĭn'də-jənt)
infinite (ĭn'fə-nĭt)
ingenuous (ĭn-jĕn'yōō-əs)
intricacy (ĭn'trĭ-kə-sē)
irreparable (ĭ-rĕp'ər-ə-bəl)
irrevocable (ĭ-rĕv'ə-kə-bəl)
lamentable (lăm'ən-tə-bəl, lə'mĕn'- )
machination (măk'ĭ-nā'shən,
   măsh'ĭ-)
maintenance (mān'tə-nəns)
minuscule (mĭn'ə-skyōōl',
   mĭ-nŭs'kyōōl)
mischievous (mĭs'chə-vəs)
naive (nä-ēv')
obese (ō-bēs')
onerous (ŏn'ər-əs, ō'nər-əs)
plebeian (plĭ-bē'ən)

plethora (plĕth'ər-ə)
preferable (prĕf'ər-ə-bəl)
pseudo (sōō'dō)
qualm (kwäm, kwôm)
redolent (rĕd'ə-lənt)
respite (rĕs'pĭt)
ribald (rĭb'əld)
schism (sĭz'əm, skĭz'əm)
scion (sī'ŏn)
secretive (sē'krə-tĭv, sĭ-krē'tĭv)
solace (sŏl'ĭs)
specious (spē'shəs)
subtle (sŭt'l)
succinct (sək-sĭngkt')
taciturn (tăs'ə-tərn)
ultimatum (ŭl'tə-mā'təm)
vagary (vā'gə-rē, və-gâr'ē)

# Choosing the Right Word

The exercise below provides practice in making discriminations between words that look or sound alike but cause confusion if used incorrectly. The teacher can use this pattern as a quick check on the vocabulary skill of the student. He or she might note those students who score high and be ready to prepare additional, more challenging work for them.

Using the same form but less difficult words, the elementary teacher might present appropriate key words for the class. The exercise can be used to emphasize word recognition, meaning, and letter discrimination (spelling).

Choosing from the three words under each sentence, the student writes the correct word in the blank.

philatelist    1. A conscientious _____ really prizes his stamps.
philosopher, philatelist, philanthropist

censure    2. The committee voted to _____ the senator's behavior.
censor, censure, sensor

empathy    3. One who feels another's misfortune has _____.
antipathy, apathy, empathy

baccalaureate    4. The dean spoke at the _____.
bacchanalia, baccalaureate, bacillary

imminent    5. An eruption from the live volcano above the village is _____.
imminent, immanent, eminent

facade    6. The _____ of a Grecian temple often tells a story.
faucet, facade, facet

56

indolent   7. An _____ person usually avoids work.
           indigent, indolent, indigenous
efflorescent  8. In May the fields are _____.
           efficacious, effervescent, efflorescent
supercilious  9. The pompous lady gave us a _____ look.
           superfluous, superficial, supercilious

## Spelling and Context

Vocabulary instruction aimed at helping students understand how language develops can contribute to their spelling skills. Linguists divide the study of language structure into three areas: (1) *phonology,* the system of sounds used in a language (Latin *phon,* sound); (2) *syntax,* the arrangement of words to form sentences (Greek *syn-,* together, + *taxis,* arrangement); and (3) *morphology,* the forms of words brought about by inflection and derivation (Greek *morphe,* form, + -*logy,* study of).

Recent studies indicate the following:

1. Spelling is a more consistent symbolic representation of speech than was formerly believed. Eighty percent of the time, a phoneme is consistently represented by a grapheme.

2. The arrangement of phonological (sound) elements is consistent in consonant-vowel, vowel-consonant, and consonant-vowel-consonant positions. The speller does not have an unlimited number of choices for letter placement.

3. These consonant-vowel, vowel-consonant patterns are really learned through the teaching of meaningful syllables and word elements (morphological elements): prefixes, roots, and suffixes.

Too often students are asked to learn the spelling of each word as a separate task, unrelated to former learning. For effective learning the students must see the word *jumping* as an inflected form (morphological change) of *jump.* They must note the morphological aspects of language: compounds, roots, prefixes, suffixes, and derivatives that point up the relationships between words. They must get the idea that every word they spell is not a new experience.

Students can learn to generalize about spelling as they generalize about words and derivatives. They can learn that words such as *mate, fate, rate* (having the long *a* sound) generally have a final silent *e.* The same is true of other vowels in words with a long sound: *kite, rote, cute.* Exceptions can be discussed after the concept is learned. (Additional generalizations and rules that can help students spell correctly are offered within appropriate chapters.)

Students who relate spelling practice to word study, who are taught to recognize certain syllables as meaningful units, readily recognize these units when they turn up in new words. (The *anti* in *antifreeze* is spelled the

57

same as the *anti* in *antidote.*) If a student can spell *circus* and is taught to recognize *circu* (around) as a unit, it is a short step to the spelling of harder words — *circuit, circuitous,* and so on.

## Predicting Spelling Difficulties

Students need to be reminded that certain words are often misspelled and thus be alerted to check these words after spelling them. Spelling not only involves the ability to put letters together in the correct form; it also requires the attitude or concern to see that it is done. We need, in other words, a spelling conscience. We must care whether we spell correctly or not.

Sometimes we can use memory devices such as rules, but they do not always work. And even if we improve our spelling by learning certain principles and by using memory devices such as noting roots and affixes, we will still misspell words unless we are able to predict and double-check the words which we might misspell.

Included here is a list of words often misspelled. In developing this list we have made use of Arthur I. Gates's *Spelling Difficulties in 3,876 Words* and Harry A. Greene's *The New Iowa Spelling Scale,* [1] listing only those words scored below 50 percent on the Iowa Spelling Scale at the eighth-grade level.

The list has implications for other grades also. The word *bicycle,* with a spelling score of 45 percent at the eighth-grade level, will be difficult for students below this level. The word *counsel* (17 percent at the eighth-grade level) will still be difficult for students beyond the eighth grade.

Teachers may put together a shorter list of commonly misspelled words that would be appropriate for their students. Each student might be asked to check the words in the list that he or she thinks might be hard to spell. The words checked are probably the ones the student needs to look up when writing.

After the student has checked this master spelling list, which should be kept in a notebook, the teacher might give a series of spelling tests on words taken from it. After each test the student can check against the master list to see which words are actually his or her spelling "demons." The master list can be expanded or changed periodically to meet students' needs.

By using this list, the teacher will be prewarned about the spelling-difficulty level of certain words. Foreseeing students' probable spelling problems, the teacher can then plan ways to eliminate them.

---

[1] Arthur I. Gates, *Spelling Difficulties in 3,876 Words* (New York: Columbia University, 1937). Harry A. Greene, *The New Iowa Spelling Scale* (Iowa City: State University of Iowa, 1954) revised by Bradley M. Loomer (University of Iowa, 1977).

| Word (% Correct) | Most Common Misspelling | Word (% Correct) | Most Common Misspelling |
|---|---|---|---|
| abandon (49%) | | children's (45%) | |
| absolutely (41%) | absolutly | chocolate (48%) | |
| abundant (47%) | abundent | chorus (44%) | |
| acceptable (48%) | | Christian (49%) | Christain |
| acceptance (44%) | acceptence | circuit (27%) | |
| accepting (49%) | | circumstance (45%) | curcumstance |
| accommodate (24%) | accomodate | civilization (42%) | civilazation |
| accompanied (42%) | | cocoon (45%) | |
| accordance (49%) | accordence | collateral (12%) | |
| accustomed (30%) | | colonel (31%) | |
| achievement (36%) | | columns (40%) | |
| acknowledgment (25%) | | commencement (42%) | commencment |
| acquaint (28%) | | commercial (49%) | |
| acquire (35%) | aquire | commission (45%) | commision |
| adequate (22%) | | committed (37%) | |
| adjourned (43%) | | committee (34%) | |
| administration (45%) | addministration | communicate (48%) | |
| advertisement (46%) | advertisment | communication (48%) | comunication |
| affidavit (15%) | | compel (43%) | |
| agricultural (40%) | | competition (39%) | |
| all right (41%) | | compliment (39%) | complement |
| amendment (43%) | ammendment | conceive (39%) | |
| analysis (22%) | | condemn (33%) | condem |
| annual (43%) | anual | congratulations (41%) | |
| anticipate (27%) | antisipate | conscience (24%) | concience |
| anxiety (21%) | | conscious (13%) | |
| appetite (36%) | appitite | consequence (33%) | |
| applicant (43%) | | continuous (25%) | |
| appreciated (48%) | | controversy (27%) | |
| approximately (21%) | | convenience (23%) | |
| artificial (38%) | artifical | correspond (42%) | |
| association (47%) | | correspondence (34%) | |
| attorney (40%) | | council (40%) | |
| authority (45%) | | counsel (17%) | |
| available (41%) | | courteous (34%) | courtious |
| bankruptcy (19%) | | courtesy (41%) | curtesy |
| bearing (46%) | | crisis (31%) | |
| benefit (39%) | benifit | criticism (12%) | |
| bicycle (45%) | | curiosity (35%) | curiousity |
| bough (36%) | | cylinder (25%) | |
| boundary (49%) | boundry | day's (46%) | |
| bouquet (45%) | | debtor (38%) | |
| boys' (39%) | | deceive (49%) | |
| bulletin (38%) | bullitin | definite (38%) | |
| bureau (32%) | | definitely (21%) | |
| campaign (28%) | campain | definition (40%) | |
| cancellation (30%) | | delegate (41%) | |
| candidate (41%) | | deny (48%) | |
| capacity (44%) | | descend (29%) | decend |
| ceased (40%) | | despair (35%) | |
| challenge (49%) | | discipline (14%) | |
| characteristic (28%) | | discussed (49%) | |

59

| Word (% Correct) | Most Common Misspelling | Word (% Correct) | Most Common Misspelling |
|---|---|---|---|
| distinguish (36%) | | imagination (46%) | |
| distribution (49%) | | immediately (33%) | |
| doctrine (36%) | | immense (28%) | |
| dormitory (24%) | | immortal (44%) | imortal |
| earnestly (48%) | | incident (46%) | |
| economy (42%) | | incidentally (12%) | |
| edition (47%) | | inconvenience (33%) | |
| efficiency (13%) | | indefinitely (10%) | |
| efficient (25%) | | individual (41%) | |
| elapsed (46%) | | inevitable (24%) | |
| eligible (31%) | | initial (35%) | |
| eliminate (36%) | | initiation (23%) | |
| embroidery (34%) | | innocent (43%) | inocent |
| employees (42%) | | inquiry (46%) | |
| enclosure (47%) | | inspiration (45%) | |
| encouraging (38%) | | installation (33%) | |
| enthusiastic (41%) | | instinct (44%) | |
| epistle (18%) | | institutions (46%) | |
| equipped (24%) | equiped | intellectual (22%) | |
| exceptionally (37%) | | intelligence (37%) | |
| excessive (37%) | | interrupt (43%) | interupt |
| execute (42%) | | interval (49%) | |
| executive (31%) | | intimate (33%) | |
| exercise (49%) | | jealous (48%) | |
| exhaust (42%) | | laboratory (38%) | labratory |
| exhibition (29%) | exibition | legislation (48%) | |
| existence (23%) | | legislature (44%) | |
| experienced (46%) | | leisure (43%) | |
| extension (49%) | extention | liability (46%) | |
| extraordinary (33%) | | license (31%) | |
| extremely (43%) | | lieutenant (18%) | |
| facilities (31%) | | liquor (43%) | |
| faculty (48%) | | loyalty (48%) | |
| familiar (40%) | | luxury (43%) | |
| fascinating (20%) | | magnificent (49%) | magnificient |
| February (47%) | Febuary | manufacturer (37%) | |
| financial (34%) | | materially (44%) | |
| flu (41%) | | mathematics (35%) | |
| foliage (26%) | | maturity (46%) | |
| foreign (48%) | | mechanical (44%) | |
| fortunately (36%) | | merchandise (45%) | merchandize |
| gratitude (40%) | graditude | merely (49%) | |
| grieve (47%) | | minimum (38%) | |
| guarantee (16%) | | mortgage (16%) | morgage |
| guardian (47%) | gaurdian | mountains (44%) | |
| Halloween (49%) | | multiplication (41%) | |
| handkerchiefs (49%) | | murmur (38%) | murmer |
| heir (48%) | | mutual (41%) | |
| hygiene (31%) | | necessarily (22%) | |
| icicles (31%) | | niece (47%) | neice |
| ignorance (47%) | ignorence | occasionally (32%) | |
| illustration (44%) | | occurred (28%) | occured |

| Word (% Correct) | Most Common Misspelling | Word (% Correct) | Most Common Misspelling |
|---|---|---|---|
| offense (39%) | | regretting (41%) | |
| official (46%) | offical | reign (35%) | |
| opportunities (34%) | | remembrance (36%) | rememberance |
| oppose (49%) | | remittance (41%) | |
| ordinarily (29%) | | representative (36%) | representitive |
| originally (37%) | | requisition (14%) | |
| ornaments (47%) | | responsibility (40%) | |
| pamphlet (29%) | pamflet | restaurant (21%) | resturant |
| pamphlets (32%) | | reverence (49%) | |
| paradise (46%) | | scarcely (43%) | |
| parliament (16%) | parliment | schedule (37%) | |
| partial (29%) | | scheme (43%) | |
| particularly (47%) | | scholarship (46%) | |
| patience (44%) | | scissors (40%) | |
| patronage (42%) | | sensible (49%) | |
| peasant (47%) | | separate (41%) | |
| peculiar (36%) | pecular | separately (37%) | |
| perceive (28%) | | shepherd (39%) | |
| peril (27%) | | similar (43%) | similiar |
| permanent (46%) | | sincerely (49%) | sincerly |
| petition (35%) | | skiing (43%) | |
| philosophy (21%) | | skis (29%) | |
| physical (47%) | | solemn (30%) | |
| physician (38%) | | sorority (18%) | |
| pigeon (45%) | | specific (35%) | |
| pilgrims (41%) | | squirrel (41%) | |
| politician (21%) | | statistics (35%) | |
| positively (44%) | positivly | statues (28%) | |
| possess (31%) | | straightened (45%) | |
| possibility (45%) | posibility | substitute (49%) | subsitute |
| practically (36%) | | succeeded (42%) | succeded |
| precious (48%) | | successfully (46%) | |
| precisely (23%) | | succession (42%) | |
| preference (43%) | | sufficient (22%) | sufficiant |
| preferred (42%) | | sufficiently (29%) | |
| presence (46%) | presense | supplement (34%) | |
| principle (39%) | principal | survey (42%) | |
| prior (38%) | | suspicion (22%) | |
| privilege (22%) | | sympathy (45%) | |
| probability (45%) | | temporarily (20%) | |
| professional (46%) | | temporary (41%) | temperary |
| psychology (7%) | | tendency (42%) | |
| pursuit (33%) | | they're (40%) | |
| quantities (45%) | | thorough (24%) | |
| receipt (33%) | | thoroughly (22%) | |
| receiving (45%) | recieving | tongue (48%) | |
| recognized (45%) | | tournament (39%) | |
| recommend (30%) | | tradition (47%) | |
| recommended (31%) | | tragedy (30%) | |
| references (41%) | | transferred (37%) | transfered |
| referred (48%) | | unanimous (25%) | |
| refrigerator (44%) | | undoubtedly (25%) | |

| Word (% Correct) | Most Common Misspelling | Word (% Correct) |
|---|---|---|
| unfortunately (40%) | | veil (38%) |
| universal (49%) | | vein (43%) |
| unnecessary (25%) | unecessary | vicinity (45%) |
| urgent (43%) | | whether (49%) |
| utilize (37%) | | wholly (46%) |
| vacancies (39%) | | woman's (46%) |
| vague (37%) | | wretched (25%) |
| variety (42%) | | wrought (33%) |

# Chapter Six

# Context Clues

Context clues are words in a sentence that help the reader understand any unfamiliar words. By using context clues, the reader can often figure out the meaning of a word without looking it up in the dictionary. There are external context clues, which are within the sentence but outside the unknown word, and there are also internal context clues, which are roots and affixes that have meaning and can give the reader an idea of word meaning. In this chapter we discuss various kinds of context clues and strategies for teaching context-clue methods of word attack.

## External Context Clues

Students grow in their ability to use context clues when they are able to recognize the various kinds they might find within sentences. In their reading they may come across the following:

**Formal definition,** the meaning of a word expressed in direct statement. "Sportsmanship is the ability to get along with people not only in athletic competition but in daily life as well."

**Definition by example,** the meaning of a word expressed through a sample or representative of the word. "Sportsmanship is often demonstrated by two opposing players who shake hands after a contest."

**Definition by description,** the meaning of a word expressed in a description of the characteristics or physical qualities of the object or idea for which the word stands. "Sportsmanship is evidenced by a person who is enthusiastic and alert, who works together with teammates, and accepts the rules and conditions of the game."

**Definition by comparison and contrast,** the meaning of a word expressed by what it is like or not like. "A good sport, like a modest person, does not seek praise or try to attract attention." "A person who boasts, behaves in a disorderly fashion, or offers excuses in competition is not a good sport."

**Definition by synonyms and antonyms,** the meaning of a word expressed in terms of words which are similar or opposite in meaning. This is often one of the best and shortest defining devices. "Sportsmanship is fair play, winning or losing gracefully."

**Definition by apposition,** the meaning of a word expressed in a parenthetical word or phrase used to clarify or define. "Sportsmanship, a quality exhibited by Chris Evert-Lloyd, is encouraged by our coach."

To introduce elementary students to the use of different context clues, the teacher may structure a lesson through a number of different steps. To start, students may be shown several words they may not know. The teacher provides the meanings of the words and then asks students to answer questions that use the unknown words. Students learn the unknown words by using the definitions and clues in the sentences.

discover — find          escape — get free
miserable — unhappy      capture — take

1. Could someone **discover** a hidden treasure?
2. Would an animal want to **escape** from a cage?
3. Would you feel **miserable** if you were sick?
4. Could someone **capture** a snake?

To reinforce the concept of word meaning and context clues, the teacher can provide picture clues and a story for the students to complete using the words just discussed. Again, the teacher can point out words and phrases in the story that give clues to correct use of the new words.

| discover | capture |
| miserable | escape |

John and Amy were in the backyard. They lifted a rock to _____ a little bug hiding there. They wanted to _____ the bug and put it in a jar. They made holes in the jar lid. Then they caught the bug and put it inside. The bug felt _____. It wanted to be free. After a short time, they let the bug _____, and it quickly ran away.

## Clues to Word Meaning

The ability to infer the meaning of a word from its context depends on the clues given. It is important that students first read and use all the sentence or sentences for clues. For example, students might read, "Juan wore a warm sarape over his shoulders." The word "wore" gives one clue, but "over his shoulders" gives important additional information.

To give students practice in looking for context clues, the teacher may use the following pattern. Students are given sentences using words they may not know. Students are to mark the meaning of the underlined word in each sentence and circle the clue or clues that helped them.

1. We read the instructions for the kit, but the directions were not clear.
   (a) pieces of a puzzle    (b) an explanation of what to do
2. This sapling will grow into a beautiful dogwood tree.
   (a) a tree with flowers    (b) a young tree
3. The Mayas in Mexico used a system of hieroglyphics to write books and keep records.
   (a) a system of eating    (b) a system of writing

The following activity encourages students to use word clues in sentences by having them replace a nonsense word with a word that fits within the context of the sentence. Students are to cross out the nonsense word and choose a, b, or c to complete the sentence.

1. The principal will skibist the contest winner this afternoon.
   (a) speak    (b) announce    (c) collect
2. Look in the pribib to find information on giraffes.
   (a) encyclopedia    (b) package    (c) drawer
3. The plants will grow best on the ubinflot.
   (a) gravel    (b) windowsill    (c) leaves

Teachers can also provide a complete paragraph for students to read. Students then write the meanings of underlined words, using context clues and a dictionary if they need help.

The job of removing, 1. dismantling, and putting back together an entire engine seemed 2. formidable to me, so I was surprised by Phil's 3. nonchalant attitude toward the project. I felt some worry and 4. apprehension about getting the job done correctly. Phil, however, didn't shrink or 5. flinch from getting started.

Using context clues will also help students understand sentences that include words with multiple meanings. In the pattern below, students choose the meaning of the underlined word in each sentence.

1. The plane will land at the airport.
   In the sentence, land means ___?___.    (a) come to a stop
                                           (b) ground
2. I have some change in my pocket.
   In the sentence, change means ___?___.    (a) switch    (b) coins
3. Squirrels store nuts for the winter months.
   In the sentence, store means ___?___.    (a) shop    (b) put away

A variation of this activity also gives students practice in the format of standardized tests. Students are given a word and five meanings. They are to choose the meaning that fits the word as it is used in each sentence. Students mark the letter of the meaning.

**board**    a. a flat piece of lumber    b. a cardboard surface for playing a game    c. food or meals    d. a group of people in charge of a company or club    e. to live at a school or other place where meals are provided

1. We set up a checkerboard on the table.    ⓐ ⓑ ⓒ ⓓ ⓔ
2. My sister is going to board at school.    ⓐ ⓑ ⓒ ⓓ ⓔ
3. The board of directors of the theater group is meeting today.    ⓐ ⓑ ⓒ ⓓ ⓔ
4. We paid for our room and board when we were on vacation.    ⓐ ⓑ ⓒ ⓓ ⓔ
5. Amy put a board across two blocks to make a book shelf.    ⓐ ⓑ ⓒ ⓓ ⓔ

# Using Precise Words

Through activities such as the above, students learn that the more they know the exact meanings of words, the more they will understand what they read. The teacher should also point out to students that it is important to use the right word when they are speaking and writing. Words that are very general don't give much information. If students use precise words when they speak and write, they will convey their meaning all the more clearly.

The following exercises give students practice in using exact words. Such exercises not only help students think about word meaning, but demonstrate how precise language makes writing more colorful and interesting.

Students match the words with their meanings and then choose the best word to write in each space to complete a paragraph.

fresh  •    • never used before
young  •    • in the early part of life
new  •    • in the present time
modern •    • just made or grown

A class of _____ children visited the city's bakery. This was a _____ experience for these children. They saw the _____ equipment that is used to make the baked goods. Each child was given a _____ loaf of bread to take home.

Students write the word from the box that fits best in each sentence.

> The words **just, suitable,** and **correct** all mean "right."

1. Is my answer to this math problem _____?
2. Did the judge make a _____ decision?
3. Will my green shirt be _____ for the party?

Students circle the word that best replaces the word **move** or **moved** in each sentence.

1. The peacock moved proudly across the lawn.
       stumbled    strutted    hurried

2. Tired and hungry, Josh moved down the road.
   galloped     swooped     trudged
3. The frightened deer moved across the field.
   bounded     tiptoed     plodded
4. In autumn it is fun to move through the woods.
   limp     wander     lope

Students write a more precise word to replace the word in parentheses in each sentence. They may be encouraged to use a thesaurus if they need help finding words.

1. Tim was (sad) when his dog was lost for two weeks.
2. We thought it was (funny) when the circus clowns threw buckets of water at each other.
3. The glowing reflection of the sunset on the water was (pretty).
4. Luke gave a practical, (smart) solution to our problem.

## Comparison and Contrast

Comparison and contrast are context clues that students can look for to help them figure out the meanings of words. Comparative definitions often extend beyond simple comparisons to implied ones, using various figures of speech. The comparison clue may range from a simple simile, "the moon is shaped like a ball," to Shakepeare's personification, "the inconstant moon, that monthly changes in her circled orb." Thus comparison allows the writer to be creative in his or her descriptions and gives the reader meaning beyond a direct definition.

Contrast may help the reader by telling him what a word is not. While it does not give the reader an exact meaning, it can be a helpful device. For example, in the sentence "A whale is not a fish," the reader learns to classify whales apart from tuna, sharks, and swordfish. It does not tell what a whale is, how long it is, what it looks like. However, in a paragraph describing the whale, this clue helps the reader remember to file whales under mammals rather than under fish.

To teach comparison and contrast as context clues, the teacher might follow the pattern below. Students read each sentence and circle the correct answer.

1. The spectral tower loomed out of the mist like a phantom.
   **Spectral** could mean ___?___.     ghostly     made of stone
2. Although the manatee is not a fish, it spends much of its life swimming underwater.
   The **manatee** could be ___?___.     a shark     a mammal
3. A seemingly endless horde of ants moved across the path like an army.
   A **horde** could be ___?___.     a small group     a large group

Comparison and contrast can also show what a word cannot mean.
1. The plot of the story was as intricate as a complicated knot.
   **Intricate** could not mean ___?___.     simple     puzzling

2. While the sun beat down on the <u>macadam</u>, the parking lot seemed as hot as an oven.
   **Macadam** could not be ___?___.      pavement      an ice rink
3. The <u>potpourri</u> made my closet as fragrant as a meadow full of flowers.
   **Potpourri** could not be ___?___.      a fish      dried flower petals

In the following activity, students circle the phrase that gives the best clue to the meaning of the underlined word. Students may use a dictionary if needed.
1. Jason's body was as <u>supple</u> as ___?___.      an acrobat's
                                                       a tree trunk
2. The big package was as <u>unwieldy</u> as ___?___.      a boulder      a book
3. Pam felt as <u>exuberant</u> as ___?___.      a statue
                                                  a fan of a winning team

A particular kind of comparison is called an *analogy*. Analogies are comparisons of words or ideas that have something in common or are allike in some way. Practice making analogies will help students think about word meanings.

To introduce students to analogies, the teacher might ask how two words such as *lead* and *pencil* go together, then how *ink* and *pen* go together. Students can complete a sentence using the two pairs: Lead is to _____ just as ink is to _____ .

To continue, students can match words that go together and use the words to finish the sentences.

1. sleep      chair      You sit in a _____ just as you would sleep in
   sit        bed        a _____ .
2. birds      fly        _____ can fly just as _____ can swim.
   fish       swim
3. room       tree       A room is part of a _____ just as a _____ is
   branch     house      part of a tree.

Students circle the correct words to complete each analogy.
1. Air conditioning is to (summer   large) as heating is to (loud   winter).
2. Stove is to (metal   cook) as car is to (ride   wash).
3. Enter is to (exit   door) as come is to (visit   go).

The teacher will want to point out that analogies can compare many different things. They can compare synonyms, antonyms, objects and their use, parts to the whole, things and groups they belong to. In the next activity, students mark the word that correctly completes each analogy. Then they indicate the kind of comparison being made.

1. Heel is to shoe as kickstand is to: (a) foot (b) bike (c) ride.
   compares antonyms
   compares parts to the whole
2. Always is to never as many is to: (a) forever (b) few (c) much.
   compares antonyms
   compares parts to the whole

3. Shriek is to scream as cry is to: (a) sniff (b) weep (c) soft.
   compares synonyms
   compares an object and its use
4. Ruler is to measuring as shears are to: (a) cutting (b) writing (c) cooking.
   compares synonyms
   compares an object and its use

# Appositives

Appositives provide easily recognized information defining or clarifying words in context without breaking the flow of the reading content. Nonrestrictive appositives are set off by commas: "I invited Mrs. Kellerman, my neighbor, to our school play." When appositives are restrictive and necessary to the meaning of the main clause commas are not used: "My cousin Christopher is coming to visit (but not my cousin Lisa)."

Authors often use appositives to avoid verbosity. The teacher may show students how three sentences can become one:

a. Abraham Lincoln was our sixteenth president. He was assassinated by John Wilkes Booth in a theater. Booth was a Shakespearean actor.
b. Abraham Lincoln, our sixteenth president, was assassinated in a theater by John Wilkes Booth, a Shakespearean actor.

Students can read sentences and paragraphs containing appositives and then answer questions about what they read.

1. The tortoise, a land turtle, can grow to be very large.
   What is a tortoise?     (a) a land animal     (b) a large fish
2. The pumpkin, a yellowish-orange fruit, grows on a vine.
   What is a pumpkin?     (a) a vine     (b) a fruit

Mrs. Howard, our teacher, took our class on a hike. We followed the trail, a small path, through the woods. We stopped to pick buttercups, small yellow flowers, to take home with us. An old oak, a very tall tree, was fun to climb. We even fed some ducks in the pond.
1. Who is Mrs. Howard?     (a) a mother     (b) a teacher
                           (c) a neighbor
2. What is a trail?     (a) a forest     (b) a pond     (c) a path
3. What are buttercups?     (a) trees     (b) bushes     (c) flowers
4. What is an oak?     (a) a tree     (b) a bird     (c) a duck

## Connective Words and Phrases in Context

One reliable test of a person's reading skill is the ability to understand the meaning of a conjunction or a preposition in context. Often we must study the context of the sentence to know what meaning to ascribe to prepositions and conjunctions. Note the following examples:

1. Around the campfire, the scouts used tree stumps and logs <u>for</u> (in place of) stools.
2. The boys had a surprise birthday party <u>for</u> (in honor of) Don.
3. He was happy with his present—a book called *Science Fiction Tales for* (suited to) *Boys and Girls*.

The word *since* is another example:

1. I have not seen her <u>since</u> (from then until now) Christmas.
2. I have not seen her, <u>since</u> (because) Christmas is the only time we get together.

Such discriminations may not become apparent without considerable practice. Teachers are advised to present conjunctions such as *before* (previously, in front of), *but* (only, except that, yet), *as* (because, during the time that) and other connecting words in a variety of contexts until students can read and use them effectively.

Conjunctions show how ideas are related, and there are times we use a pair of conjunctions to express a particular meaning. Conjunction pairs are called correlatives and usually connect parallel constructions. The teacher may present correlatives and have students complete sentences:

> **as/as** means "equally"
> **both/and** means "one and the other"
> **either/or** means "one or the other"
> **neither/nor** means "not one or the other"
> **not only/but also** means "in addition to"
> **whether/or** means "if this or that happens"

1. I will see you this summer _____ you go to camp _____ stay home.
2. Because of the rain, _____ Mike _____ Pat could come over.
3. _____ I do my chores this afternoon _____ I cannot go to the game.
4. We played _____ hard _____ the other team.
5. Mr. Thornton _____ grows peas and carrots in his garden _____ cultivates roses and tulips.
6. While touring the country we traveled _____ by bus _____ by train.

## Internal Context Clues

In addition to the external clues discussed above, students should be taught to look for internal context clues. Our studies indicate that many students from the fourth to the twelfth grades have not learned to use internal clues to figure out word meaning. The internal context-clue method is not used because students are not taught early and regularly that prefixes, roots, and suffixes have meaning. However, through a systematic approach to the study of roots and affixes as described in Chapters 2 and 3, the student can learn a number of key word parts and can easily acquire the habit of analyzing whole words by breaking them into their meaningful parts.

The importance of learning to use the internal context clue can be seen by scanning typical material read by elementary, high school, and college students. As the material becomes more abstract, and therefore more difficult, the number of words that are compounds of key roots and affixes becomes greater. Names of inventions, the areas of politics, medicine, and so on, often use Greek or Latin words, or compounds of Greek and Latin combining forms (roots): *television* (from Greek *tele,* distance, + Latin *vis,* see); *appendicitis* (from Latin *appendic,* hang on, + Greek *-itis,* inflammation); *bursitis* (from Latin *bursa,* purse, sac, + Greek *-itis*).

Our study of children's knowledge of words indicates that, in general, students are not making associations between words such as *reduce* and *reduction* or *receive* and *reception.* Our studies show that 74 percent of fourth-graders know *pretend;* but *pretense,* the noun form of *pretend,* is not commonly known until the twelfth grade (at a score of 78 percent).

The authors believe that the skillful, systematic presentation of key roots and affixes can, over a period of time, increase the general level of vocabulary by half a grade.

A student who is led to discover that the prefixes *non-, un-,* and *in-* mean "not" immediately gets the idea of negation when he sees the words *nonvoter, nonreligious, nonfiction; unable, unfit, unalterable; inactive, inappropriate, inalienable.* Likewise, the student can be taught to notice key roots in words. For example, *scrib* or *script* in a word gives the reader a clue that the word has something to do with writing, as in *scrib*e, in*scrib*e, post*script, script*ure, and pre*script*ion.

Learning key word parts from words already known, such as *auto* (self) in *automobile,* is an effective way of using transfer of knowledge to other words: *autograph, autobiography, automotive, automatic, autocratic*— all carrying the meaning of self.

Frequent guided practice in using roots and affixes helps students in generalizing and conceptualizing. Using key word parts the student can classify objects according to a general characteristic. For example, the student can learn to categorize words ending in *-et, -ette* as referring to something small (*kitchenette, dinette, novelette*). The student can easily learn to use additional suffixes meaning "small," such as *-let* (*streamlet, booklet, droplet*); *-ling (duckling, gosling, sapling, suckling*); and *-cule, -ule, -icle* (*molecule, globule, particle*).

As we have previously suggested, exercises that help the student classify help him or her conceptualize. The learner categorizes before he or she discriminates. We can help the student gain vocabulary skills by organizing learning in advance and setting up a learning system. Once the student recognizes the meanings of key word parts in known words, he or she uses less energy learning other words containing the same word parts.

## Context Clues and Reading Skills

The particular meaning of a word generally depends on its relationship to other words in a phrase or sentence—its context. Therefore, the student needs to learn how to use these various kinds of context clues to determine meanings of words in reading, thus bringing meaning to the printed page to get meaning out of it.

But we should not assume that using context clues to determine word meaning will solve all vocabulary problems. Some teachers overestimate the power of context clues to reveal word meaning. Sometimes context does not help, as in the sentence "The boy spoke with alacrity." *Alacrity* might mean bitterness, sympathy, cheerfulness—any number of things.

Throughout this book we stress the need for attention not only to the context within which words are found but also to the structure and analysis of the word itself. The relative importance of the word *per se* as pointed out by Charles H. Judd many years ago still holds true:

> It has been said that a word which does not call up some past experience is an utterly barren item in the pupil's mental life. The truth is that many words when first heard do not arouse interpretive experiences. It is enough in these cases if the word becomes a motive for seeking an idea. If the pupil is aroused by a word to look for further experiences to attach to it, then the word which is at first without meaning may be a very potent instrument of instruction.[1]

One of the fundamental aims of an effective vocabulary program is to draw the student's attention to words. Heavy reliance on context clues alone as a word-study method may defeat this purpose. Therefore, we suggest that in teaching vocabulary the teacher be aware of many ways of making students word-conscious, of helping them develop a conscience about word discrimination and precision in somewhat the way they develop a spelling conscience.

In developing word sensitivity students need to make use of context clues in relation to other methods of vocabulary study. They need to see the relationship between cognates, derivatives, and word families. They need to learn the significance of word inflection, the process of word formation by means of roots, prefixes, suffixes, and compounds. And they need to be aware of the roles of the various parts of speech, such as connectives (prepositions and conjunctions) that relate ideas and concepts.

[1]Charles Hubbard Judd, *Reading: Its Nature and Development*, Chicago: The University of Chicago Press, 1918 , p. 178.

# Chapter Seven

# Figures of Speech

Effective speakers and writers make much use of figures of speech to get their ideas across. Such rhetorical devices were used by Cicero and by Suetonius, the Roman novelist who used *figūra* to mean a hint or an allusion. A figure of speech is picturesque, imaginative language used to heighten effect by comparing or identifying a particular thing with another, more familiar thing. Notice how the use of figurative language changes connotation, as in the two sentences below:

1. That fullback is much bigger than the halfback.
2. That fullback is a giant beside the halfback.

In the first sentence the comparison is *literal* (made between nouns in the same class—persons who are football players). In the second sentence the comparison is *figurative*—the fullback is made to appear like something else. The comparison of the fullback to a giant exaggerates the size of the fullback for effect. (This figure of speech, hyperbole, is discussed later in this unit.)

In this chapter we will discuss the following figures of speech:

**Personification:** "Resolved to take Fate by the throat and shake a living out of her." (Louisa May Alcott gives Fate personal qualities.)

**Simile:** "But pleasures are like poppies spread—You seize the flow'r, its bloom is shed." (Robert Burns makes a direct comparison.)

**Metaphor:** "Robed in the long night of her deep hair." (Alfred, Lord Tennyson makes an implied comparison.)

**Hyperbole:** "Bowed by the weight of centuries he leans upon his hoe and gazes on the ground." (Edwin Markham exaggerates.)

**Onomatopoeia:** "You'd hear the thunder let go with an awful crash, and then go rumbling, grumbling, tumbling down the sky." (Mark Twain uses words that sound like their referent.)

**Slang:** "What really knocks me out is a book that, when you're all done reading it, you wish the author that wrote it was a terrific friend of yours." (J.D. Salinger uses nonstandard language for effect.)

**Euphemism:** "Into the darkness they go, the wise and the lovely. Crowned/ With lilies and with laurel they go; but I am not resigned." (Edna St. Vincent Millay euphemizes death.)

These are the most common figures of speech. Others listed below will be covered in this text and can be discussed in class when appropriate.

**Oxymoron:** "A likely impossibility is always preferable to an unconvincing possibility." (Aristotle combines contradictory or incongruous terms.)

**Metonymy:** "The pen is mightier than the sword." (Edward Bulwer-Lytton uses *pen* and *sword* to stand for literature and physical force.)

**Synecdoche:** "'Tis God gives skill,/But not without men's hands: He could not make/Antonio Stradivari's violins/Without Antonio."(George Eliot [Marian Evans Cross] uses a part to represent the whole man and his talent.)

**Litotes:** "There is no little enemy." (Benjamin Franklin makes a statement by denying its opposite.)

# Personification

Personification is from the Latin *persona,* meaning person, actor, or mask worn in a drama, + *fic,* meaning to make. Hence when we use personification we give human or personal qualities to inanimate things or ideas. Thus a ship is referred to as *she.* Its foghorn *moans.*

We often personify the forces of life, nature, and civilization. We speak of *Father* Time and *Mother* Earth, the *mother* country and the *father*land. We say that "Justice is blind," representing justice as a blindfolded woman holding a balance scale.

Personification may run through a whole poem or story. Young children grow up with rhymes and stories that make things and animals seem like people—*Winnie the Pooh* by A.A. Milne, *Frog and Toad* by Arnold Lobel, *Peter Rabbit* by Beatrix Potter, *Charlotte's Web* and *Stuart Little* by E.B. White, and many others.

Personification continues to be used at all levels of literature. In Shelley's poem "The Cloud," the personified cloud speaks:
I bring fresh showers for the thirsting flowers . . .
I sift the snow on the mountains below . . .
I am the daughter of Earth and Water,
And the nursling of the Sky.

Longfellow says,
The green trees whispered low and mild.

In *Romeo and Juliet,* Friar Lawrence says,
The gray-eyed morn smiles on the frowning night.

In "The First Snowfall," Lowell says,
Every pine and fir and hemlock
Wore ermine too dear for an earl.

In classroom instruction, discussion about personification can help young students separate real from make-believe as well as stretch their vocabularies. At the elementary level students should be able to identify examples and create their own examples of personification.

# Simile

Another example of figurative language is *simile*. Simile (from Latin *similis*, like) is a direct comparison between things, often using the clue words *as, like, than, as . . . as,* or *so . . . as.* Notice the simile in "He fought like a tiger." His fighting is likened to that of a tiger.

Similes help us illustrate our thoughts and ideas with references to external things: persons, objects, nature. Thus a heavy person may be said to be "as big as a house." Someone else may be "as sly as a fox."

Before students can use similes effectively in speaking and writing, they must be able to recognize them. One approach is to have them work with similes that are phrases they already know but do not associate with similes. Students may be asked to match parts of a simile, or to write the name of something to fit a description.

| | | | | |
|---|---|---|---|---|
| 1. as tall as | a clown | 4. as quiet as | silk |
| 2. as funny as | grass | 5. as fast as | a mouse |
| 3. as green as | a tree | 6. as smooth as | the wind |

What could be . . . as bright as the sun? . . . as light as a feather? . . . as straight as an arrow?

To emphasize the colorful and interesting quality of similes, students can be given multiple-choice phrases to replace words in similes.

1. Jason looked as happy as a <u>clam</u>.
   a. bent stick     b. dog with a bone     c. hungry lion
2. Tina moved as slowly as a <u>turtle</u>.
   a. wagon with square wheels     b. rusty nail     c. jet plane
3. Tom's boots felt like <u>lead</u>.
   a. two cement blocks     b. fluffy clouds     c. falling leaves

Students can also be given similes that have become clichés and asked to create original comparisons.

# Metaphor

A figure of speech often adds punch to a sentence. *Metaphor,* for example, can help a speaker or writer paint a clear picture through comparison or contrast. *Metaphor* comes from Greek *metaphora,* meaning "transfer," from *meta,* over, + *pherein,* to carry. A metaphor draws a comparison between two things to create a vivid mental image, although it is not introduced by the *like* or *as* of the simile. For example, Shakespeare says, "All the world's a stage." John Donne wrote,

No man is an island, entire of itself;
Every man is a piece of the continent,
a part of the main.

People often make the mistake of assuming that metaphors are rare. On the contrary, metaphors are so abundant and we use them so frequently that it is often hard to judge whether a word is really a metaphor or not. Almost every word we use is metaphorized to some extent. For example, the word *fall* ranges in meaning from "dropping down from a higher place" to the metaphorical meaning of the *Fall of Man* as used by Milton. Several other meanings *fall* in between: his eyes *fell;* he *fell* into sin; he has *fallen* from high estate.

In addition, a city may *fall* to the enemy; a soldier may *fell* his enemy; one may *fall* asleep or *fall* in love or *fall* into a bad habit. In the word *fallen,* the accent *falls* on the first syllable. Longfellow says, "The shades of night are *falling* fast." These phrases, like the *fall* (autumn) of the year, are metaphorical extensions of the original concept of *fall:* to drop down.

It might be argued that while metaphor is applicable to literature, sociology, and art, you must choose accurate terms when dealing with the cold, clear logic of a science. Consider the subject of magnetism, for example: Like poles *repel* each other; unlike poles *attract* each other. *Repel* and *attract* are used metaphorically. Gravity is often described metaphorically as the force that pulls an object toward the earth. Newton said in his law of gravitation that "all objects *attract* one another."

Teachers might provide sentences with metaphors and have students identify the two things being compared and the meaning of the metaphor in each.

1. The storm clouds were dark giants.
   a. very loud     b. huge and dark     c. rolling across the sky
2. After a summer without rain, our backyard was a desert.
   a. windy     b. hot and dry     c. muddy
3. After I walked through the snowstorm without my gloves, my fingers were icicles.
   a. hard     b. very cold     c. broken

Like similes, many metaphors have become clichés through overuse. Students can become more aware of metaphors and language by writing the meaning of familiar metaphors.

1. When I asked the question, Paula clammed up.
2. Why is Charlie such an eager beaver?
3. Bob let the cat out of the bag when he told Pam about the party.

Metaphors involving parts of the body are common to our daily language, so much so that we may not even think about their meaning. Students can discuss some of the metaphorical words and phrases listed below and what they mean.

| | |
|---|---|
| keep an eye on | heads up |
| give me a hand | lend an ear |
| has a green thumb | stick your neck out |
| was up to her chin | you said a mouthful |
| face grew red | he got an earful |
| caught her eye | splitting hairs |
| break my heart | back on her feet again |

see eye to eye    face the music
won by a nose    foot the bill
put your foot in your mouth    get it off your chest

In the exercise below, the student chooses the phrase that best defines the metaphorical expression.

1. "Putting your nose to the grindstone" means __?__ .
   a. to be punished    b. to work hard    c. to have a nose operation
2. People with a "finger in every pie" are __?__ .
   a. big eaters    b. selfish    c. involved in many activities
3. "To get something off your chest" means __?__ .
   a. to take off your coat    b. to tell something    c. to realize a goal
4. "Thumbs down" means __?__ .
   a. to disapprove    b. to approve    c. to consider

Other familiar metaphors involve color words and dimension words. Children learn the names of colors early. Therefore, reference to color is an easy and fruitful way of teaching students to recognize metaphors. Well-known sayings can be used to introduce the concept of metaphor; then students can be encouraged to create their own metaphors.

green with envy    once in a blue moon
purple with rage    silver-tongued orator
in a blue mood    in the red; in the black
a red-letter day    yellow journalism
in the pink of condition    a black sheep

narrow-minded    short-sighted
broad-minded    in narrow straits
high hopes    thick-headed person
low in spirits    a tall tale
deep in thought    through thick and thin
a narrow point of view    a slim chance of winning

It might be pointed out to students that we can make metaphors by adding the suffix -ine to certain words. The Latin word for *dog* is *canis.* Add -ine and the word becomes *canine,* meaning "like a dog." Other words that might be familiar to students include *aquiline, asinine, bovine, elephantine, equine, ermine, feline, leonine,* and *serpentine.*

## Hyperbole

*Hyperbole* is a Greek word meaning "extravagance," from *hyper-,* beyond, + *ballein,* to throw. Hyperbole is an exaggeration for effect, a figure of speech in which truth is stretched. Some examples of hyperbole are as follows:

I haven't seen him in a million years.
I was scared to death.
She is up to her neck in work.
He hits the ball a mile.

Students can have fun with exaggeration by choosing the phrase that best demonstrates hyperbole. The teacher may also provide sentence starters for students to complete on their own.

1. I am ten years old and I am the best baseball player in
   a. the school.     b. the neighborhood.     c. the country.
2. I usually hit a home run
   a. twice in a game.     b. once a week.     c. every five seconds.
3. The wind was so strong it could knock down a _____ .
4. It snowed a lot yesterday. The snow was _____ feet deep.

Students can also be given factual statements and asked to rewrite the sentences using hyperbole. For example:
   My cat is big.
   My cat is so big that I can sit on her back and take a ride.
Students can rewrite sentences such as:
   I can run fast.
   My desk is a mess.
   I ate a lot of pizza.

An interesting lesson can be structured around the use of hyperbole in advertising. Teachers can point out how TV and magazine advertisements use exaggeration for effect: "We make the best sandwiches in the world!" "This is the scariest movie you will ever see!" "Everyone loves these pickles!" Students can be asked to write their own advertisement for a particular product, exaggerating its qualities.

## Onomatopoeia

Some words are the names of sounds. These are called *onomatopoeia,* from the Greek *onomat,* name, + *poiein,* to make. The word *purr* sounds like a noise made by a contented cat. The word *tick-tock* sounds like the noise a clock makes.

Young students will be familiar with the words that name animal sounds. They can make animal sounds and match the sound words with pictures of the appropriate animals: *baa*/sheep; *moo*/cow; *oink*/pig; *cluck*/chicken; *quack*/duck; *neigh*/horse; *bark*/dog.

Slightly older students can be introduced to onomatopoeia by being told to listen to the sounds around them, or to imagine the sounds they hear in the morning as they wake up. The teacher can ask students to write the words that name the sounds they hear. Some possibilities might include the *hum* of lights overhead, the *squeak* or *click* of shoes as someone walks down the hall, the *whiz* of cars outside, the *pitter-patter* of rain, the *sizzle* of bacon, and the *popping* of toast.

Teachers might point out that some birds were named for the sounds they make. If students were to listen closely to a *bobwhite,* a *chickadee,* a *whip-poor-will,* or a *cuckoo,* they would think the bird was saying its name.

Students should understand that onomatopoeia helps us see and hear things in our minds, gives us clues to help us understand what we are reading, and makes writing and reading more interesting. Students can be given sound words and asked to imagine who or what might make the sounds. For students with a strong visual sense, it can be fun to write sound words in a way that illustrates the sound:

1. s-c-r-i-t-c-h s-c-r-a-t-c-h

2. creak

3. bubble-pop-bubble

4. ≤ROAR≡

## Slang

*Slang* expressions are nonstandard figures of speech, popular words and phrases used in ways not yet acceptable in formal writing or speaking. Students should understand that slang is a way of experimenting with the language. Most slang expressions—*twenty-three skidoo; Oh, you kid*—die out after a period of time. But each slang word or expression (often a metaphor) has a chance to become an accepted word if it stands the tests of time and utility. Some words make it: *blackmail, lynch,* and *hoax.* The word *okay,* or *O.K.,* is firmly set in the language in an informal sense. *Lousy* (bad; of low quality) has been a "permanent" slang word for over two hundred years. Slang is not necessarily bad usage. The best speakers and writers find themselves using slang for effect.

For students, slang is an interesting subject and one that makes language fun. Teachers can illustrate the shift in meaning between standard usage and slang by providing sentences and different interpretations.

"That movie was cool!" What does the speaker mean?
a. The theater was chilly.     b. The film was very good.
"You're right, it was great!" Here, the word **great** means __?__ .
a. very good     b. very large

Some slang expressions are shortened forms of longer words. The dictionary eventually classifies many of these words as "informal": *gas, phone, bike, hi, lab, gym.*

Compounds are another source of slang expressions: *copycat, butterfingers, bookworm, lazybones, hothead.* Metaphors are clearly seen in slang expressions such as "The car was a lemon," "He's a good egg," and "I don't have enough bread to buy the record."

Teachers should emphasize that while slang makes our language more colorful, it is not always correct to use. When students are talking to a friend, slang is all right. But when they are giving a talk in class, writing a letter to a company, describing a problem to a doctor, or writing an essay, slang is not correct.

In the exercise below, students are asked to circle the slang expression in each sentence, then write the sentence again using a standard word or phrase for the slang expression.

1. I had to work my head off to finish in time.
2. I saw a neat baseball game last night.
3. It bugs me when my brother borrows my bike.
4. The class picnic was a real blast.

## Euphemism

While figures of speech such as personification, simile, and metaphor are based on similarity, *euphemism* is based on contrast. We use euphemism to express a disagreeable or unpleasant fact indirectly. Death, for example, is described in a variety of ways: "passed away," "passed on," "expired," "breathed his last," "is taken back to God."

The word *euphemism* itself is from the Greek *euphemizein,* meaning "to speak with fair words," from *eu,* good, + *phanai,* speak. The Greeks used euphemism to placate the Erinyes (the Furies), three females who avenged unpunished crimes. Afraid to call them by their original, older name, and hoping to avoid unpleasantness by saying something pleasant, the Greeks called the Erinyes *Eumenides,* a euphemism which means "the well-meaning," "the soothed goddesses."

We use euphemisms for every occasion. We *stretch the truth* instead of *tell a lie;* we buy a *previously owned car* instead of a *used car;* a room is *extremely untidy* instead of *messy.* Students can practice writing euphemisms for direct words or expressions. They may also write direct words for euphemisms.

rude _____          not very becoming _____
out of work _____   somewhat worn _____
very sick _____     exceedingly exhausted _____
sweat _____         not very appetizing _____

## Oxymorons

One of the literary devices writers use to get an effect is the *oxymoron.* The word *oxymoron* comes from two Greek words, *oxys,* sharp, + *moros,* foolish; it is the use of contradictory or incongruous words together.

In *Romeo and Juliet,* Juliet says, "Parting is such *sweet sorrow.*" In conversation some people might refer to an act of *cruel kindness.* At first students may think such phrases are nonsensical. Teachers may use the examples listed below to discuss the effect of oxymorons and to determine which have meaning for the students. Students may be asked to make up oxymorons of their own or to find examples in their reading.

| | |
|---|---|
| thunderous silence | open disguise |
| trained incapacity | gentle strength |
| studied imprecision | orderly chaos |
| exquisite torture | humble pride |
| a hotbed of apathy | hopeful pessimist |
| priceless unessentials | creative anxiety |
| sad laughter | planned spontaneity |
| bittersweet | sublime folly |

## Metonymy

*Metonymy,* from the Greek *meta,* change, + *onym,* name, is the use of the name of one thing for that of another which it suggests. In metonymy one thing is said but another thing is meant. "I like to read Poe" means "I like to read Poe's works." *The Crown* might mean *the king. The press* can mean *newspaper and television reporters.*

Metonymy is so commonly used it is often unrecognized as such. "Put on your glasses" means "Put on your spectacles" (a word seldom used now). Here metonymy allows us to use the name of the material (glass) to represent the object made from the material (spectacles). Likewise, "I'd like a glass of milk" means "I'd like a drinking glass full of milk."

Other examples are as follows:

"The world is shocked" really means "The people of the world are shocked."

*City Hall* can refer to the mayor and his administration. *The court* can refer to the judge and jury.

When we pledge allegiance to the flag we really mean to the country which the flag symbolizes.

In the following exercise, students are to write what the underlined word or words actually mean.

1. A watched pot never boils.
   (a pot of liquid such as water, broth, or soup)
2. France was competing against Spain for the soccer championship.
   (the teams or team players of France and Spain)
3. The town prepared for the expected hurricane.
   (the people of the town)

## Synecdoche

*Synecdoche* (sĭ nĕk' də kē) literally means to supply something to what's been said. For example, if someone says, "India has too many mouths to feed," you must supply the rest: whole bodies, human beings, Indians. Synecdoche is a figure of speech in which a part is used for the whole.

Synecdoche is a kind of metonymy, but it is sufficiently different to be classified as a separate figure of speech. The teacher should not insist on the student making a neat distinction between metonymy and synecdoche although an explanation might, on occasion, be necessary. An easy way to illustrate the distinction follows:

*Metonymy:* Let out more *canvas.* (Actually refers to the *sail,* which is *made of canvas.*)

*Synecdoche:* They saw a hundred *sail* on the horizon. (The *sail* is a *part of the whole ship.*)

Additional examples of synecdoche are:

All *hands* on deck (all sailors on deck).

Two hundred *head* of cattle (two hundred animals).

The British Museum houses the Elgin *Marbles* (Greek statues).

In the exercise below, students are to circle the word that describes the underlined figure of speech in each sentence.

1. Many <u>great minds</u> of history have debated the question endlessly.
   hyperbole     synecdoche     simile
2. If I hear that joke once more, I'm going to go <u>stark raving mad.</u>
   hyperbole     synecdoche     simile
3. The coach counted <u>noses</u> to see if the entire team was present.
   hyperbole     synecdoche     simile

## Litotes

The opposite of hyperbole is *litotes* (līt' ə tēz'), from the Greek *litos,* plain, simple. Litotes is a figure of speech that makes an assertion about something by denying its opposite. For example, "London is *no mean city*" means "London is a *great* city."

Since we often tend to overlook or discount hyperbolic claims such as those of advertising agencies (*the greatest, superb, outstanding, gigantic,* and so on) we may use litotes to catch attention, or to emphasize a point by stating it negatively.

Other examples of litotes, or understatement, are as follows:

Leo Durocher *wasn't a bad ballplayer* when he was young.

Mary is *not unhappy* with her job.

I've just read *Kon-Tiki.* Crossing the Pacific Ocean on a forty-foot raft is *no small achievement.*

The teacher may ask students to write either litotes or hyperbole to complete sentences. The letter *L* or *H* in parentheses tells the students which figure of speech to use.

(**L**) 1. Winning the race demonstrated that June was __?__ swimmer.
(**H**) 2. The strawberry pie at my favorite restaurant is __?__ .
(**L**) 3. The team that won the championship is certainly __?__ .
(**H**) 4. Patrick began to regret having to take on the __?__ work.
(**L**) 5. The exotic flowers in the greenhouse have a __?__ scent.

# Chapter Eight

# Synonyms, Antonyms, Homophones

*Synonym* and *antonym* are words formed from the Greek root *onoma*, *onym*, meaning "name." Synonyms (from *syn*, together, like, + *onym*) are words that have the same or similar meanings: *fast, quick; tiny, little; frightened, terrified; boring, dull, tiresome.*

Synonyms not only help us convey general ideas, they also help us make fine distinctions between the meanings of words. Although the words *under, below,* and *beneath* are generally synonymous, we do not say we are living "beneath a democratic form of government"; we say "under a democratic form of government." A sunken ship is not 200 feet under sea level; it is 200 feet below sea level.

Contrasted with the synonym is the antonym (*anti* or *ant*, against), a word that means the opposite of another word: *open, shut; good, bad; genuine, imitation; harmony, discord.* Like the study of synonyms, the study of antonyms can help students learn words through the process of classification by helping them think of words in terms of comparative and contrasting relationships.

Words that sound the same but differ in spelling, origin, and meaning are called *homophones* (from the Greek *homo*, same, + *phon*, sound): *knew, new; won, one; bough, bow; mist, missed; sight, cite, site.*

## Synonyms in Vocabulary Development

Studying synonyms is an excellent time-saving approach to vocabulary study. Comparing synonyms helps the student see the relationship between words of similar meaning. It also helps the student generalize and classify words and concepts.

Synonyms are substitute words. They allow us to express the same idea in a variety of ways, although the overall context, the setting, the mood, and the tone of the speaker or writer may dictate the choice of the synonym to be used. Although the study of lists of synonyms helps the student to classify general concepts, of greater value is the development of the student's ability to make fine distinctions between synonyms.

But making fine distinctions is not easy. Students can best learn to distinguish the fine shades of meaning of words by (1) noting words that belong to within an overall concept such as "big" (*large, great, huge, enormous, bulky, massive, corpulent, monumental, prodigious, titanic, elephantine, herculean, leviathan, behemoth, gargantuan, macroscopic, Brobdingnagian*), and then (2) using them as the situation demands.

## Denotation and Connotation

The study of synonyms offers the teacher an excellent opportunity to teach concepts relating to the denotative and connotative aspects of vocabulary development. Dictionaries generally list the denotation (literal meaning) of a word. Such definitions (approximate at best) may be expanded by illustrative material such as pictures and synonyms.

But definition by synonym is useful only if the synonym is less difficult than the word being defined: *density* is *thickness* (the latter word is easier). David Berlo points out, in regard to denotative defining, that "when words are equally unfamiliar, we have gained nothing—and we probably have lost the receiver in the process."[1]

As opposed to the denotation, the connotation of a word is the circle of ideas and feeling surrounding that word and the emotions that the word evokes. We can see the difference between denotation and connotation in the synonyms for a given word. Each of the following synonyms for *prison*, for example, carries a different connotation: *house of correction, workhouse, jail, lockup, dungeon, hoosegow, calaboose, jug, pokey, clink, penitentiary, correctional facility.*

Note also that these connotative meanings involve varying experiences. Each synonym for *man*, for example, has, in addition to its denotation, its own special connotation: *male, husband, father, son, uncle, grandfather, brother, widower, gentleman, fellow, chap, beau, buddy, guy, blade.*

## Making Discriminations

It is clear that students cannot easily make fine distinctions between synonyms without a great deal of experience and practice. In vocabulary study, it is impractical to assume that fine discriminations can be made before gross discriminations are conceptualized.

Therefore, we suggest that students be provided with ample opportunity to make gross discriminations. They need to hear and see broad relationships between synonyms, see how words can be classified in broad categories or filing systems. They need to work with various forms of classification exercises.

The following are examples of activities on synonyms.

The student circles the two words that could finish each sentence.
1. The __?__ ladybug sat on a leaf.    top    little    tiny
2. I like to play with my __?__.    pal    friend    cup
3. Who lives in this __?__?    home    tree    house

The student chooses a synonym for each underlined word.
1. Please shut the door.    a. open    b. close    c. clock
2. This roast beef is tasty.    a. delicious    b. raw    c. tough
3. This is a great book!    a. scary    b. new    c. wonderful

---

[1] David Berlo, *The Process of Communication*, New York: Holt, Rinehart & Winston, 1960, pp. 193-194.

The student circles the words in each line that are synonyms.
1. jump        push        shove        start
2. huge        full         vacant       empty
3. limb        bush        leaves       branch
4. treat       stunt       picture     trick

The student crosses out the word in each line that is not a synonym.
1. fake        false        original     imitation
2. durable   strong     delicate    tough
3. clear       plain        apparent   confused
4. damage   bandage   injury     harm

For the following activities, students should be reminded that many words have more than one synonym, and the meanings of the synonyms may be slightly different. Choosing the right synonym depends upon how the word is used.

The student writes the best word to use in place of **get**.
**Buy, catch,** and **win** are synonyms for **get**.
1. I will get the ball you throw.
2. The fastest runner will get a prize.
3. Will you get a new sweater at the store?

The student circles the best synonym for the underlined word in each sentence.
1. When the nation finally became free, its citizens celebrated.
   generous       untied       independent
2 Mr. O'Hare is very free with his good advice.
   released      costless      generous
3. I heard that an elephant has gotten free from the zoo.
   independent     loose      generous
4. We decided to go when we found out the show was free.
   loose      costless      uncaged

Students replace each word in parentheses with a synonym from the box. They will use each synonym twice, and it will have a different meaning each time.

| keen    slim    serious |
| --- |

The hikers were (eager) _____ to reach the cabin. The approaching storm could be (dangerous) _____ . Already, a (sharp) _____ wind was blowing, and the possibility of finding a cave to shelter in was (unlikely)_____ . "Come on," said the guide, a tall, (thin) _____ woman. Her expression was (solemn) _____ .

## Variability of Language

The teacher can stress the variability of language by pointing out that many common objects have different names. In Maine, if you ask for a milk shake, you get it without ice cream. If you want ice cream in it, you ask for a frappe. Depending on the region, a sandwich on a long, crusty roll is called a hero, a hoagie, a submarine, or a grinder.

Some people sit in the living room; others in the front room. Some sit on a sofa; others on a couch. A chest of drawers may also be a bureau or a dresser. Some fry in a skillet; others use a frying pan. One person uses a saltshaker; another a saltcellar. Some people eat dinner; others call the same meal supper. The following exercise emphasizes the use of synonymous expressions.

The student writes an appropriate noun in each blank.

**Answers**

| | |
|---|---|
| cellar | 1. Another name for basement is c_____ . |
| carpet | 2. Another name for rug is c_____ . |
| lamp | 3. You can turn on a light or a l_____ . |
| faucet | 4. You can turn off a spigot or a f_____ . |
| nails | 5. Carpenters often use brads or small n_____ . |
| abdomen | 6. Another word for belly is a_____ . |
| pail | 7. A bucket is also known as a p_____ . |
| bureau | 8. A chest of drawers may be called a b_____ . |
| sofa | 9. A couch is sometimes called a s_____ . |
| drumstick | 10. The leg of a cooked chicken or turkey is called a d_____ . |
| fee | 11. The charge for a service is a f_____ . |
| gift, tip | 12. A gratuity is a g_____ , or t_____ . |
| hamlet | 13. He lived in a small village, or h_____ . |
| hide | 14. An animal's skin is called a h_____ . |
| cassette | 15. The film was in a cartridge, or c_____ . |

## Antonyms in Vocabulary Development

Another effective way to expand students' vocabulary skills is through the study of antonyms. Although the term *antonym* might not be used in the primary grades, first and second-graders can master the concept of opposites—*up, down; hot, cold; high, low.* Antonyms range from easy words such as *first, last* and *brave, cowardly* to harder ones like *pessimism, optimism* and *authentic, counterfeit.*

Just as no two synonyms are exactly the same in meaning, few antonyms are the exact opposite of other words. We can conveniently group synonyms according to their general meaning, and so, too, we can classify certain terms as being opposite or nearly opposite in meaning. Learning the concept of opposites helps students extend the concept of negativism in language, the concept first met in the use of conjunctions such as *but, however,* and so on. Classifying antonyms, therefore, helps the student to think in terms of contrasting or contradictory concepts and statements.

At the elementary level, teachers may use visual clues to help introduce antonyms. Here the student draws lines to match the words that mean the opposite.

1.  fast •                    • a. off

2.  on •                      • b. from

3.  wet •                     • c. slow

4.  to •                      • d. dry

Using words appropriate to the level of the class and the subjects being studied, the teacher can present exercises in which the student gets practice in recognizing antonyms.

The student chooses an antonym for the underlined word.

1. Hang the second picture <u>above</u> the first one, not ___?___ it.
   a. below          b. next to          c. beside
2. The wind is <u>warm</u>, but the lake water feels ___?___.
   a. hot            b. chilly           c. dirty
3. The dancer was <u>graceful</u>, not ___?___.
   a. small          b. awkward          c. tired
4. The bread was <u>stale</u>, so we had to buy a ___?___ loaf.
   a. fresh          b. burned           c. large
5. Were apples <u>plentiful</u> this year, or were they ___?___ ?
   a. large          b. delicious        c. scarce

The student circles the two antonyms in each sentence.

1. Andy looks weary, but Pam seems rested.

2. Grace was willing to make the climb but felt reluctant to begin.

3. As fast as Mark uncovered the path, the falling snow buried it again.

4. Did the legislators meet in harmony, or was there some discord?

The student circles the antonym of each word on the left.

| **humble**    | mean        | meek      | conceited |
| **displeased** | angry      | delighted | unhappy   |
| **tender**    | gentle      | cruel     | tough     |
| **simple**    | complicated | easy      | tiresome  |

The following exercise gives students practice in recognizing antonyms and classifications. Students draw a line to connect antonyms.

|      **Touch**      |          |   **Size**   |          |
|---------|----------|---------|----------|
| soft    | hard     | immense | tiny     |
| damp    | smooth   | long    | plump    |
| rough   | dry      | slender | short    |

| Time | | Appearance | |
|---|---|---|---|
| prompt | brief | beautiful | clean |
| long | slow | filthy | shiny |
| swift | tardy | dull | ugly |

Students should understand that not all words have antonyms. In the pattern below, students determine which word in each group has an antonym; then they should write the antonym.

1. high    round    jump          3. night    snore    bed

2. fly    rise    eagle            4. clean    soap    bucket

Studying antonyms can be a part of word analysis. The teacher might present pairs of words to illustrate how their antonymy evolves from the addition of certain prefixes and suffixes to roots or to base words. Students can be provided one word and asked to form antonyms by changing or adding a prefix or suffix.

| | |
|---|---|
| indoors - outdoors | interior - exterior |
| inhale - exhale | import - export |
| encourage - discourage | approve - disapprove |
| thoughtless - thoughtful | useful - useless |
| careful - careless | worthy - unworthy, worthless |
| underrate - overrate | prewar - postwar |

Note: Purists may suggest that a true antonym must be formed from a root word rather than through the addition of affixes. For example, it might be said that an antonym of *kind* is *cruel,* not *unkind;* that an antonym of *happy* is *sad,* not *unhappy.* However, the majority of persons view *unhappy* as an antonym of *happy* and on the whole have chosen through usage to disagree with the purists.

Notice, however, that the prefix *in-* does not always mean "not." *Inactive* is the opposite of *active,* but *invaluable* is not the opposite of *valuable.* Here, the *in-* is called an intensive (an emphasizer of the root word). In the words *inside* and *income, in-* means "in" or "within."

# Homophones

Students often experience confusion between the terms *homophone, homograph,* and *homonym.* Focusing their attention on the root of each word will help. When students see *phone* they should think of *sound;* when they see *graph* they should think of *write.* Homophones sound the same but differ in spelling. Homographs are spelled the same (i.e., written the same) but differ in sound. *Homonym* uses the same base as *synonym* and *antonym*—the Greek *onoma, onym,* meaning "name." The prefix *homo-* is from the Greek *homos,* meaning "same." Homonyms have the same sound and often the same spelling, but they differ in meaning.

Note: The teacher may want to point out the similar Latin word *homo* (meaning "man") if there is any confusion about the derivation of *homonym* or words related to it. *Homo,* same, is the base for *homogeneous, homogenize,* and *homologous.* Words formed from the Latin word *homo,* man, are spelled *homi* or *hom,* as in *homicide, hominid,* and *homage.*

Homophones are phonemically identical words—words identical in pronunciation but different in meaning and derivation. Although homophones are pronounced alike (*pear, pair*), the context generally indicates the meaning. When one person tells another, "My aunt is coming for a visit," it's clear the speaker is not referring to an insect.

One of the chief problems with homophones involves correctly transferring them from spoken language to print. Confusion of homophones such as *there, their; to, too, two; principle, principal; sum, some; whose, who's; new, knew;* and *minor, miner* is the cause of many spelling difficulties.

As with synonyms and antonyms, the student needs much practice discriminating between homophones. Students in the early grades can work with homophones like *no, know; bear, bare; one, won;* and *write, right.* At the higher levels students can deal with homophones such as *assent, ascent; strait, straight;* and *right, rite.* Some students might be challenged by *rye, wry; leaf, lief; hue, hew; freeze, frieze; fold, foaled; brooch, broach; metal, mettle; throws, throes;* and *sign, sine.*

Teachers can use written exercises to give the student an opportunity to discriminate between homophones by learning their spellings and meanings. Adequate practice with an ample number of examples can help the student become sensitive to the different spellings of two or three words that sound alike, such as *air, heir, ere* and *sent, cent, scent.* We suggest several approaches for presenting homophones in the activities that follow. To introduce homophones at the first and second grade levels the teacher might present sentences containing pairs of homophones so that students have the words in context: "We rode our bikes down the dirt road." "We were so hungry we ate eight apples!"

Then the teacher can have students match each homophone with its meaning:

| | |
|---|---|
| rode | a place for people, cars, and trucks to travel |
| road | did ride |
| ate | one more than seven |
| eight | did eat |

The teacher might also supply definitions and ask the students to write the appropriate words. In the following exercise, students read the definition and write a homophone for the underlined word.

1. A word that means "fastened" and sounds like tide. _____
2. Writing paper whose name sounds like stationary. _____
3. A grain or seed inside a shell; it sounds like colonel. _____

Short practice periods of this kind can help the students fix the spellings and meanings of troublesome homophones and can help them avoid errors such as *pane* for *pain, rein* for *reign,* and *vain* for *vein.*

Teachers might also provide pairs of homophones and have students complete sentences with the correct words. Sentences can be written to use one or both homophones.

| | |
|---|---|
| roll<br>role | I played the _____ of a Pilgrim in the class play. |
| weight<br>wait | Will you _____ for me after the game? |
| heard<br>herd | Lauren was sure she _____ the sound of a stampeding _____ of cattle. |
| lessen<br>lesson | Adam decided to study the _____ thoroughly, because that would _____ problems with the test. |

A variation of this exercise is to give students a complete paragraph containing sets of homophones. Students select the correct word in each group according to the context.

Not ( so sew ) many years ago, people shopped differently from the way we ( dew do ) today. Shoppers ( would wood ) give the list of what they needed ( two too to ) the shopkeeper. The customer had to ( wait weight ) for the items.

# Chapter Nine

# Semantics

Semantics is the study of meanings. It deals with symbols or signs that denote meaning, their relationships with one another, and their influence on man and society. Semantics, therefore, involves word meanings, their development and change. Aptly named, the word *semantics* is originally derived from the Greek *semantikos,* meaning "significant," which comes from *sema,* meaning "sign," as in the word *semaphore.*

Semantics has to do with the meanings of words and the meanings people get from words. "Meaning" may refer to the etymology of words. For example, the word *dismal* comes from Latin *dies,* day, + *malus,* bad: literally "a bad day." "Meaning" may also refer to the denotative and connotative meanings as found in the dictionary. The denotation of a word is its exact literal meaning. For example, *blue* denotes a particular color. However, the connotation of the word *blue* might be "sad" or "gloomy." The word *cool* literally means "moderately cold." But when someone describes a movie as *cool,* he or she usually means to imply that it is excellent.

## Semantics and Vocabulary

What is the relationship of semantics to the teaching of vocabulary? For one thing, the study of semantics suggests to the teacher the importance of experience in word interpretation. Tennyson's Ulysses says, "I am a part of all that I have met." Experience influences both perception and conception.

Students interpret words in the light of their past experiences. Students with a rich background of experience bring more to the words they meet, decode the symbols in terms of what they already know. They interpret the abstract symbol and then reapply it in usable, concrete terms.

Teachers can help students grow in semantic skill by helping them associate what they already know with what they are learning. The best approach in teaching vocabulary is to get students to classify new words and to make finer discriminations about words they already know.

For example, some critics have attacked the long definition of *door* in *Webster's Third International Dictionary.* Surely everybody knows what a door is, so why the long explanation? The reason is that we must make sure our definition includes anything that in fact *is* a door and excludes what clearly *is not* a door. What about metaphorical extensions: "His curt remark closed the door on our negotiations"; "She strove to keep scandal from her door"? These must also be included in the definition of a word.

In short, semantics can be the basis for discussion with students about the *what* and *why* of words. Why, for example, can we say "bask in the sun" but not "bask in the shade"? Can we get "long shrift" as well as "short shrift"? Why does *cleave* mean "to split" as well as "to stick or cling to"? It is apparent that a certain usage becomes standard because it satisfies a particular meaning. If we vary the usage, the meaning is lost.

## Gaining Semantic Skill

We can best help students gain skill in semantics by enriching their experiences. This can be done in a variety of ways: conducting adequate oral language activities, promoting stimulating conversation both in and out of the classroom, and encouraging students to listen critically to their own recorded conversations and to those of others on television, radio, films, filmstrips, and other audiovisual media.

Success in semantic skill is often related to enjoyment. Students should play more with language, get involved with puns, riddles, jokes, rhymes, puzzles, and other word games (see Chapter 12). Students should be encouraged to manipulate and combine word parts to "create" words.

Class discussion helps in semantic study. The teacher can encourage discussions about the meanings of words in context, their origins, their changes, and their general or particular uses. Discussion about word meanings helps build concepts. It stimulates students to observe likenesses and differences, to generalize and discriminate, to weigh words and their meanings. In short, we can help build interest in vocabulary by talking about what we say and about how and why we say it.

In the following activities, the student gets an opportunity to examine the meanings of words in terms of their likenesses and differences, their relationship to context (see Chapter 6), their origin and structure, and their tendency to change and take on new meanings.

## Shortened Word Forms

We are constantly looking for shorter ways of saying what we want to say. Thus we drop superfluous letters from words and words from various expressions until our language rolls easily off the tongue—or pen. In the exercises that follow, students can gain some insight into word meaning, origin, and change through a study of these shortened forms.

### Contractions

Jonathan Swift in No. 230 of the *Tatler* was worried about the "corruption of the English tongue." He was against the practice of using contractions such as *he'd, she's,* and *I'd.* But such contractions typify the tendency of speakers and writers to shorten the forms of the words they use. The following list illustrates this point. Some of these contractions are used only in stories to illustrate a given dialect or period of time. Some are used only in verse. Others are used regularly.

The list might be used to check the students' knowledge of contractions. They might be asked to write in the blank the meaning of each contraction or to check those they don't know. Activities to teach contractions include matching the long form with the contracted form, writing contractions given the long form, and using contractions in original sentences.

Note: The difference between *its* and *it's* should be clarified: *its* is the possessive; *it's* is the contraction. Students may be surprised to find that some contractions have more than one meaning; for example, *one's* means either *one is* or *one has*.

## List of Contractions

| | | | |
|---|---|---|---|
| can't | cannot | aren't | are not |
| doesn't | does not | could've | could have |
| e'en | even | didn't | did not |
| hadn't | had not | won't | will not |
| hasn't | has not | haven't | have not |
| he'd | he had/would | she'll | she will |
| there's | there is/has | you'd | you had/would |
| I'll | I will/shall | I'm | I am |
| isn't | is not | that's | that is/has |
| it'll | it will | let's | let us |
| we've | we have | they're | they are |
| o'clock | of the clock | | |

## Additional Contractions

| | | | |
|---|---|---|---|
| ain't | that'll | they'll | what'd |
| daren't | needn't | they've | what's |
| don't | o'er | this'll | what'll |
| e'er | one's | 'tis | what've |
| he'll | she'd | 'twas | who'd |
| he's | she's | 'twasn't | who'll |
| I'd | shouldn't | 'twill | who's |
| I've | should've | 'twon't | who've |
| it'd | that'd | wasn't | wouldn't |
| it's | there'd | we'll | would've |
| mightn't | there'll | we'd | you'd |
| might've | there've | we're | |
| mustn't | they'd | weren't | |

## Contracted Forms

The teacher might point out to the class that the principle of contraction has always been at work in the development of the language. Polysyllabic words contain syllables that are accented and those that are unaccented. As a result, unstressed sounds often drop out, and so do their corresponding letters. For example, words such as *king* and *lady* were

93

longer in their Old English forms: *cyning* and *hlaefdige* (literally "loaf kneader"). Note also that *lord,* discussed later in this unit (See *Amelioration*), is an example of a contracted word. In Old English, *lord* was spelled *hlaford* (literally "loaf ward or guard").

Here are some other clipped forms:

*Sham* is a shortened form of *shame.*

*Curio* is a clipped form of *curiosity; tend* came from *attend,* and *mend* from *amend.*

*God be with you* has become *goodbye.* From *St. Audrey* comes *tawdry. Fence* is a variant of *defense.*

*Fall* refers to the "fall of the leaf" in autumn. *Private* comes from *private soldier.* A *lyric* is a *lyric poem.*

*Canter* is from *Canterbury gallop.* (Pilgrims going to Thomas à Becket's shrine in Canterbury rode at this easy gait.)

*Alarm* is a contracted form of *all'arme,* an old Italian phrase meaning "to arms."

Contracted words are often a part of slang. When first used, those words may be considered by some to be unrefined, unworthy of the language. But many of these clipped forms persist, and in time they are recognized as bona fide words. For example, *perk* is used as often as *percolate* to describe a way of making coffee. *TV* in the United States and *telly* in Britain are used as often as the word *television.*

*Miss* is short for *Mistress. Hack* is used for *hackney.*

Latin phrases are often clipped: *mob* is short for *mobīle vulgus,* the fickle common people. *Confab* comes from Latin *confābulārī,* to tell tales or fables. Although the latest dictionaries indicate that the origin of *nincompoop* is unknown, some scholars believe that *nincompoop* is a corrupted form of *non compos mentis,* not of sound mind.

Teachers may provide both short and long forms of words for students to match.

1. gas          caravan
2. mike        gasoline
3. movies     microphone
4. van          moving pictures

Another activity would be to have students rewrite sentences using the contracted form of specified words.

1. Kelly put the lemonade in the <u>refrigerator.</u> (fridge)
2. The history <u>examination</u> was not easy. (exam)
3. Did you see the <u>advertisement</u> for the <u>zoological garden?</u> (ad; zoo)
4. We're going to try out for the <u>coeducational university</u> swimming team. (coed varsity)

Other examples of contracted words are as follows:

| Short Form | Longer Form |
| --- | --- |
| bike | bicycle |
| cute | acute |
| piano | pianoforte |
| pram | perambulator |
| auto | automobile |
| flu | influenza |
| con | convict; confidence |
| Halloween | all hallow even (evening) |
| isle | island |
| scram | scramble |
| pep | pepper |
| bus | omnibus |
| chemist | alchemist |
| cello | violoncello |
| cop | copper ("catcher") |
| sax | saxophone |
| math | mathematics |
| gym | gymnasium |
| fan | fanatic |
| clerk | cleric |
| pants | pantaloons |
| mum | chrysanthemum |
| cab | cabriolet |
| trump | triumph |
| gab | gabble |
| togs | togas |
| cent | centum (100) |
| petrol | petroleum |
| knickers | knickerbockers |
| lube | lubricating oil |
| mart | market |
| wig | periwig |
| cafe | cafeteria |
| taxi | taxicab |
| sub | submarine |
| vet | veteran |

## Portmanteau Words

Other language shortcuts are found in portmanteau words. A *portmanteau* is a folding traveling bag. Some words "fold" or "blend" together like a portmanteau to form new words.

We blend *smoke* and *fog* to get *smog*.

*Chuckle* and *snort* become *chortle* (coined by Lewis Carroll).

*Gallop* and *triumph* telescope to form *galumph* (also coined by Carroll).

*Brunch* comes from *breakfast* and *lunch; motel* from *motor* and *hotel.*

*Tangelo* comes from *tangerine* and *pomelo,* grapefruit.

We blend *dumb* and *confound* to get *dumfound.*

*Fourteen nights* becomes *fortnight.*

## Acronyms

The word *radar* comes from radio detecting and ranging. What is a *scuba* diver? He or she is a deep-sea diver. Why *scuba?* It comes from self-contained underwater breathing apparatus.

*Radar* and *scuba* are acronyms. The word *acronym* comes from the Greek *akros,* highest, + *onym,* name. An acronym is generally formed from the first letters or syllables of a compound term.

Submarines are detected by *sonar* (sound navigation ranging).

Scientists often talk about light amplification by stimulated emission of radiation. It's commonly called *laser,* a thin, intense beam of light that can burn a hole in a diamond. *Zip* Code is used to speed mail delivery. It means zone improvement plan.

We often use acronyms for titles of national and international businesses, agencies, and organizations because many of these names are long. People who use computers use acronyms for terms such as *CRT* (Cathode Ray Tube) and for languages such as *COBOL* (Common Business Oriented Language) and *FORTRAN* (Formula Translation).

An acronym frequently becomes an accepted word. In fact, the acronym is often known when the words for which it stands are not. For example, many students know the general purpose of the organization called *CARE,* but they may not know what the letters stand for (Cooperative for American Relief Everywhere). Some persons will recognize *LEM* as the Apollo lunar module but may not know that this acronym stands for Lunar Excursion Module.

The following list is a sample of some familiar acronyms and their meanings. Students may have noticed other acronyms in local and national magazines and newspapers. Many students may have parents or friends who work for companies that are known by their acronyms. The names of regional utilities are usually abbreviated, as well as the names of businesses such as International Business Machines and American Telephone and Telegraph. Teachers may provide full names and acronyms for students to match, or they may provide full names and have students make up appropriate acronyms.

| CAT | Computerized Axial Tomography |
| emcee | Master of Ceremonies |
| Gestapo | Geheime Staatspolizei (Secret State Police) |
| HUD | Housing and Urban Development |
| lox | liquid oxygen (rocket fuel) |

| maser | microwave amplification by stimulated emission of radiation |
| NASA | National Aeronautics and Space Administration |
| NATO | North Atlantic Treaty Organization |
| RAM | Random Access Memory |
| UNESCO | United Nations Educational, Scientific, and Cultural Organization |
| UNICEF | United Nations International Children's Emergency Fund |
| VISTA | Volunteers in Service to America |
| WAC | Women's Army Corps |
| WHO | World Health Organization |

## Multiple Meanings

As we have pointed out, semantics deals with meaning. But meaning is sometimes unclear because we often use the same word for different objects, acts, or ideas. Thus a pipe may *leak* and let water *out,* a boat may *leak* and let water *in,* or a government agency may *leak* a story to the press. The context controls the meaning.

But the listener or reader also helps create the meanings of words. You hear or mishear, read or misread, interpret or misinterpret according to your background of experience and beliefs. To the liberal, a *conservative* statement may sound *reactionary.* You may be *thrifty* where another is *tightfisted.* You are *bold,* but your opponent is *reckless.* In dealing with semantics, therefore, we are dealing not only with the origin, structure, and context of words but also with the use of words changed by time and by the experiences of people.

The teacher may present a word in a number of phrases to emphasize its variant meanings in idiomatic expressions. For example, the word *lean* can be used in various ways: to lean on the desk; to lean on (rely on) someone; to lean toward a political party; a lean pork chop, a lean harvest, a lean fuel mixture in the carburetor. Class discussion can elicit the specific meaning for the word in each instance.

One activity for teaching multiple meanings is to provide students with a number of definitions for a word and a sentence using each meaning. Students then choose the meaning that fits in each sentence.

**beat**   a. to strike again and again   b. to overcome; to defeat
c. to mix by stirring rapidly
1. The blue team beat the red team at soccer.
2. Be sure to beat the eggs well.
3. I am tired of hearing Jack beat his drum.

**spring**   a. a season of the year   b. to leap forward
c. a natural flow of water from underground
1. We are going to the spring for a drink of cool water.
2. Did you see the frog spring into the pond?
3. The flowers will bloom in spring.

Note: Teachers may provide more definitions and sentences to challenge students or may ask students to think of other uses of the words. For example, *beat* may also refer to the rhythm in music or the area regularly covered by a police officer or reporter; it can mean to flap (wings) or to make flat by pounding; and it is used in informal phrases such as *beat around the bush* and *beat a retreat*.

In the exercise below, the student reads each sentence and writes a meaning for each underlined word. (There may be a variety of acceptable answers.)

1. There are birds in the air. (sky)
2. Open the door and air the room. (ventilate)
3. Air your opinion. (speak)
4. He sang an old air. (song)
5. He has a strange air about him. (way)

Note: Students may be encouraged to think of and discuss other uses of the word *air,* such as "putting on airs," "hot air," "on the air," and others.

## Compound Words

One of the characteristics of semantic change and variation in the language is found in the process of compounding. The teacher may point out the tendency of the language to form different compounds from the same base word. Thus we easily form new words from known words.

At the elementary level, compound word formation can be taught with the help of visual clues. Students can study the clues and then write the words.

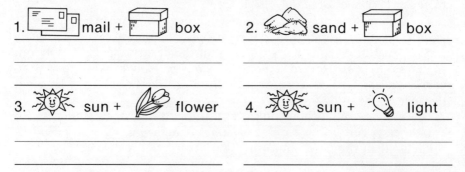

Students can also be given words they know to match and use to form compounds.

| 1. wall | line | 5. green | mark |
|---------|------|----------|------|
| 2. shoe | paper | 6. back | pack |
| 3. under | lace | 7. flash | house |
| 4. basket | ball | 8. book | light |

A slightly more advanced form of this activity is shown below. Students make compound words using the word in the middle of the box. They draw a line from the word in the center to each of the words in the box that they can use to form a compound. The word in the center can be the first or last part of the compound. (In the example, answers are *underwater, waterproof, waterfront, watermelon, waterfall, rainwater.*)

| whale | | front |
|-------|-------|-------|
| under | water | melon |
| proof | | fall |
| drink | | rain |

Teachers may point out that knowing the meaning of part of a compound can help students understand the meaning of the compound itself. Also, students can discuss how a word takes on specific meanings when used as part of different compounds, such as the *light* in *sunlight, lighthouse, headlight,* and *flashlight.*

Many compound words are sometimes formed from a single term. The word *head* might be used as an example. The teacher may use the following list to prove this point. It may be helpful to see how many words the class knows and to discuss their meanings.

| | | | |
|---|---|---|---|
| arrowhead | hothead | spearhead | headland |
| beachhead | letterhead | subhead | headline |
| blackhead | loggerhead | thunderhead | headlong |
| bulkhead | masthead | headache | headphone |
| bullhead | overhead | headband | headquarters |
| copperhead | pinhead | headboard | headrest |
| forehead | redhead | headdress | headstrong |
| hammerhead | sleepyhead | headfirst | headwaters |
| hardhead | sorehead | headgear | headway |

Note: Teachers may wish to show how certain suffixes can form compound adjectives and other nouns. The addition of *-ed* to existing compounds can form adjectives such as *bullheaded* and *hardheaded.* Suffixes *-ing* and *-er* can be used to form new compounds such as *slow-moving* and *laborsaving, doubleheader, six-footer,* and *forty-niner.*

## Classifying

The ability to group words can help students understand meanings and learn new words. At the elementary level, teachers need to point out that words can be grouped in different ways: things that have the same shape or color or location, things that have the same use or the same meaning, and so on. Even in the first and second grades students can begin to discriminate at different levels. Students can be provided a group of pictures and asked to circle the pictures of animals. Then from the group of animals they can choose those which can be pets. Finally they can select sentences that describe the different pets. In the following activity, students (1) cross out the word that does not belong in each group, then (2) select the name of the group.

1. hands    head    feet       (a) types of clothing
       legs    shoes          (b) body parts
                            (c) names of bones

2. basket    board    box    (a) containers for carrying things
       bag    pail           (b) plastic things
                            (c) round things

3. spoon    bowls    pots    (a) things used in a bathroom
       frying pan    bushes    (b) things used in a kitchen
                            (c) things used in a garden

For another classifying activity, show groups of pictures and/or words to the students and have them write the name of each group.

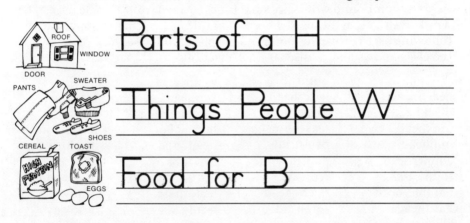

Students read each group of words and determine what the words have in common. They write a name that describes each group.

1. cub  gosling  colt  calf  _____
2. tambourine  clarinet  cymbals  oboe  _____
3. navy  peacock  royal  indigo  _____
4. corduroy  chintz  linen  denim  _____

Students at a more advanced level need practice in recognizing synonyms and antonyms, but they should also be challenged to recognize minor but semantically important differences in words related to general meaning, for example: *hurry, speed, streak, skitter, pace.* In the exercise below, students cross out the word that does not belong in each group and then state the meaning of the other three words.

1. blaze, glow, extinguish, kindle
   The other words are synonyms for _____ (burn).
2. temper, wrath, contentment, rage
   The other words are synonyms for _____ (anger; being upset).

3. cardinal, paramount, salient, trivial
   The other words are synonyms for _____ (importance; significance).
4. renowned, glorious, celebrated, obscure
   The other words are synonyms for _____ (fame).

# Semantic Change

Words and their meanings change with the changing times. Semantic change often accompanies social change brought about by wars, migrations, technological advances, and other factors.

To maintain student interest in word study, the teacher might discuss with the class four forms of semantic change: (1) specialization, (2) generalization, (3) amelioration, and (4) pejoration.

## 1. Specialization

*Specialization* (restriction) refers to the process by which the meaning of a word becomes more limited in its application. A given word may at one time be applied to a general class and may later become restricted or specialized in its meaning. For example, the word *hound* (from Old English *hund*) once referred to any dog. Now the word is used for a certain hunting breed with drooping ears.

Note the following examples of specialization:

*City* at one time referred to a fortified place but now refers to any urban area.

*Maid* used to mean any girl. Now, except in poetry, a maid is a domestic employee in the home or in a hotel.

*Century,* originally any group of 100, now means 100 years.

*Cattle,* once any group of quadrupeds, now refers only to bovines.

*Deer,* like *cattle,* changed its meaning from any four-legged animal to a certain species.

*Success,* originally any kind of outcome, now generally means a favorable one.

*Corn* used to be the name for grain or cereal in general. Now, in the United States, corn is the name of a particular grain.

*Typewriter* once meant either the machine or the typist; now it refers only to the machine.

*Corpse* is a doublet of *corps* (body) and once meant any body at all, but now *corpse* refers only to the body of a deceased person. (A doublet is one of two words derived from the same source but coming into the language by different routes. Other examples of doublets are *frail* and *fragile, choir* and *chorus, influenza* and *influence, canal* and *channel, warden* and *guardian.*)

101

*College* used to mean "company, assemblage, or crowd"; now it usually refers to a university.

*Popular* used to mean "public" or "gregarious." (Julius Caesar belonged to the *Popular* Party, the party of the common people in Rome.) The narrowing process has given *popular* the meaning of "has the acceptance of the public" or "liked by one's associates."

## 2. Generalization

Changes in meaning also take place through the process of *generalization,* the opposite of specialization. Through generalization, or expansion, a word loses its specialized or restricted meaning and becomes the symbol for a general class of objects. For example, *boycott* once had a specialized meaning relating to the action against Captain Boycott. It is now applied worldwide and has a more generalized meaning: combining against or refusing to do business with a firm or a nation.

Note the following examples of generalization:

*Graphic* has expanded from its original meaning "written" to "depicted" to "colorfully concrete."

*Lady* once referred only to the wife of a lord, and then to any woman who behaved like the former. The term came to include almost all women.

*Coke* was once short only for Coca-Cola; *coke* now (whether authorized or not) generally refers to all soft drinks with a cola base.

In the early days of the record player, the brand name *Victrola* became synonymous with the phonograph itself.

*Vaseline* is a trade name that is widely substituted for the generic name of the product petroleum jelly.

*Manuscript* has now been extended from "handwritten" to include typed material as well.

*Kleenex,* like Victrola and Vaseline, is another example of a specific trade name that became the term used for a general class of products.

*Ghetto,* which in former times named the part of a city set aside for Jewish people, is coming to mean a place occupied primarily by any minority group due to economic and social disadvantages.

*Realm,* once restricted to mean "kingdom," has taken on more vague dimensions. For example, in Shakespeare's *Richard II,* John of Gaunt uses *realm* in the restrictive sense:
This blessed plot, this earth, this *realm,* this England.
But *realm* has an extended meaning in Bryant's "Thanatopsis":
The innumerable caravan, which moves
To that mysterious *realm,* where each shall take
His chamber in the silent halls of death.

## 3. Amelioration

The meaning of a word is often changed through *amelioration* (making better, from Latin *melior,* better). Ameliorative change refers to the elevation of a word in meaning. For example, *knight* (Old English *cniht*) at one time meant boy or youth, but by extension came to mean a follower or servant who moved up the social ladder from page to squire to *knight,* a servant of a lord or a king.

*Queen* (from Old English *cwen*) didn't always refer to royalty. Originally *queen* merely meant woman. Later it came to mean the "woman of the country," that is, the female monarch or the king's wife.

A *lord* used to be literally a "bread keeper." Old English *hlaf* (loaf) and *weard* (keeper; ward) contracted to form the word *lord.*

A *mansion* is now a large, stately residence; originally *mansion* referred to a farmhouse or to a modest dwelling or building.

*Chemise* has been upgraded so that now it has fancier connotations than its original French meaning, a shirt. *Lingerie* also now connotes more than its original meaning, a linen garment (from Latin *linum,* flax).

*Chiffon* meant not the light, silky fabric of today, but merely a rag. And before *chiffonier* came to refer to a high chest of drawers, it meant ragpicker.

Country *squire* now indicates more dignity than did the original *squire,* which meant servant or shield-carrier.

A *marshal* (now an officer) at one time merely groomed horses (from Old High German *marah,* horse, + *scalc,* servant).

*Angel* in its religious sense now occupies a loftier position than it did formerly. It used to mean merely a messenger.

## 4. Pejoration

We have already described three main forms of semantic change: (1) *specialization,* in which a word takes on a limited use; (2) *generalization,* in which a word loses its limited meaning and signifies a general class; and (3) *amelioration,* in which a word becomes elevated, or more favorable in its meaning.

The fourth form of semantic change is *pejoration* (making worse, from Latin *pejor,* worse). Pejoration (or degeneration) refers to the lowering in esteem of a word's meaning. For example, *knave* once meant merely boy (from German *knabe,* boy) but now means "a rogue or rascal." Thus through time the meaning of a particular word often degenerates, or takes on less favorable meaning.

Here are some examples of pejoration:

*Persecute* once meant to follow persistently. Now it means to follow persistently with an evil purpose, or to treat badly or oppress.

*Temper,* once simply a state of mind, now when used as a noun without an adjective often means an angry state of mind.

*Stench* originally meant any kind of smell, but now its meaning has degenerated to "a bad smell."

*Problem* (from Greek *proballein,* to propose or put forth, from *pro-,* forward, + *ballein,* to throw) originally referred merely to a proposal, but now generally refers to a troublesome question, one that causes difficulty.

*Silly* once meant blessed (from Old English *saelig,* happy), but now it refers to childish or immature behavior.

*Rash* didn't always mean too hasty or reckless. *Rash* (Middle English *rasch*) at one time merely meant quick.

*Dame,* except when specifically used as a title (feminine counterpart of *knight*), is now slang for woman.

*Bourgeois* once represented the new middle class (merchants or businesspeople below aristocrats but wealthier than the proletariat), but now often connotes commonness, lack of dignity or refinement.

*Villain* once meant farmer (from Latin *villanus,* farmhand; originally from *villa,* farmhouse), but *villain* now has degenerated to mean a wicked person or a scoundrel.

*Cunning* (from Old English *cunnan,* knowing how) once meant clever but now means clever in deceiving.

*Sly,* which once meant skilled or wise, now means tricky, cunning, or underhanded.

*Collaborate* (to work together) took on a pejorative or unfavorable meaning during World War II, when *collaborators* were traitorous cooperators with the Nazi regime. The meaning of the word is now probably losing its tinge of treason.

*Pious* (from Latin *pius,* dutiful) may still describe a true reverence or religious characteristic, but it may also connote a pretended or hypocritical quality.

*Propaganda* is a Latin form meaning "must be propagated" (the ending *-nda* is also found in words such as *agenda,* "must be done"). Basically, *propaganda* meant a systematic effort to spread an opinion or belief, but propaganda has also taken on the unfavorable connotation of swaying public opinion by spreading slanted or incomplete information.

*Counterfeit,* now meaning a copy made to deceive, a forgery, once meant merely a copy, an image, or a likeness. Thus we find Hamlet comparing his father's and uncle's portraits:

Look here, upon this picture, and on this
The *counterfeit* presentment of two brothers.

104

And in *The Merchant of Venice*, Bassanio opens the leaden casket to find a picture of Portia:
    What find I here?
    Fair Portia's *counterfeit*

The teacher might use some of the following words as a basis for discussion. It will help the student become aware of the tendency of certain words to change their meanings over the years. The teacher could ask for a current definition of each word below and then explain to the class the earlier meaning of the word. Some etymological information has been included to show the relationship between meanings.

| Word | Then | Now |
|------|------|-----|
| painful | painstaking; careful | hurting |
| amuse | to cause to muse (think); to occupy one's mind with | to make one smile or laugh |
| wretched | wicked (from Anglo-Saxon *wrecca*, outcast) | miserable |
| hobby | small walking horse (from Middle English *hobyn*, small horse) | favorite pastime |
| awkward | heading in the wrong direction (from Middle English *awk*, contrary) | clumsy |
| usury | money paid for using something | charging very high interest |
| brave | showy; excellent | courageous |
| palliate | to cover with a cloak (from Latin *pallium*, cloak) | to ease but not cure |
| adamant | very hard rocks (from Old French *adamaunt*, the hardest metal or stone, such as a diamond) | unyielding; firm |
| snob | a commoner | a stuck-up person |
| bachelor | a young knight (from Latin *baccalārius*, originally a farm helper or tenant) | unmarried man |
| gossip | friend; godparent (from Old English *godsibb*, godparent, from *god* + *sibb*, relative) | idle talk or talker |
| havoc | a battle cry (In *Julius Caesar*, Antony says, "Cry 'Havoc,' and let slip the dogs of war.") | great destruction |

| Word | Then | Now |
|---|---|---|
| sloth | slowness (from Old English *slaw*, slow) | laziness; an animal |
| iconoclast | an image-breaker (from Greek *eikon*, image, + *klas*, break) | one who attacks cherished or traditional ideas or institutions |
| sinister | left; on the left hand (from Latin *sinister*, left. Omens appearing on the left side were considered ominous.) | threatening; evil |
| craven | vanquished; defeated | cowardly |
| farce | stuffing for fowl or roast (from Old French *farce*, comic intermission in a mystery play) | comical play |
| urbane | to live in the city (from Latin *urbs*, city) | civilized; refined |
| carriage | whatever was carried; a burden or load | a conveyance |
| unkind | unnatural (from Old English *gecynde*, natural) | lacking in kindness |
| censure | opinion (from Latin *cēnsēre*, to think, judge) | to express disapproval |
| uncouth | unknown (from Old English *un*, not, + *cuth*, known) | crude |
| pencil | artist's small brush (from Latin *pēnicillus*, painter's brush) | writing tool |
| clumsy | stiff from the cold (from Middle English *clumsen*, numb with cold) | awkward |
| quaint | skillful (from Old French *queinte*, clever; originally from Latin *cognitus*, known. In *The Tempest*, Prospero refers to Ariel disguised as a water nymph: "Fine apparition! My *quaint* Ariel.") | strange; odd |
| tuition | guardianship; custody (from Latin *tuitiō*, protection, and *tuērī*, to watch over) | instruction or the charge paid for it |
| conceit | thought; wit; concept | too much pride |
| trivial | commonplace; ordinary | trifling; not important |

| Word | Then | Now |
|------|------|-----|
| | (from Latin *trivia,* where three roads meet: *tri,* three, and *via,* road) | |
| tarpaulin | sailor (from *tar* + *pall* + *ing,* a combination meaning tar-covered, as a sailor's tarred canvas suit. *Tarpaulin* was later shortened to *tar,* which even now refers to a sailor.) | waterproofed canvas |
| danger | jurisdiction; having power over (In *The Merchant of Venice,* Portia asks Antonio, "You stand within his *danger,* do you not?") | chance of harm |
| perspective | an optical glass instrument, such as a magnifying glass (from Latin *per,* through, + *specere,* to look) | the view from a distance; the appearance of distance; an outlook |
| novelist | an innovator; one who likes *novelty* | writer of novels |
| spices | kinds (from Latin *speciēs,* kind, sort. *Spices* is a doublet of the English word *species;* that is, both words came from the same root but along different paths. *Species* is direct from Latin; *spices* came through French.) | flavorings; seasonings |
| fond | foolish (from Middle English *fonned,* foolish) | having strong affection |
| plausible | worthy of applause (from Latin *plaudere,* to applaud) | appears reasonable or fair |
| explode | to drive an actor from the stage; to hoot off by clapping the hands (from *explōdere,* to clap the hands). *Explode* was the opposite of *applaud* (from *plaudere,* to clap hands in approval.) | to blow up; burst |

107

| Word | Then | Now |
|------|------|-----|
| generous | high-born of noble lineage (from Latin *genus,* race) | unselfish |
| polite | polished (from Latin *politus,* refined, and *polire,* to polish) | having good manners |
| handsome | apt; easy to handle; skilled with the hands | good-looking |
| pomp | a procession (from Latin *pompa,* procession, display) | splendor |
| peevish | obstinate | cross; complaining |
| harbinger | person sent ahead to secure a *harbor* (lodging) for royalty | forerunner; announcer |
| insolent | unusual (from Latin *in,* not, + *solēre,* to be used to) | boldly rude |
| nephew, niece | grandchildren (from Latin *nepōs,* grandson, and *neptis,* granddaughter. Note also *nepotism,* hiring relatives.) | children of one's brother or sister |
| miscreant | unbelieving (from *mis-,* wrongly, + Latin *creant,* believing; from *crēdere,* to believe) | base or one who is depraved; villain |
| miser | wretched person (from Latin *miser,* wretched, miserable) | one who stores up money |
| prevent | to go before (from Latin *pre-,* before, + *venīre,* to come) | to keep from |
| heathen | one who lives on a *heath,* outside the society (from Old English *haethen,* heath dweller) | a pagan; one regarded as unenlightened or uncivilized |
| punctual | careful about details, about small points (from Latin *punctum,* point) | on time |
| preposterous | to put the last first (from Latin *pre-,* before, + *post-,* after) | absurd; contrary to |

# Chapter Ten

# Reading and Vocabulary

Reading and building a vocabulary go hand in hand. One is dependent on the other. Reading is one of the greatest contributing factors to building an extensive vocabulary.

Of course, we do not read literature to build a vocabulary, but we need an adequate vocabulary to appreciate and learn from literature. An acquaintance with literature broadens students' understanding of the world and their knowledge of human nature. The teacher can use literature to show the importance of words, their varied meanings, and the importance of style in getting ideas across.

Much of the pleasure of reading escapes the student with a meager vocabulary. Any student may get some pleasure from the jingle of a stanza of poetry because he or she feels the rhythm or hears the rhyme, but enjoyment and understanding increase when the student also recognizes the poet's meaning and the use of such devices as metaphor, imagery, and allegory as integral parts of the versification.

The most important factor in building a vocabulary is rich experience. Our vocabulary is the residue of our experiences. But, in addition to firsthand experiences, much is gained from vicarious experience through listening, observing, and reading. Literature provides important vicarious experiences. The reader may relive the exciting adventures of Jim Hawkins in *Treasure Island* or of David Balfour in *Kidnapped.* A student might sense the warm relationship between human and animal in stories such as Jack London's *The Call of the Wild* or Marjorie K. Rawlings's *The Yearling.*

## Children's Literature and Vocabulary

Children's literature once dealt predominantly with religion and conduct but now covers a wide variety of subjects. Children's literature includes standard books such as *Tales of Mother Goose* by Charles Perrault; *Grimm's Fairy Tales,* collected by the linguist Jacob Grimm; and *The Adventures of Tom Sawyer* by Mark Twain. And there are a great many more appropriate, exciting, well-written, and well-illustrated books aimed at children's tastes and reading levels.

The list of books written especially for children continues to grow. By reading these books, elementary students gain pleasurable experience in reading and vocabulary skills. They learn to "read" pictures, to weigh words, to think critically. They get some understanding of human nature.

Sensitive and skillful teaching of children's literature can create in students an interest in words and a lasting enjoyment in reading that will remain with them throughout high school and beyond.

The planned reading of literature can help young people get a better understanding of their schoolmates, regardless of differences. For example, a child who reads *Crow Boy* sees a reason for accepting persons who are "different." Crow Boy's problems become the reader's problems. Through reading literature children may learn the need to stand by one's values in the face of great odds.

In general, children's literature reflects life. It presents words spoken by a variety of characters in a variety of situations, and, most important, it presents words not in artificial but in natural contexts. Thus the elementary teacher can emphasize in a variety of ways the effective use of vocabulary in any of the books he or she uses. The teacher might note the phrasing used by certain characters. For instance, here are a few examples of the imaginative use of words found in *Dorp Dead* by Julia Cunningham:

"ferociously intelligent"
"overstuffed woman"
"bongs that bounce off my eardrums"
"calm as a boulder in a blizzard"
"leaf through my memories"
"barrenness of the nothinglandscape"

## Children's Literature and Word Origin

A significant aspect of word study as it relates to general language development is the origin or history of words. Word history often makes interesting reading for young students. Films, filmstrips, and slides on word history are available in many school and college film libraries.

Perhaps the most productive way to have elementary students study word origins as a technique for building vocabulary and critical awareness about what is read is through the examination of children's literature. A fifth or sixth-grade teacher might read aloud some well-known nursery rhymes and then ask the students to analyze their vocabulary. For example, in the rhyme "Little Miss Muffet sat on a tuffet eating her curds and whey," what is a tuffet? What is whey? *Tuffet* (a diminutive of *tuft,* meaning "a small stool") and *whey* (the watery part of milk) are not known by most twelfth-graders. Although poetry is read not for word study but for enjoyment and meaning, key words in certain poems can be selected for discussion of meaning and origin.

The elementary teacher might also use stories in literature as a point of departure for word origin. Short original stories by the children may be used as exercises in creating new words or presenting fanciful origins for established words.

For example, one teacher asked a group of students about the origin of the word *vinegarroon.* One student gave the name *vinegarroon* to a group of persons marooned on an island with nothing but a cargo of vinegar to drink. Another student gave the name to a special coconut macaroon cookie originally made with vinegar that was accidentally added to the recipe. Its unique taste developed into a famous recipe. Still another said that *vinegarroon* is the name for a special salad dressing.

When given the hint that a *vinegarroon* is an animal, the students created a story about a fisherman and a loon. The waterfowl was causing such a disturbance on the lake, the fisherman called the loon with a sour disposition a "vinegarroon." The definition given in the *World Book Dictionary* is "a large whip scorpion of the southwest United States, mistakenly believed to be poisonous, and when alarmed, having an odor like that of vinegar."

The students may be invited to try writing and then sharing their own made-up word origins about familiar objects: household items, people's names, animals' names, kinds of boats, buildings, tools, and so on. The class may later want to find out the true word origins (if available in the dictionary or encyclopedia) and compare them with their own creations.

After reading Helen F. Orton's *Mystery in the Apple Orchard,* the reader may be asked to find the origin of such words as *haunted, treasure, detective, mystery.* Will James's *Smokey the Cowhorse* or Marguerite Henry's *King of the Wind* may lead the reader to look for the origins of such words as *palomino, mesa, mesquite, lariat, mustang,* and *fetlock.*

Animal stories give the teacher an opportunity to discuss the origins of the names of animals. The teacher may illustrate on the chalkboard the relationship between the words *lion* (from Latin *leo,* from Greek *leon,* lion) and leopard (from Greek *leon* + *pardos,* leopard or large cat).

Fanciful tales (such as the excellent story *The Wind in the Willows* by Kenneth Grahame) provide the teacher and students with a great number of words to analyze in terms of meaning and origin. Grahame's context will often enhance the student's interest in an otherwise flat word. He says, at one point, that Mole (tunneling up through the ground) "scraped and scratched and scrabbled." Other phrases in the story include "Something up there was calling him *imperiously"* (from the Latin *impero,* command), related to *imperative* mood and to *emperor* (commander); "fond of a *bijou* riverside residence" (*bijou* is French for a jewel, or trinket); "drawing after them the long bobbing procession of casks, like a mile of *porpoises"* (Latin *porcopiscis,* hogfish, from *porcus,* pig, + *piscis,* fish).

The area of word origin is broad enough to be linked to any subject matter being studied. In its relation to children's literature, a great deal of word-origin study can be spontaneous—if the teacher is prepared to encourage it.

However, there are two essential points for the success of word-history study in the lower grades: (1) The children must be personally involved, suggesting, contributing, experimenting in terms of history or etymology (at their level), and thereby seeing the relationship of word history to their everyday lives. This goal can be reached by encouraging the children to use key words studied in discussion and conversation. (2) The teacher must become as expert as possible in words and word origin as they relate to general language development. The teacher must, in effect, become "word-conscious," bringing to the classroom a knowledge of the "new" words to be discussed and having at his or her fingertips sufficient background information to sustain the interest of the students as they proceed through a story or poem.

Children who listen to or read Maxine Kumin's *The Beach Before Breakfast* take part in a meaningful relationship—a father taking his son on an adventurous, thoughtful expedition to a beach inhabited by interesting sea creatures. Readers easily get inside the character and identify with him as they live his experiences on the sand and water. They meet vivid adjectives like "creamy" sand, and similes such as "the dunes sit up like fat camels." Words like *dunes, whelks,* and *conch* form essential parts of the story, within the context of beach surroundings. These words belong in the story. It is no accident that they are there; they are an integral part of the mood and the setting. They are in natural context—an excellent way to learn words.

## Underlining Unfamiliar Words in Reading

As noted previously, vocabulary growth is achieved by rich experiences, by conversation, by wide reading of various kinds of literature, and by systematic study. A good part of the systematic study should be devoted to ways of developing a filing system for remembering and retrieving words.

Many students today buy paperback books, perhaps as members of a class book club. To help students become more word-conscious, the teacher should encourage them to underline unfamiliar words they meet while reading their own paperbacks. A marked personal book is not a spoiled book. In fact, it becomes more useful.

When underlining unfamiliar words in reading, the student will note the following: (1) If the word is a key word, it will occur again. The student will be alerted to it and not skip it. (2) The student becomes conscious of marked words and the way they are spelled. (3) The student becomes uncomfortable if he or she skips over a hard word without a quick try at inferring its meaning. (4) The student faces a decision—to learn or not learn a given word. (5) The student becomes conscious of how many important words he or she does not know. (6) The student finds that word study is a rewarding learning experience, a challenge rather than a chore.

Students can effectively increase their vocabulary skills by wide reading of school magazines. Many such magazines contain interesting word-study games and challenging quizzes. Words may be taken from articles for purposes of defining, noting construction and spelling, and determining their use in the context of the article.

## Vocabulary and Periodicals

One way to extend the reading horizon of students is to enrich their recognition vocabulary. The teacher and the class can scan current newspapers and magazines for definitions or explanations of new or unfamiliar words currently used in domestic, scientific, national, and international affairs.

From a newspaper clipping, for example, students may learn that some scientists believed the Apollo 11 astronauts had found *biotite* (a form of mica) on the moon. *Biotite* is named after the French mineralogist Jean Biot. Commander Armstrong noted that certain rocks were *vesicular* (having little cavities, from Latin *vesicula,* little blister; bladder).

A magazine article may explain that a laser beam is a thin, intense beam of light that can send signals to and from the moon. The teacher may read from an article explaining that the word *laser* is an acronym formed from the words light amplification by stimulated emission of radiation. Articles in other sources might explain how lasers are used in medicine, construction, manufacturing, and photography.

There are a number of excellent children's periodicals that expose children to new and interesting vocabulary words and concepts. There are magazines on nature, science, history, health, literature, and general interest. One issue of the magazine *Highlights for Children,* for example, contains articles on moths and bats (*sonar, echo, detect, instinct*), the magnetic sense in animals (*compass, magnetism, observant, sensitive*), and short fiction with phrases such as the following:

"howl and yowl and growl like a mighty lion"
"rolling and twirling and whirling"
"mystery-prize raffle"
"purple detective beanie"

Using the available sources in the classroom and at home, students might keep a notebook or "Word Log" for new words and definitions. For many children the act of writing a word and its definition will help in remembering it later. The notebooks will also become a resource for sharing new words in class discussion. If a student records a word and then has trouble finding a definition for it, he or she can ask the teacher for help.

## The Vocabulary of Journalism

Newspapers are a part of our current literature, providing excellent materials for vocabulary and reading growth. Each day a newspaper prints thousands of words, some easy, some hard. Newspapers are responsible for many of the new words that appear in our language. Newspaper reporters often coin words because they need words that are short, to the point, vivid, and graphic.

Students can enrich their vocabularies by noting the way journalists use words. Words in newspapers, especially those in headlines, often have a different flavor from those in books. Because headlines must fit a certain space and tell the story at a glance, headline writers use words and phrases that are short and colorful. Sports writers have been particularly inventive: "Twins Take Two," "Cubs Cinch Flag," and so on.

Below are pairs of words. The student chooses the one a headline writer might be more likely to use. (Correct answers are underlined.)

| | | | | |
|---|---|---|---|---|
| 1. agreement | pact | 6. jolt | earthquake |
| 2. catch | net | 7. location | site |
| 3. curb | restrict | 8. prevent | bar |
| 4. hail | welcome | 9. probe | investigation |
| 5. hike | increase | 10. slash | decrease |

## Vocabulary and Essay Style

We do not consider the learning of "big" words the goal of vocabulary development, but from time to time there are students who want to increase their vocabularies and who consider the learning of big words important. This desire should not be dampened. Such students can profit greatly from reading Macaulay's *Life of Samuel Johnson*. From its vocabulary alone, high school students can learn the art of using an extensive vocabulary with style (the way we put sentences together). Macaulay is an excellent model. A look at a few of his pages shows a broad, varied vocabulary: *discernible, morbid, propensity, procrastination, malady, indolent, desultory, opulent, effigy, haranguing, absolving, felons, torpid, squalid, ceruse, extolling, tawdry, munificently, sinecure, rancid, sycophancy, obloquy, septennial, turgid, emendation, scurrilous, triads, casuistry, garrulous.*

There is, of course, virtue in short words, and we do not recommend the learning of sesquipedalian words (Horace's term for a long word) just for the sake of learning them. Samuel Johnson sometimes favored big words (as in his novel *Rasselas*) and did not avoid using them when the occasion arose. Macaulay in his biography notes Johnson's natural inclination to use long words and points out that many readers considered Johnson "a pompous pedant, who would never use a word of two syllables where it was possible to use a word of six."

## Allusions in Literature

Writers allude to historical or literary characters, events, or geographical locations (1) on the assumption that the reader knows the characters, (2) with the knowledge that the allusion carries with it rich associations, and (3) with the understanding that the allusion will have a dramatic effect or will clarify a point.

In literature and in conversation, we come across such expressions as "carrying coals to Newcastle," "meeting his Waterloo," being "shanghaied." Prose and poetry are filled with allusions to Greek and

Roman mythological characters. In order to understand the point of the allusion in context, the reader or listener must have some knowledge of the expression or its source.

To point up the importance of literary allusions the teacher can discuss the great number and variety of these allusions. They are found at every level of written material. For instance, the teacher can put clippings of advertisements with pictures on the bulletin board. The classical name Atlas might be found in an advertisement with a picture of Atlas holding up the world, thus connoting the product's strength and dependability. A car manufacturer uses the name Mercury, connoting swiftness.

The teacher may find short articles to read to the class to illustrate the use of allusions in writing. An article might point out that a person or country has achieved a pyrrhic victory. At this point the teacher can explain that a pyrrhic victory is one gained at too great a cost to the victor, with too many lives lost, for example.

It is important for students to recognize that they cannot simply "learn" allusions and that, in their reading, they will come across allusions they do not understand. Just as students should be comfortable about asking for help in pronunciation of new or difficult words, they should be comfortable about asking for an explanation of an unknown allusion. Asking for help is a sign of learning, not a sign of ignorance.

The appreciation of allusions can be doubly beneficial for students. When students find an allusion they do not understand, it can lead them to reading about the origin of the expression or reading the source of the expression itself. A reference to "meeting one's Waterloo" might interest students to read about Napoleon and his military exploits. Likewise, the more reading students do, the more they are exposed to the people and places that make up our allusions and the more they will appreciate the expressions when they see them again.

Students may be given the names of people and places often alluded to in speaking and writing and asked what they mean. Easier or harder proper nouns may be used, or references may be included from current subject material. The teacher may use this type of exercise to initiate a class discussion about certain words and about allusions in general.

1. *Mars* represents ___?___.

   a. hate   b. love   c. war

2. *Ulysses* is a symbol of man's ___?___.

   a. joy   b. wanderings   c. fear

3. *Pandora's box* represents ___?___.

   a. happiness   b. evils   c. love

4. *Ambrosia* is ___?___.

   a. the food of the gods   b. a thick woods   c. a shady glen

5. A *Gordian knot* __?__ .

   a. a deep hole  b. a crooked branch  c. a tough problem

## Associations in Literature

The teacher may use the following pattern to emphasize the importance of association in learning vocabulary. Primarily, the lesson is meant to help the student remember a word by associating one word with another. The teacher might point out that certain people's names bring the name of their partner to mind. Thus, we seldom see the name *Romeo* without thinking of *Juliet,* or vice versa.

Depending on the student's background and interests, the teacher might present one of two closely associated literary characters and ask the student to supply the other. Initial letter clues can be furnished as needed. Many of the following pairs are found in English and American literature.

**Answers**

| Answers | |
|---|---|
| Cleopatra | 1. Antony and C _____ |
| Knights of the Round Table | 2. King Arthur and the K _____ |
| Remus | 3. Romulus and R _____ |
| Charybdis | 4. Scylla and C _____ |
| Sancho Panza | 5. Don Quixote and S ____ P _____ |
| Pocahontas | 6. Capt. John Smith and P _____ |
| Caliban | 7. Ariel and C _____ |
| Eliza Doolittle | 8. Professor Higgins and E ____ D _____ |

The teacher may use the same form to present character pairs from stories read by younger students. In the following activity, note that without initial letter clues there may be more than one correct answer for some characters (Peter Pan and Tinkerbell, Robin Hood and Maid Marian).

| | |
|---|---|
| Jill | 1. Jack and J _____ |
| Pussy Cat | 2. The Owl and the P ____ C _____ |
| Captain Hook | 3. Peter Pan and C ____ H _____ |
| Tiny Tim | 4. Bob Cratchit and T ____ T _____ |
| Huck Finn | 5. Tom Sawyer and H ____ F _____ |
| Little John | 6. Robin Hood and L ____ J _____ |
| Mr. Hyde | 7. Dr. Jekyll and M ____H _____ |
| Dr. Watson | 8. Sherlock Holmes and D ____ W _____ |

Books may also be listed:

| | |
|---|---|
| Willows | 1. The Wind in the W _____ |
| Beauty | 2. Black B _____ |
| Big Woods | 3. The Little House in the B ____ W _____ |

Note: These exercises are not aimed to teach these names to those who have never heard of them. They are meant to remind, to revive dim memories, and occasionally to stimulate students to find out more about these persons.

### Nursery Rhyme Quiz

The elementary teacher might test the students' recall of words used in nursery rhymes and other poems and stories.

1. The _____ was in the counting house. (king)
2. A ten o'clock _____ . (scholar)
3. Simple Simon met a _____ . (pieman)
4. Little Jack Horner sat in a _____ . (corner)
5. All the King's _____ and all the King's _____ . (horses; men)
6. Old King Cole was a _____ old soul. (merry)
7. There was an old woman who lived in a _____ . (shoe)
8. Mary, Mary, quite _____ . (contrary)
9. To _____ , to _____ , to buy a fat pig. (market; market)
10. Three little kittens lost their _____ . (mittens)

## Choosing the Right Word

Students in composition classes can often learn from models of style by noting the words writers use to express an idea or set a mood, a time, a locale, and so on. Using selections from literature, the teacher can give students an opportunity to choose concrete, vivid words.

Below are some quotations from *Silas Marner* in the form of a multiple-choice exercise. Students underline the word they think the author used, then check the answer. Other choices are not necessarily wrong, merely different from those selected by the author. Thus, the teacher may wish to discuss with the class the appropriateness of the author's choice of words to fit the character, setting, and mood.

**Answers**

| | |
|---|---|
| hummed | 1. In the days when the spinning wheel *hummed, droned, sang, buzzed* busily in the farmhouse . . . |
| bosom | 2. . . . deep in the *center, bosom, heart, core* of the |
| pallid | hills, certain *wan, pallid, pale, colorless,* undersized |
| brawny | men who, by the side of the *strong, muscular,* |
| remnants | *brawny* countryfolk, looked like the *fragments, remnants, remainders, residue* of a disinherited race. |
| fiercely | 3. The shepherd's dog barked *fiercely, viciously, threateningly* when one of these alien-looking men appeared on the upland . . . |
| protuberant | 4. . . . these large, brown *bulging, protuberant* eyes in Silas Marner's pale face really saw nothing. |
| rude | 5. . . . for the *rude, rustic, crude* mind with difficulty |

117

benignity          associates the idea of power and *goodness, kindness, benignity* . . .

barren          6. Not that it was one of those *bare, barren, poor* parishes lying on the outskirts of civilization . . .

vibrations      7. It was never reached by the *blare, vibrations, tooting call* of the coach horn.

# A Vocabulary of Literary Terms

Any evaluation of literature, made either by the student or by a professional critic, is more understandable if the student is familiar with the technical vocabulary of literary criticism and analysis. The items below deal with some of these terms and can be used as both a diagnostic and a teaching device.

The student checks one of three choices. Notes in parentheses after certain items are for the teacher's convenience and may be used in class discussion. The teacher should discuss the key words after the lesson.

1. A *ballad* is ___?___.
   a. ___ meter
   b. _X_ a song (also a narrative poem)
   c. ___ a rhyme scheme

2. A *motif* is ___?___.
   a. ___ a play acted out
   b. ___ a subplot
   c. _X_ a dominant theme (*Romeo and Juliet* has a love motif.)

3. A *simile* is ___?___.
   a. ___ a portrait
   b. _X_ a direct comparison (using *like* or *as*)
   c. ___ a theme

4. A *paradox* is ___?___.
   a. ___ a rephrasing
   b. _X_ a seeming inconsistency (as in Wordsworth's statement "The Child is father of the Man.")
   c. ___ a strict belief

5. *Alliteration* is ___?___.
   a. ___ the study of literature
   b. _X_ the repetition of a beginning consonant ("Nor cast one *longing, lingering look* behind?"—Gray)
   c. ___ the use of the same final sound

6. *Assonance* is ___?___.
   a. ___ the use of the same endings
   b. ___ the use of words that imitate sounds
   c. _X_ the repetition of the same vowel sounds (often in consecutive words: "mad as a hatter")

7. *Onomatopoeia* is ___?___.
   a. ___ unrhymed poetry
   b. ___ an Italian sonnet
   c. _X_ words that imitate sounds (In addition to words such as *buzz*, whiz, fizz, and *murmur*, note words such as *Minnehaha*, Laughing Water.)

8. *Free verse* ___?___.
   a. ___ has no rhythm or rhyme
   b. _X_ has neither rhyme nor consistent length (It has rhythms that change with the mood.)
   c. ___ has a regular rhythm pattern

9. A *fable* is ___?___.
   a. _X_ a story with a moral, often using animals as characters
   b. ___ a kind of formal essay
   c. ___ a funeral song

10. A *diary* is ___?___.
    a. ___ a direct comparison
    b. _X_ a person's own account of day-to-day events in his or her life
    c. ___ a story in the form of dialogue

11. *Blank verse* ___?___.
    a. ___ has rhyme but no rhythm
    b. _X_ is unrhymed verse with a meter (the meter is iambic pentameter)
    c. ___ has no rhyme or rhythm

12. *Apostrophe* is ___?___.
    a. ___ the use of rhyming couplets
    b. _X_ a kind of personification
    c. ___ a kind of meter

13. An *allegory* is ___?___.
    a. _X_ an extended metaphor (as Bunyan's *Pilgrim's Progress*)
    b. ___ a refrain or chant
    c. ___ a short stanza

14. An *elegy* ___?___.
    a. ___ is a lyrical ballad
    b. ___ describes a battle
    c. _X_ laments or honors the dead

15. An *epic* is ___?___.
    a. _X_ a long poem about a hero's deeds (as *Beowulf* and *Paradise Lost*)
    b. ___ a funeral song
    c. ___ a short poem in free verse

# Some Mythological Information

The following provides some background on mythological characters often cited in allusions and associations. It is not expected that students know all of these, but the information may be useful in vocabulary discussion and as a resource for teachers.

*Achilles.* This Greek warrior (hero of *The Iliad*) was invulnerable except in the heel. His mother had dipped him into the River Styx to make him invulnerable. It worked except in one place—the heel by which she had held him. Achilles died after an arrow pierced his heel. A person's weak spot is often called his or her *Achilles' heel.*

*Adonis.* A handsome youth loved by Aphrodite, Adonis was killed on a boar hunt. A flower sprang up from his blood—the *anemone,* "wind flower" (from the Greek *anemos,* wind, as in *anemometer,* a wind gauge).

*Aegis.* A magic shield made for Jupiter by Vulcan. Jupiter's daughter Minerva (Athena) is often portrayed carrying it. "To be under the aegis of" means to be under the protection or sponsorship of someone.

*Aeolus.* The Greek god of the winds, viceroy of the gods. The *Aeolian Harp* is a box fitted with strings that produce a musical tone when the wind blows through them. It is one of the foremost symbols of Romantic poetry.

*Agamemnon.* Commander in chief of the Greek army attacking Troy, he agreed to sacrifice his daughter in exchange for a good wind for his ships held in port by a calm.

*Alcyone.* The daughter of Aeolus, she was turned into a sea bird. According to Greek mythology, the halcyon bird nested at sea, so at this time the seas were calm. "Halcyon days" are calm, peaceful days.

*Amazons.* A nation of female warriors who were strong and skilled in battle.

*Ambrosia.* Originally the food of the gods, it has come to mean any food that is particularly delicious and special.

*Apollo.* The god of light, poetry, medicine, music, and prophecy. In Roman mythology his twin was Diana, goddess of the moon, hunting, and childbirth. In Greek mythology his twin was Artemis. Apollo was considered to represent the perfect young man.

*Arachne.* The proud Arachne, a mortal woman, challenged the goddess Athena to a weaving contest. Punished for her boldness, Arachne was changed into a spider so that she would have to spend the rest of her life spinning. *Arachne* is the Greek word for "spider" or "web." Note also English *arachnid* — an invertebrate of a class including mites, scorpions, and spiders.

*Atlas.* One of the Titans, Atlas was condemned to hold up the world on his shoulders.

*Aurora.* The goddess of the dawn. (Often pictured driving a chariot drawn by swift horses to announce the arrival of the sun.) The *aurora borealis* is the northern lights.

*Bacchus.* The Roman god of wine. Called Dionysus in Greek mythology.

*Cassandra.* This daughter of King Priam of Troy had the gift of prophecy, but the curse of not having anyone believe her prophecies about the doom of Troy. Hence a Cassandra is a person who prophesies disaster but is not heeded.

*Castor and Pollux.* Castor was a tamer of horses, and Pollux was known for his boxing skill. They were transformed into the constellation *Gemini* by Zeus.

*Centaur.* A wild mythological creature, half man and half horse.

*Ceres.* The Roman goddess of grain and agriculture (note: *cereal*). In Greek mythology she was called Demeter.

*Chaos.* The vast disordered matter that existed before the formation of the universe. The opposite of Chaos is *Cosmos* (order).

*Cupid.* The god of love who was the son of Venus, goddess of love. He often went about blindfolded, aiming his arrows indiscriminately. In Greek mythology he was called Eros.

*Cyclopes.* The Cyclopes were a race of giants who had only one eye in the middle of their foreheads. *Cyclops* means "round eye."

*Elysian Fields* or *Elysium.* In Greek mythology, the home of the blessed after death. It can refer to a place or condition of bliss and happiness.

*Furies.* The Furies were three goddesses who punished people who had committed crimes. They were pictured with snakes in their hair.

*Gordius.* The father of Midas. He once tied a knot that no one could untie. *Gordian knot* stands for an especially complicated or intricate problem. *To cut the Gordian knot* is to solve a problem by taking bold measures.

*Graces.* Three goddesses who gave out charm and beauty. Young men would take an oath of loyalty by the Graces.

*Hercules.* The strongest man on earth. He had to perform twelve great labors after having killed his wife in a fit of madness. One of these was to clean in one day the Augean stables, which housed 3,000 oxen and hadn't been cleaned for thirty years. Hercules changed the course of the rivers Alpheus and Peneus and let the water run through the stables. The phrase *Augean stables* refers to something dirty or corrupt. *Herculean labors* are extremely difficult tasks.

*Hermes.* In Greek mythology Hermes was the messenger of the gods, usually pictured with winged shoes and a winged hat. In Roman mythology he was called Mercury.

*Icarus.* One of the first aviators, and the son of the skilled architect Daedalus, who constructed a pair of wings for Icarus and himself. Despite his father's warning, Icarus flew too close to the sun, the wax holding the wings melted, and Icarus fell into the sea and drowned.

*Jupiter.* In Roman mythology, the king of the gods. Also called Jove. In Greek mythology he was called Zeus.

*Labyrinth.* A building with many winding passages and dead ends originally built as a prison for the Minotaur, a monster that was half man and half bull. The word *labyrinth* can refer to a construction that is highly complicated and confusing.

*Mars.* The Roman god of war. The word *martial* comes from Mars; *martial law* refers to the enforcement of laws by the military. In Greek mythology the god of war was called Ares.

*Medusa.* A glance at this creature turned a person to stone. Her head was covered with snakes instead of hair.

*Mentor.* An old, trusted friend of Odysseus and teacher and adviser of Odysseus' son Telemachus.

*Midas.* Bacchus gave King Midas his foolish wish—that everything he touched would turn to gold. Since even his food and drink turned to gold, he soon asked to be rid of the "Midas touch." Today, a financially successful person may be described as having the "Midas touch."

*Minerva.* The Roman goddess of crafts, war, and wisdom. In Greek mythology she was called Athena.

*Morpheus.* The son of Somnus (Sleep) and the god of dreams. Morpheus is related to Greek *morphe* (form; shape) because of the shapes or forms he presented to the dreamer.

*Narcissus.* He fell in love with his own reflection in a pool, stayed there gazing at it until he died, and changed into a flower—the narcissus. Note also the *Narcissus complex* — love of one's self.

*Nemesis.* The Greek goddess of retribution. She also measured out happiness and misery to each person.

*Neptune.* The Roman god of the sea. Called Poseidon in Greek mythology.

*Olympus.* The highest mountain in Greece, believed to be the home of the gods. Later, as the summit became accessible to man, Olympus became an imaginary mountain in the sky.

*Orpheus.* The son of the Muse Calliope, Orpheus could charm gods, men, and inanimate objects with his musical ability. His talent even got him past the gates of Hades to visit his beloved wife, Eurydice.

*Pan.* The god of the forest, flocks, and shepherds, who is often portrayed with the horns, hooves, and legs of a goat and playing a pipe or reed.

*Pandora.* In mythology, the first woman on earth. She became curious and opened a box from heaven, which released all the evils into the world. Only Hope remained in the box. Pandora means "all-gifted," from the Greek *pan,* all, + *doron,* gift.

*Paris.* The prince of Troy who abducted Helen, wife of Menelaus, the King of Sparta. For revenge, the Greek chiefs attacked Troy, beginning the Trojan war.

*Pegasus.* Mythological winged horse that flew to the heavens and is now a constellation.

*Phoenix.* A mythological bird that would set itself on fire when it was about to die. A new young bird would then rise from the ashes. The phoenix is a symbol of rebirth and immortality.

*Phobos.* The god of fear, the son and attendant of Mars, god of war. Phobos is Greek for *fear* (fear accompanies war). Note that Phobos still "attends" Mars—it is one of the moons of Mars.

*Pluto.* The Roman god of the underworld, identified with the Greek god Hades.

*Procrustes.* In Greek his name means "the stretcher." He made his victims "fit" his bed either by stretching the short ones or by lopping the limbs off the tall ones. A *Procrustean bed* refers to a preconceived, arbitrary idea being forced on someone.

*Prometheus.* Prometheus and his brother Epimetheus had the job of creating man and the animals and furnishing them with means of self-preservation. Epimetheus gave all his gifts to the animals and had none left for man, so Prometheus stole fire from heaven and gave it to man. A *Promethean act* is something daring and bold.

*Pygmalion.* He fell in love with a statue he had made. The statue came to life. Note George Bernard Shaw's play *Pygmalion* (and the musical version, *My Fair Lady*).

*Saturn.* The Roman god of the universe until overthrown by his son Jupiter. He is identified with the Greek god Cronus.

*Scylla and Charybdis.* Scylla, a mythical monster on one side of a narrow strait, and Charybdis, a treacherous whirlpool on the other, menaced ships sailing between them.

*Sirens.* Sea nymphs whose singing drew sailors to destruction on the rocky shore. The word *siren* has come to mean a seductive woman.

*Sisyphus.* A cruel king of Corinth who tricked the gods repeatedly. He was punished in the underworld by being made to roll a huge boulder to the top of a hill. As he reached the top the boulder would always roll back down again.

*Styx.* The river Styx was believed to encircle the darkness of Hades. The word *stygian* refers to something dark, dismal, or hellish.

*Tantalus.* This king's punishment after death was to have a great thirst while standing in a lake whose water receded each time he tried to drink. Fruit that hung above his head was always just out of his reach. Note the word *tantalize,* to tease.

*Trojan horse.* According to Virgil, the end of the Trojan war was brought about through the use of the Trojan horse. The Greeks hid in an enormous hollow wooden horse to sneak into Troy. The horse, thought to be a sacred gift, was pulled within the walls of the city. While the Trojans were asleep the Greeks climbed out of the horse, let the rest of the Greek warriors into Troy, and defeated the Trojan army. The phrase "Trojan horse" refers to a device introduced through treachery and intended to overthrow the enemy.

*Venus.* The Roman goddess of love and beauty. In Greek mythology she was called Aphrodite.

*Vulcan.* The Roman god of fire and the blacksmith for the gods.

**Word Entries**

**Pronunciation**

**Derivations**

**Parts of Speech**

**Phrases**

**Usage Notes**

**Definitions**

**Levels of Usage**

**Synonyms**

**Examples
of Usage**

**bib|li|o|thèque** (bē blē ō tek′), *n. French.* **1** a library. **2** a bookcase.

**bick|er¹** (bik′ər), *v., n.* —*v.i.* **1** to take part in a petty, noisy quarrel; squabble: *The children bickered through the long, hot afternoon.* **SYN:** fight, argue. **2** to babble; patter: *Streamlets . . . bickered thro' the sunny glade* (James Thomson). **3** to flash; flicker.
—*n.* **1** a petty, noisy quarrel. **2** a babble; patter. [Middle English *bikeren*] —**bick′er|er,** *n.*

**bick|er²** (bik′ər), *n. Scottish.* a wooden bowl. [variant of *beaker*]

**bi|col|or** (bī′kul′ər), *adj., n.* —*adj.* having two colors; bicolored. —*n.* a two-colored blossom.

**bi|col|our** (bī′kul′ər), *adj., n. British.* = bicolor.

✻**bi|cy|cle** (bī′sə kəl, -sik′əl), *n., v.,* **-cled, -cling.**
—*n.* a metal frame on two wheels, one behind the other, that supports a rider. The rider sits on a seat and steers with handles attached to the front wheel. . . . —*v.i.* to ride a bicycle.
[< *bi-* two + Greek *kýklos* circle, wheel]
▶**bicycle, bike.** Informal speech often uses the shortened form *bike.*

✻**bicycle**

brake lever
derailleur
chainwheel
chain
pedal

**bi|cy|clic¹** (bī sī′klik, -sik′lik), *adj.* **1** consisting of or having two circles. **2** *Botany.* in two whorls: *bicyclic stamens.* **3** *Chemistry.* containing two rings of atoms in the molecule: *bicyclic alcohol.* [< *bi-* two + Greek *kýklos* circle, wheel + English *-ic*]

**bi|cyc|lic²** (bī sik′lik, bī′sə klik), *adj.* of or having to do with bicycles.

**bid** (bid), *v.,* **bade, bid,** or (*Archaic*) **bad, bid|den** or **bid, bid|ding,** *n.* —*v.t.* **1** to tell (someone) what to do or where to go; command; instruct; direct: *Do as the law bids. The judge bid the witness sit down.* **SYN:** order. **2** to say; tell (a greeting or the like); wish: *His friends bade him good-by.* **3** (*past tense and past participle* **bid**) **a** to offer to pay (a certain price): *She bid five dollars for the table. He then bid seven dollars.* **b** to offer to charge a certain price: *The builder bid $1,000 to repair the porch.* **SYN:** proffer, tender. —*v.i.* to make an offer; offer a price: *to bid at an auction.*
—*n.* **1** the action of bidding: **a** an offer to pay a certain price: *She made a bid of seven dollars on the table.* **b** an offer to charge a certain price: *The painter made a bid of $100 to paint the room.* **2** the amount offered or stated: *Her bid was seven dollars. The painter's bid was too high.* **3a** the amount bid in a card game. **b** the turn of a player to bid: *Whose bid is it?*

**bid for,** to try to secure, obtain, or win: *Several companies will bid for the contract. The candidate is bidding for votes.*

**bid in,** to buy at auction to keep for the owner: *The costly books . . . were bid in at the sale of 1878* (Joseph F. Daly).
[Middle English *bidden,* Old English *biddan* ask for, influenced in sense by *bēden* < *bēodan* command, proclaim] —**bid′der,** *n.*
▶In the sense "command," now somewhat archaic, **bid** in the active voice usually takes an infinitive without *to: You bade me forget what is unforgettable.* With the passive *to* is used: *They were bidden to assemble.*

# Chapter Eleven

# Using the Dictionary

In 1755 Samuel Johnson published an English Dictionary which became the standard for decades in both England and America. In the Preface he states, "I applied myself to the perusal of our writers . . . noting whatever might be of use to ascertain or illustrate any word or phrase. . . ." He goes on to say, "[I] do not form, but register the language. [I] do not teach men how they should think, but relate how they have hitherto expressed their thoughts."

The dictionary is more than the recorder of a word's meaning. It is in a sense the depository of our labeled experiences and as such is a useful instrument for the teaching of vocabulary. The dictionary gives information on word derivation, meaning, spelling, and pronunciation. Dictionary study increases the student's understanding of general, technical, and literary terms. It also supplies information on the formal and informal use of words, idioms, foreign words, proper nouns, and abbreviations.

A surprisingly large number of students get as far as college without knowing how to use a dictionary to its fullest extent to increase their vocabularies. Unfortunately, the definition of an unfamiliar word (or as much of it as the student cares to read) may be comprehended at the time of reading but will quickly fade into obscurity unless the student, through careful analysis of the entire definition, can find sufficient keys to (1) understand it fully, (2) remember it, and most important, (3) use it intelligently.

Opposite are sample word entries from a dictionary page. This unit will discuss the labeled items in terms of how they might be helpful in vocabulary development.

## Word Entries

**bick|er¹** (bik′ər), *v., n.* —*v.i.* **1** to take part in a petty, noisy quarrel; squabble: *The children bickered through the long, hot afternoon.* SYN: fight, argue. **2** to babble; patter: *Streamlets . . . bickered thro' the sunny glade* (James Thomson). **3** to flash; flicker.
—*n.* **1** a petty, noisy quarrel. **2** a babble; patter. [Middle English *bikeren*] —**bick′er|er,** *n.*
**bick|er²** (bik′ər), *n. Scottish.* a wooden bowl. [variant of *beaker*]

It is important that students be able to find quickly the entry they are looking for. Recognition of word entries should come easily with a little practice, although knowledge of the system of entries will eliminate much trial-and-error searching.

Students should know, for example, that

1. all main entry words are listed in strict alphabetical order.

2. all entries are set in boldface type.

3. biographical entries are listed according to surname and alphabetized, if necessary, by given name: *Jackson, Andrew,* followed by *Jackson, Bruce,* and *Jackson, Ralph.*

4. each variant spelling has its own entry in alphabetical order. If two variant spellings are alphabetically close to each other, they may appear together as a joint boldface entry. Variant spellings alphabetically close to the main-entry spelling and pronounced exactly like it are given at the end of the entry block in small boldface. Example: **par·a·keet** . . . Also, **paraquet, paroquet, parrakeet, parroket, parroquet.** If the two entries are somewhat removed alphabetically, they are cross-referenced.

5. main entries may be single words, compounds, proper nouns, phrases, abbreviations, prefixes, suffixes, or roots. Proper nouns are capitalized. Other words begin with lower-case letters.

6. main entries that are spelled alike but differ in meaning and origin (homographs) are entered separately and marked by superscript numbers. Example:

   **pen**[1] . . . an instrument with a point to use in writing or drawing in ink.

   **pen**[2] . . . a small, closed yard for cows, sheep, pigs, chickens or other animals.

7. entries are syllabified by means of slashes or raised dots. The stressed syllable may be indicated by an accent mark ('), which replaces a syllable dot.

8. foreign entries are usually marked in a way that sets them off from English entries. The entry *au naturel* may be preceded by a double dagger (‡) or followed by *Fr.* placed in brackets.

## Using Guide Words

Although the sample column does not show them, each dictionary page contains two guide words in its top corners, indicating the first and last entries on the page. If, for example, a page contains the guide words *eternal* and *eulogy,* the reader will find *ethics* but not *evaluate.*

Students who need practice can be provided with many different guide-word exercises like the sample shown here. Given these guide words and the pages on which they are found, students are asked to indicate the pages on which they would expect to find the words listed in the second column.

| Guide Words and Page | Word | Page |
|---|---|---|
| flagpole—flat, 102 | gimmick | 132 |
| flourishing—flush, 104 | hayloft | 143 |
| genial—genus, 130 | gentle | 130 |
| gild—give, 132 | flamethrower | 102 |
| harmonica—haste, 140 | hash | 140 |
| hawk—heading, 143 | flush | 104 |

## Pronunciation and Parts of Speech

**bi|col|or** (bī′kul′ər), *adj., n.* —*adj.* having two colors; bicolored. (—*n.*) a two-colored blossom.
**bi|col|our** (bī′kul′ər), *adj., n. British.* = bicolor.
\* **bi|cy|cle** (bī′sə kəl, -sik′əl), *n., v.,* -**cled, -cling.** (—*n.*) a metal frame on two wheels, one behind the other, that supports a rider. The rider sits on a seat and steers with handles attached to the front wheel. On an ordinary bicycle the rear wheel is turned by a chain connected to pedals; on a motor bicycle the chain is attached to an engine. (—*v.i.*) to ride a bicycle.
[ < *bi-* two + Greek *kýklos* circle, wheel]

The pronunciation of a word, given in phonetic symbols, appears immediately after the word entry. Sometimes several correct pronunications are listed. Dictionaries generally provide a key to phonetic symbols at the bottom of the page, with more detailed explanations at the front of the book.

Parts of speech notations describe the word's grammatical use. The parts of speech are abbreviated, as in *adj.* for *adjective* and *n.* for *noun.* Verbs are shown as transitive or intransitive by *v.t.* (or *tr.v.*) and *v.i.* (or *intr.v.*).

When the same word can be used as more than one part of speech, the dictionary will list each definition separately. Students should notice, for example, that the entry *bid* (p. 126) can have a different denotation as a verb than it has as a noun. If students are weak in parts-of-speech recognition, practicing with simple sentences may help them to learn this skill. For example, using the word *alert* as a noun, an adjective, and a verb, we can construct sentences:

1. The *alerts* lasted ten minutes each.
2. The most *alert* boy was first to notice the smoke.
3. They *alerted* us of a change in plans.

We can ask ourselves the following questions:
1. Testing for the noun:
   Can we insert a noun determiner (*the, a,* or *an*) and still be understood?

2. Testing for the adjective:
   Can we insert *more* or *most* before the word (or add the suffix *-er* or *-est*) and still make sense?
3. Testing for the verb:
   Can we add *-ed* (or *-ing*) to the word and still make sense? (In other words, can we change the tense?)

Obviously, these tests are inconclusive, but they can often solve problems quickly when students are looking up words in the dictionary.

# Definitions

* **bi|cy|cle** (bī′sə kəl, -sik′əl), *n., v.,* **-cled, -cling.**
  —*n.* a metal frame on two wheels, one behind the other, that supports a rider. The rider sits on a seat and steers with handles attached to the front wheel. On an ordinary bicycle the rear wheel is turned by a chain connected to pedals; on a motor bicycle the chain is attached to an engine. —*v.i.* to ride a bicycle.
  [ < *bi-* two + Greek *kýklos* circle, wheel ]

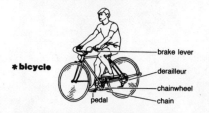

* **bicycle**

brake lever
derailleur
chainwheel
pedal
chain

**bi|cy|clic**[1] (bī sī′klik, -sik′lik), *adj.* **1** consisting of or having two circles. **2** *Botany.* in two whorls: *bicyclic stamens.* **3** *Chemistry.* containing two rings of atoms in the molecule: *bicyclic alcohol.* [ < *bi-* two + Greek *kýklos* circle, wheel + English *-ic*]
**bi|cyc|lic**[2] (bī sik′lik, bī′sə klik), *adj.* of or having to do with bicycles.

Definitions give the exact meanings of words. When a word has more than one meaning, the definitions are numbered. Generally, the most common definition is listed first. (Some dictionaries present definitions in historical order, beginning with the earliest known meaning.) Illustrations are often used to clarify the definitions. A label shows which definition is being illustrated.

One of the greatest sources of vocabulary development lies not so much in learning new words as in learning other meanings for words already known. For example, many students recognize the word *about* as a preposition (She wrote a book *about* dinosaurs) but may not realize that the same word as an adverb means "nearly" (The jar is *about* empty). *About* may also mean "somewhere in" (His tame raccoon was always wandering *about* the house). Thus, *about* has many meanings and is used in many common phrases, such as "up and about," "about to leave," "about face."

A group of first-graders, for example, would probably know the meaning of *above* in "Put that *above* the other book." But they would not be likely to know the meaning of *above* in the sense of something written before, as in "the *above*-mentioned problem." They would also not be likely to understand "She is *above* telling lies," since the literal sense of *above* fails to tell the reader that *above* carries with it the idea of moral superiority and integrity.

The word *battery* has a wide range of dictionary meanings. The young child will know it as something to put in a flashlight or in a car. Perhaps the sixth-grader will know that a battery stores electricity but not know *battery* in "The *battery* for today's game" (the pitcher and catcher). Indeed, some college students do not know the separate and joint meanings of the words in the expression "assault and *battery*."

The teacher might select certain words from the dictionary to put on the chalkboard, such as the word *bill*, and ask the students to list the various meanings found in the dictionary (a bird's beak; front part of a cap; theater entertainment, and so on). Another word, *bit,* will be known by most students as the past tense of *bite,* or as a small part of something. But its other meanings (something attached to a drill to bore holes; the part of a bridle that is placed in the horse's mouth) may be known to relatively few. The same may be true of the slang expression "two bits."

## Examples of Usage

**bick|er¹** (bik′ər), *v., n.* —*v.i.* **1** to take part in a petty, noisy quarrel; squabble: *The children bick-ered through the long, hot afternoon.* sʏɴ: fight, argue. **2** to babble; patter: *Streamlets ... bick-ered thro' the sunny glade* (James Thomson). **3** to flash; flicker.
—*n.* **1** a petty, noisy quarrel. **2** a babble; patter. [Middle English *bikeren*] —**bick′er|er,** *n.*
**bick|er²** (bik′ər), *n. Scottish.* a wooden bowl. [variant of *beaker*]
**bick|er|ing** (bik′ər ing), *n.* **1** wordy sparring or wrangling: *eternal bickering over German unifica-tion* (New York Times). **2** a skirmish.

The dictionary also provides examples of how a word is used in actual phrases and sentences. Such examples appear in italics to set them apart from the definition. Sometimes these examples may be quotations from well-known authors or publications. The source of the quotation appears in parentheses. The sample above includes a quote from Scottish poet James Thomson and a quote from the *New York Times*. For the student faced with a number of different definitions or definitions that are themselves difficult, examples may be the key to unlocking word meaning.

Students may enjoy finding their own examples of usage. Given certain words from the dictionary, students can read newspapers, magazines, stories, and poems in search of phrases and sentences that include the words. The teacher should provide ample opportunity for the students to share their quotations. Discussion may revolve around where certain words were found, how they were used, and the feelings evoked in each particular context.

# Phrases in the Dictionary

**bid** (bid), *v.*, **bade, bid,** or (*Archaic*) **bad, bid|den**
or **bid, bid|ding,** *n.*
—*n.* 1 the action of bidding: **a** an offer to pay a
certain price: *She made a bid of seven dollars
on the table.* **b** an offer to charge a certain price:
*The painter made a bid of $100 to paint the
room.* 2 the amount offered or stated: *Her bid
was seven dollars. The painter's bid was too
high.* **3a** the amount bid in a card game. **b** the
turn of a player to bid: *Whose bid is it?* 4 *U.S. Informal.* an invitation: *She has three bids to the
prom.* 5 an attempt to get or achieve: *She made
a bid for our sympathy by saying she was lonely.*
**bid fair,** to seem likely; have a good chance:
*The plan bids fair to succeed.*
**bid for,** to try to secure, obtain, or win: *Several
companies will bid for the contract. The candidate is bidding for votes.*
**bid in,** to buy at auction to keep for the owner:
*The costly books . . . were bid in at the sale of
1878* (Joseph F. Daly).
**bid up,** to raise the price of by bidding more:
*They bade them up until they reached 10,000
livres* (John H. Burton).
[Middle English *bidden,* Old English *biddan* ask
for, influenced in sense by *bēden < bēodan*
command, proclaim] —**bid'der,** *n.*

Many word entries list special meanings that depend on usage. The word *account* assumes a different meaning in each of these phrases:

a. to take into *account* (make allowance for)

b. to turn to *account* (make profit from)

c. to call to *account* (reprimand)

d. to *account* for (give a reason for)

e. on your own *account* (for yourself)

f. on no *account* (under no conditions)

g. on *account* of (because)

h. on *account* (on credit; partial payment)

i. of no *account* (of no use)

In the dictionary, these phrases are listed in boldface under the entry word, defined, and often placed (in italics) in sentence context.

Phrases like these can be used by the teacher for illustrating the concept of metaphor. The word *card*, for example, might be metaphorized in several ways in dictionary phrases:

a. He has a *card* up his sleeve. (holding back a plan)

b. Put your *cards* on the table. (be perfectly frank)

c. It's in the *cards*. (likely to occur)

## Word Pairs in the Dictionary

Illustrative phrases and sentences found in the dictionary often associate an entry word with certain other words. For example, the adjective *bumper* often appears with *crop* in "bumper crop." *Brand* may appear with *new* in "brand new." Such associations may be a basis for class discussion. Here is a sample list:

*kith and kin:* friends and relatives (from Old English *cyth,* known, and Old English *cyn*)

*null and void:* not binding (from Latin *nullus,* not any; French *voide* from Latin *vocāre,* to be empty)

*flotsam and jetsam:* things thrown overboard and floating on the sea; articles that drift ashore (*flotsam,* floating; *jetsam,* jettisoned, or cast overboard)

*assault and battery:* successful carrying out of a threat to do physical harm (*assault,* to threaten to beat; *battery,* to beat)

## Keys to Dictionary Definitions

Students using the dictionary to find the meaning of a word often discover that certain key words in the definition are harder than the word they are looking up. These defining, or key, words may be difficult, for example, because they involve technical labels for classes: *genus, species, implement, order.* In one dictionary, *dogwood* is defined as "any of a genus of various trees"—a definition of doubtful help to the student if he or she doesn't know what *genus* means. And some words may be unfamiliar to students at a particular grade level: a fourth-grade student looking in the dictionary for the word *cloth* may find that it is "*material* made from wool, cotton, etc." The key word *material* in this case may be harder for the student to understand than *cloth.*

In dictionary work, therefore, the student often needs help with the meanings of certain key words and phrases as they pertain to descriptions of people, places, actions, processes, qualities, geographic locations, functions, and physical appearances. In order to alert the teacher to some of these key words, the authors have included here a short list of key words and grade levels at which we can generally expect students to be familiar with them.

| Key Word | Grade of Key Word | Known by Students | Key Word in Definition |
|---|---|---|---|
| 1. article | 6 | 77% | hardware—article made from metal |
| 2. body | 4 | 87% | ocean—a great body of water |
| 3. body | 6 | 77% | law—body of rules recognized by a state |
| 4. form | 4 | 74% | hoop—a flat band in the form of a circle |
| 5. material | 4 | 69% | cloth—material made from wool, cotton, silk, etc. |

| | | | |
|---|---|---|---|
| 6. matter | 12 | 71% | gas—matter not solid or liquid |
| 7. inhabitant | 8 | 76% | Roman—an inhabitant of Rome |
| 8. pertaining | 8 | 70% | French—pertaining to the people of France |
| 9. identify | 10 | 79% | label (v.)—to identify, put into a class |
| 10. regarded | 8 | 75% | Liberty Bell—bell in Independence Hall regarded as a symbol of liberty |
| 11. represents | 6 | 74% | flag—specially designed colored cloth that represents a country |
| 12. representing | 10 | 72% | map—drawing representing earth's surface features |
| 13. study | 4 | 75% | astronomy—the study of the stars and planets |
| 14. class | 6 | 75% | reptile—any of a class of cold-blooded animals |
| 15. genus | 12 | 82% | dogwood—any of a genus of various trees |
| 16. order | 13 | 33% | fern—pteridophyte of the order of Filicoles |
| 17. species | 8 | 90% | shoveler—any of a species of freshwater ducks |
| 18. system | 6 | 67% | science—knowledge of facts in an orderly system |
| 19. unit | 6 | 74% | ampere—unit measuring strength of electric current |
| 20. variety | 6 | 72% | Sea Island cotton—long-staple variety of cotton |
| 21. character | 8 | 77% | plastic—having the character of being easily molded |
| 22. characteristic | 8 | 89% | metallic—characteristic of metal |
| 23. features | 8 | 70% | resemblance—having similar external features |
| 24. property | 10 | 85% | magnetic—having the property of attracting |
| 25. quality | 8 | 77% | beauty—the quality that pleases |
| 26. comprising | 10 | 68% | Hawaii—U.S. state comprising the Pacific islands of Hawaii, Kauai, etc. |

| | | | |
|---|---|---|---|
| 27. distinguished | 8 | 75% | hardbound (books)—as distinguished from paperback |
| 28. related | 4 | 80% | brown thrasher—songbird related to the mockingbird |
| 29. implement | 8 | 68% | tool—an implement used for working |
| 30. mechanism | 10 | 72% | gear—a mechanism for starting or changing motion |

## Derivations

*bi|cy|cle (bī′sə kəl, -sik′əl), n., v., -cled, -cling. —n. a metal frame on two wheels, one behind the other, that supports a rider. The rider sits on a seat and steers with handles attached to the front wheel. On an ordinary bicycle the rear wheel is turned by a chain connected to pedals; on a motor bicycle the chain is attached to an engine. —v.i. to ride a bicycle. [< bi- two + Greek kýklos circle, wheel]

bid (bid), v., bade, bid, or (Archaic) bad, bid|den or bid, bid|ding, n. —v.t. 1 to tell (someone) what to do or where to go; command; instruct; direct: Do as the law bids. The judge bid the witness sit down. syn: order. 2 to say; tell (a greeting or the like); wish: His friends bade him good-by. 3 (past tense and past participle bid) a to offer to pay (a certain price): She bid five dollars for the table. He then bid seven dollars. b to offer to charge a certain price: The builder bid $1,000 to repair the porch. syn: proffer, tender. 4 to proclaim; declare: He bade defiance to them all. 5 (past tense and past participle bid) to state as the number of tricks or points one proposes to make or to win in a hand of a card game. 6 Archaic. to invite: I made a feast; I bad him come (Tennyson). —v.i. to make an offer; offer a price: to bid at an auction. [Middle English bidden, Old English biddan ask for, influenced in sense by bēden < bēodan command, proclaim]—bid′der, n.

Derivations are statements of word origin. They indicate the language or languages a word has come from and show the changes in meaning and structure the word has undergone in becoming a part of our contemporary language. For example, one dictionary lists the derivation of *rhinoceros* as follows: [Latin *rhinoceros* < Greek *rhinókerōs* < *rhis, rhīnós* nose + *kéras* horn]. Notice that word-derivation statements are usually enclosed in brackets and that they often make use of symbols and abbreviations: < is the symbol for *from* or *derived from*. Some dictionaries abbreviate *from* as *fr.* and abbreviate languages (*Gr.* for *Greek* and *M.E.* for *Middle English* for example). The words *rhīnós* and *kéras* are italicized.

Dictionary derivations can be a basis for useful activities on word structure and comprehension. In an exercise on word analysis, students can use the dictionary to find the literal meanings of certain word parts (roots, prefixes, suffixes) listed in the derivation of a given word. Below is one form that might be used. Students write the prefix and root of each word, along with their meanings, in the appropriate blanks below. (Answers are provided.)

| Word | Prefix | Meaning | Root | Meaning |
|---|---|---|---|---|
| conduct | con- | together | duct | lead |
| predict | pre- | before | dict | say |
| repel | re- | back | pel | push |
| eject | e- | out | ject | throw |
| inaudible | in- | not | aud(ible) | hear(able) |

## Levels of Usage Labels

**bi|cy|clic**[1] (bī sī′klik, -sik′lik), *adj.* **1** consisting of or having two circles. **2** (*Botany.*) in two whorls: *bicyclic stamens.* **3** (*Chemistry.*) containing two rings of atoms in the molecule: *bicyclic alcohol.* [ < *bi-* two + Greek *kýklos* circle, wheel + English *-ic*]
**bi|cyc|lic**[2] (bī sik′lik, bī′sə klik), *adj.* of or having to do with bicycles.

**bid** (bid), *v.*, **bade, bid,** or (*Archaic*) **bad, bid|den** or **bid, bid|ding,** *n.* —*v.t.* **1** to tell (someone) what to do or where to go; command; instruct; direct: *Do as the law bids. The judge bid the witness sit down.* SYN: order. **2** to say; tell (a greeting or the like); wish: *His friends bade him good-by.* **3** (*past tense and past participle* **bid**) **a** to offer to pay (a certain price): *She bid five dollars for the table. He then bid seven dollars.* **b** to offer to charge a certain price: *The builder bid $1,000 to repair the porch.* SYN: proffer, tender. **4** to proclaim; declare: *He bade defiance to them all.* **5** (*past tense and past participle* **bid**) to state as the number of tricks or points one proposes to make or to win in a hand of a card game. **6** (*Archaic.*) to invite: *I made a feast; I bad him come* (Tennyson).

Levels of usage labels indicate when and where a word is most commonly used and whether the word is acceptable English usage. The labels are explained in the dictionary's introductory section.

The labels used most commonly include the following:

*Informal (Colloquial):* words generally acceptable in conversation but not in formal writing.

*Slang:* words used in new, special senses, often figurative, usually transitory, not suitable for formal writing.

*Substandard (Nonstandard, Dialectal):* words not acceptable to educated speakers. These may include forms that are results of misuse or forms that exist alongside standard forms (*ain't* for *isn't* or *aren't*).

*Vulgar:* words that carry a social taboo.

*Archaic:* words that were once common but are rarely used now. Compare with the label *Rare*, which indicates words that were never common.

Specialty labels (e.g., *Linguistics, Mathematics, Architecture, Botany, Military, Law*): words or definitions that are used within a specific field of knowledge.

Foreign-language labels (*Spanish, French, Italian*): words and expressions borrowed directly from other languages and still not belonging to English. In formal writing such words are usually set in italics. These labels may also be used to indicate definitions peculiar to another country (*bonnet,* a "hat;" or *bonnet, British,* "the hood of a car"). See section on Foreign Words and Phrases below.

## Usage Notes

**\*bi|cy|cle** (bī′sə kəl, -sik′əl), *n., v.,* **-cled, -cling.**
—*n.* a metal frame on two wheels, one behind the other, that supports a rider. The rider sits on a seat and steers with handles attached to the front wheel. On an ordinary bicycle the rear wheel is turned by a chain connected to pedals; on a motor bicycle the chain is attached to an engine. —*v.i.* to ride a bicycle.
[ < *bi-* two + Greek *kýklos* circle, wheel]
►**bicycle, bike.** Informal speech often uses the shortened form *bike.*
**bid** (bid), *v.,* **bade, bid,** or (*Archaic*) **bad, bid|den** or **bid, bid|ding,** *n.* . .
[Middle English *bidden,* Old English *biddan* ask for, influenced in sense by *bēden* < *bēodan* command, proclaim] —**bid′der,** *n.*
►In the sense "command," now somewhat archaic, **bid** in the active voice usually takes an infinitive without *to: You bade me forget what is unforgettable.* With the passive *to* is used: *They were bidden to assemble.*
►See **bade** for another usage note.

Usage notes in the dictionary deal with a variety of language skills. They discuss spelling and grammar and advise on how to use a word in speaking and writing. They may inform the student that *data* (information) is the plural of *datum* (an item of information) or that after *ability,* the infinitive of a verb is used rather than the gerund: *A lawyer needs the ability to think clearly,* not *of thinking clearly.* Or the student may learn that the preposition used after *ability* and before a noun is *in: ability in music.* Usage notes also explain problems or variations in the language, as in the example under *bicycle, bike* above.

## Synonyms

**bid** (bid), *v.,* **bade, bid,** or (*Archaic*) **bad, bid|den** or **bid, bid|ding,** *n.* —*v.t.* **1** to tell (someone) what to do or where to go; command; instruct; direct: *Do as the law bids. The judge bid the witness sit down* (**SYN:** order.) **2** to say; tell (a greeting or the like); wish: *His friends bade him good-by.* **3** (*past tense and past participle* **bid**) **a** to offer to pay (a certain price): *She bid five dollars for the table. He then bid seven dollars.* **b** to offer to charge a certain price: *The builder bid $1,000 to repair the porch* (**SYN:** proffer, tender.)

Sometimes the dictionary is of little or no help to students because the definition of a word is harder than the word itself. What good is it, ask students, if, in order to know one word, you have to look up three more to

137

understand its definition? For students with this kind of problem, many dictionary entries include synonyms. Teachers should be aware that this provision can unlock doors that formal definitions may never do, and they should promote dictionary use and point up the role of synonyms in increasing students' vocabularies.

Of course, students may need help in the areas of denotation (literal meaning) and connotation (associative or emotional meaning) in order to discriminate between synonyms. For example, the teacher might provide students with a word entry from a dictionary that includes synonyms as well as definitions. Class discussion may elicit the different feelings or associations students give the word and its synonyms. Students can also be encouraged to find their own examples of word entries and synonyms for discussion.

Some dictionaries not only provide synonyms but also explain the shades of meaning and usage for the different words. The *World Book Dictionary* provides the following for the word *ashamed:*

a|shamed (ə shāmd'), *adj.* 1 feeling shame; disturbed or uncomfortable because one has done something wrong, improper, or silly; feeling embarrassed or disgraced: *I was ashamed when I cried at the movies. The poor girl was ashamed of her ragged dress.* 2 unwilling because of fear of shame; held back by the belief that shame would be felt: *He was ashamed to tell his mother he had failed. A man should never be ashamed to own he has been in the wrong* (Alexander Pope). [Old English *asceamod,* past participle of *asceamian* feel shame < *a-* on + *sceamu* shame] —a|sham'ed|ly, *adv.* —a|sham'ed|ness, *n.*
— *Syn.* 1 Ashamed, humiliated, mortified, chagrined mean feeling embarrassed and disgraced. **Ashamed** emphasizes a feeling of having disgraced oneself by doing something wrong, improper, or foolish: *Later he felt ashamed at his lack of self-control.* **Humiliated** emphasizes a painful feeling of being lowered and shamed in the eyes of others: *Parents are humiliated if their children behave badly when guests are present.* **Mortified** means feeling greatly embarrassed and humiliated, sometimes ashamed: *He was mortified when he forgot his speech.* **Chagrined** means embarrassed and annoyed or disappointed: *I was chagrined to find that I had left the tickets at home.*

Once students are familiar with this sort of information they should be encouraged to use it. One suggested writing activity would be to have students find a word in the dictionary (*wet,* for example), list the synonyms for that word (*drench, soak*), and use each word in a sentence illustrating its particular meaning.

The point is that teachers can use the dictionary as a starting place to show students that (1) synonyms provided in the dictionary often help to unlock the meaning of a word, and (2) synonyms reflect shades of meaning, and when they are used correctly they can heighten the accuracy of verbal or written communication.

Students can use their dictionaries to help them complete exercises such as the one below. One dictionary entry may provide clues to several unknown words. They should write the answers to as many of the word clues as they can, then look up one unknown word at a time. Teachers should be aware, of course, that not all dictionary entries will provide synonyms. But students can often use dictionary definitions to arrive at an answer. The point is that students will be able to reinforce their concepts (i.e., "beginning" and "ending") as they proceed through the exercise.

The words below mean "begin" or "end". If a word means "begin", the student is to write **B** in the blank. If it means "end", the student writes **E** in the blank. (Answers are provided.)

Sample __E__ conclude (end)  __B__ origin (begin)

1. __B__ launch
2. __E__ finale
3. __B__ initiate
4. __E__ omega
5. __E__ expire
6. __B__ primer
7. __B__ alpha
8. __E__ epilogue
9. __B__ incipient
10. __B__ preliminary

11. __B__ genesis
12. __B__ initial
13. __E__ terminal
14. __B__ debut
15. __B__ prologue
16. __B__ embark
17. __B__ inaugurate
18. __B__ prelude
19. __E__ destination
20. __B__ overture

## Foreign Words and Phrases in the Dictionary

**bib|li|o|thèque** (bē blē ō tek′), n. *French.* 1 a library. 2 a bookcase.
**bick|er¹** (bik′ər), v., n. —v.i. 1 to take part in a petty, noisy quarrel; squabble: *The children bickered through the long, hot afternoon.* syn: fight, argue. 2 to babble; patter: *Streamlets ... bickered thro' the sunny glade* (James Thomson). 3 to flash; flicker.
—n. 1 a petty, noisy quarrel. 2 a babble; patter. [Middle English *bikeren*] —**bick′er|er**, n.
**bick|er²** (bik′ər), n. *Scottish.* a wooden bowl. [variant of *beaker*]

Since many words in our language originated in different parts of the world, we might say that there is a "geography" of words. Although we have anglicized the majority of these words, there are still many that have retained aspects of their original spellings and pronunciations.

The difference between the words and phrases that are recognized as part of the English language and those that remain foreign can be determined by the way they are listed in the dictionary. Words and phrases that are listed with their pronunciation, part of speech, and definition have been accepted as part of the English language. Words and phrases that are given a foreign language label (e.g., *French, Spanish, Italian*) between their pronunciation and definition are still separate from the English language, even though they may be used frequently in writing and speaking. The acceptance of certain expressions is a matter of usage and may vary from one dictionary to another or between an older edition and a newer one.

The list below provides some examples of French terms that are listed in the dictionary. The teacher may discuss the ones students are familiar with and have them look up the meanings of unfamiliar ones.

| Word | Meaning |
|---|---|
| au courant | well-informed |
| bon vivant | lover of luxury |
| flâneur | an idler |
| pièce de résistance | chief dish of a meal; something outstanding |
| joie de vivre | joy of living; enjoyment of life |
| idée fixe | fixed idea; obsession |
| coup d'oeil | a quick glance |
| coup de maître | a master stroke |
| hors de combat | disabled; out of action |

## Latin Words in the English Dictionary

The English language abounds with words of Latin origin. Many Latin phrases, unchanged from centuries ago, are standard usage in areas such as law and politics. Some commonly used abbreviations are based on Latin words. For example, *A.D.* stands for *anno Domini* (in the year of the Lord), *A.M.* for *ante meridiem* (before midday), *P.M.* is *post meridiem* (after midday), and *etc.* for *et cetera* (and the rest). The list below covers some of the most common Latin expressions students may come across.

| Word or Phrase | Meaning |
|---|---|
| addendum(-a) | to be added; an appendix |
| ad hoc | for this purpose |
| ad lib(itum) | freely; spontaneously |
| ad nauseam | to the point of nausea |
| alias | otherwise named |
| alter ego | another self |
| a priori | from the cause to the effect |
| bona fide | in good faith |
| caveat emptor | let the buyer beware |
| corpus delicti | facts that prove a crime (literally "body of the crime;" popularly known as "the murdered person") |
| datum(-a) | a fact or principle granted (from *dare*, "to give") |
| de jure | by right; by the law |
| dictum | a saying; a pronouncement |
| emeritus | retired but holding rank and title |
| erratum(-a) | an error |
| ex officio | by virtue of one's office |
| ex post facto | after the deed is done; after the fact |

| | |
|---|---|
| extempore | without preparation; offhand |
| fiat | let it be done; a decree |
| habeas corpus | a writ to release someone from unlawful restraint (literally "you shall have the body") |
| persona non grata | unacceptable person |
| sine qua non | absolutely necessary |
| status quo | way things are |
| verbatim | word for word |

## Additional Information in the Dictionary

Often a certain section of the dictionary is devoted to explaining the abbreviations used by writers and printers. An understanding of these abbreviations should be considered an important part of a student's vocabulary skills.

In writing a research paper, students need to refer to certain publications to find information. They will be confronted with technical terms and abbreviations in their research, and they may need to make use of the same in their writing. Students should know that instead of saying *for example* they can write *e.g.* (from Latin *exempli gratia,* meaning "for the sake of an example"). Another abbreviation they might see is *viz.,* short for Latin *videlicet.* The translation of this Latin term is "it may be seen; it is clear." The usual meaning of the word is "namely" or "to wit."

The following words may be used in a class discussion to help students gain an understanding of their use in books and periodicals, or simply as a reference for teachers when such abbreviations come up in class work.

| Abbreviation | Meaning |
|---|---|
| p. | page |
| pp. | pages |
| anon. | anonymous |
| ff. | following (pages) |
| vol. | volume |
| et al. | et alii (Latin "and others") |
| e.g. | exempli gratia (Latin "for the sake of an example") |
| i.e. | id est (Latin "that is") |
| ibid. | ibidem (Latin "in the same place") |
| cf. | conferre (Latin "compare") |
| loc. cit. | loco citato (Latin "in the place cited") |
| n.b. | nota bene (Latin "note well") |
| non seq. | non sequitur (Latin "it does not follow") |
| op. cit | opere citato (Latin "in the work cited") |
| viz. | videlicet (Latin "namely," "it may be seen") |
| q.v. | quod vide (Latin "which see") |
| Q.E.D. | quod erat demonstrandum (Latin "which was to be demonstrated or proved") |

In addition to material previously discussed, many dictionaries also include the following:

1. common abbreviations.

2. signs and symbols used in many fields, such as astronomy ($\ominus$ earth); biology, ($\sigma$ male, $\varphi$ female); mathematics ($\pi$ pi); medicine ($\mathbb{R}$ prescription).

3. biographical names with their pronunciations, as well as information about famous men and women.

4. a pronouncing gazetteer that lists names, locations, populations, and other information about important geographical features, countries, regions, cities, and so on.

5. common first names of men and women, including the literal meaning of each name.

6. a vocabulary of rhyming words, helpful in writing verse.

7. rules for the correct use of punctuation, capitals, compounds, parts of speech, and so on.

8. information on the preparation of bibliographies, including correct form for author names, book titles, magazines, and so on.

9. pointers about preparing a manuscript for publication.

10. proofreaders' marks and their meanings, for example: $\wp$ (delete), $\subset$ (close up); $\P$ (paragraph).

11. illustrations of word entries by means of drawings, diagrams, and photographs.

12. differentiations in usage between words such as *respectively* and *respectfully; continual* and *continuous; uninterested* and *disinterested; luxurious* and *luxuriant; flaunt* and *flout.*

13. other forms of the entry word, such as principal parts of verb forms (*bicycle, bicycled, bicycling*) and other words formed by the addition of suffixes (*bid, bidder*).

14. irregular inflectional forms: *spectrum, spectrums* or *spectra; fungus, funguses* or *fungi; children, oxen, geese, beaux,* and so on.

15. cross references to additional information elsewhere, usually marked by an arrow for attention.

# Chapter Twelve

# Using Word Games

An important objective of vocabulary instruction is developing students' interest in words. Students whose curiosity about words is aroused are likely to increase their vocabularies and to become more discriminating in using words. One way to develop students' interest in words is the use of word games to supplement vocabulary lessons.

Students generally enjoy word games and exercises. In this unit we will discuss riddles, crossword puzzles, hidden words, anagrams, palindromes, and other forms of word play. It is believed that these lessons will

1. point up the elements of enjoyment and challenge in language study and encourage word play.
2. require students to look carefully at words (an important aspect of vocabulary building).
3. give students practice in calling up words to match given clues.
4. require students to match words with definitions.
5. provide spelling practice and encourage close attention to word formation.
6. show students how the letters of many words can be manipulated to form other words.
7. emphasize the importance of letter position in relation to word meaning.
8. encourage students to classify and generalize concepts.

Grade level is significant in deciding the kinds of exercises to use. Some of the exercises require more mature thinking; others can be done at a lower grade level. However, by using appropriate words the teacher can fit the techniques of almost any exercise to the desired grade level.

## Riddles and Puns

Riddles can be used at the earliest elementary levels to show children the fun of word play. Riddles can be written as clues for guessing vocabulary words, or as clues to building words from parts. For example:

I have four legs,
But I cannot walk.
People sit around me,
But I cannot talk.
What am I? (table)

I fall in drops
From the sky.
I keep the plants
From going dry.
What am I? (rain)

Given the root words *spot* and *color* and the endings *-ful* and *-less,* students answer the following riddles.

I am red, blue, green, and yellow. I keep people warm. I am a _____ quilt.

I am white. I have no dirt on me. You can wear me with pants. I am a _____ shirt.

Words and word parts with similar or identical sounds can be used as a basis for riddles and puns. Puns play with the meanings and sounds of words; for example, "The sign on the boat said *For Sail.*" Many riddles use puns as part of the answer. (These riddles are sometimes called conundrums.) Below are some examples of riddles and puns for a slightly higher grade level. Teachers may wish to present puns and riddles in groups in which answers are based on a common theme (such as the flower riddles below) or on word structure (such as the word-ending riddles). Teachers could ask students to collect their own riddles or construct their own puns to share with the class.

### Finding Flowers

1. What flowers do you use for kissing? **tulips**
2. What flower is seen in the eye? **iris**
3. What nation has a lot of cars? **carnation**
4. What flower wants to be remembered? **forget-me-not**
5. When do sheep look like a flower? When they come in **phlox.**
6. What plant is a fake stone? **shamrock**

### Riddles and Word Endings

1. How can you help a lemon? Give it **lemonade**.
2. What log moves around? a **travelog**
3. What age does a ship have? **anchorage**
4. What age is a stamp? **postage**
5. What ant is proud? **arrogant**
6. What ant lives in a house? **occupant**

Another form of word play involving puns is called *Swifties.* To play Swifties, students use an adverb in a sentence to make a joke: "'There's no water in the well,' Ruth said dryly." Swifties provide students with a humorous and clever way of looking at words and word meaning. In each sentence below, students select the adverb that would make a joke.

1. "Do you think the lake is frozen?" Tom asked ___?___.
   icily      kindly      quickly
2. "Sharpen my pencil," Rosa said ___?___.
   flatly      pointedly      nicely
3. "There's too much lemon in the lemonade," Julie said ___?___.
   sweetly      eagerly      sourly
4. "Be careful with that knife," Mike said ___?___.
   snappily      cuttingly      rapidly

Once students understand the concept of Swifties, they can be encouraged to make up their own to share with the class.

## Stink Pinks and Spoonerisms

Stink Pinks provide practice with synonyms. To play Stink Pinks, students write a pair of rhyming words that are synonyms for a definition: "An **unhappy father** is a **sad dad.**" To introduce Stink Pinks, the teacher can give students sentences to complete.

1. A **fake horse** is a **phony** _____ .
2. An **imitation serpent** is a **fake** _____ .
3. A **simple downpour** is a **plain** _____ .
4. A **splendid musical group** is a **grand** _____ .

A variation of this is to provide lists of Stink Pinks and definitions for students to match.

1. chilly lily
2. foul owl
3. pale whale
4. bee tea

a. a light-colored ocean mammal
b. a shivering flower
c. a beverage for insects
d. a bird that is out of bounds

Students can also write Stink Pinks to fit given definitions.

1. a comical rabbit _____
2. a scary flash of light in a storm _____
3. a sneaky insect _____
4. a drooping crustacean _____

Another form of word play that can be used to illustrate the fun of language is *spoonerisms,* named after the Reverend William A. Spooner, who was noted for such slips. Spoonerisms switch the beginning sounds or parts of words to make humorous sentences. For example: "Our team suffered a blushing crow in the game." A well-known radio announcer once excitedly introduced President Herbert Hoover as "Hoobert Heever." Other bloopers heard by thousands over the radio include "a twenty-one sun galoot" and "The Duck and Doochess of Windsor."

Students may be given several puns and spoonerisms and asked to identify which is which. In the examples below, students mark a **P** if the sentence is a pun, or an **S** if the sentence is a spoonerism.

1. Allie will be ready to go at the hop of a drat.
2. My favorite book is *How I Broke My Ankle* by Jim Nastics.
3. May I sew you to a sheet?
4. Jan is tow as a slurtle this morning.
5. I'd like to read *Hit By a Bus* by Jay Walker.

Teachers could also provide examples of spoonerisms for students to rewrite so they make sense.

# Crossword Puzzles

The crossword puzzle is still the most popular word game. At the elementary level, very simple puzzles can be given to students to fill in, such as the example below, which focuses on opposites. Students read the word in each puzzle and then write a word from the box that means the opposite.

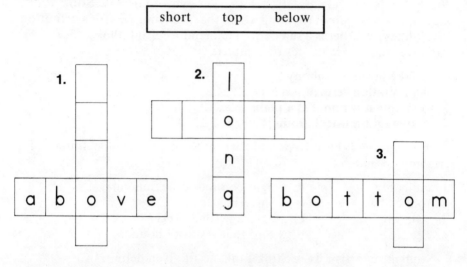

Other crossword puzzles can be devised for work on specific vocabulary words, concepts, or subjects at the appropriate grade level. An example with clues is provided here if the teacher should wish to reproduce it.

**Clues for Crossword Puzzle on Sports**

### Across

6. It is played with a ball and paddles at a table.
8. It is played with a mallet.
10. Its players dribble the ball.
12. Riding waves on a board.
13. Use of a bow and arrow.
16. Riding on the water.
17. Its players hit a puck while ice-skating.
19. Its players don't like bogeys.
22. Game played by people on horseback.
23. Its players move a ball with their feet, head, or body into the opposing team's goal.
25. He or she rides on a bridle path.

### Down

1. Rod and reel are used in it.
2. A gun is used in it.
3. Players compete in forty-yard dash on it.
4. The ball is hit with the hand.
5. All its players wear helmets.
7. The backstroke is used.
9. Its players use a racket to hit a ball over a net.
10. It is played on a diamond.
11. Its players use cues.
14. Its players use a stick with a net at one end.
15. Its players hit a ball over a net with their hands.
18. You can sit or lie on it to go down a snow slope.

27. Taking a short trip on foot.
29. A birdie is used in it.
30. It is played between wickets.

20. Swords are used in it.
21. Skimming along on top of the water.
24. Player knocks pins down.
26. Moving on little wheels.
28. Gliding across a frozen pond.

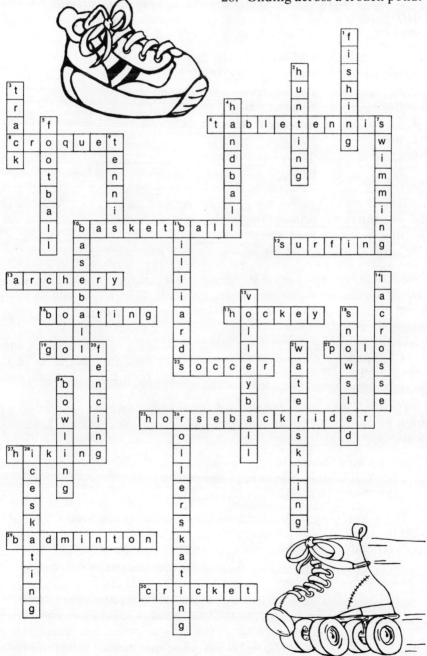

# Hidden Words

There are a number of different forms and levels of hidden word games that can be adapted to the needs of the teacher's class. At the most basic, students can be given words and asked to find words hidden in them. Definitions of the hidden words may be provided to give students clues of what to look for. This exercise gives the students practice in letter discrimination and word recognition and tests their ability to call up a word on the basis of its definition.

| Key Word | Definition of Hidden Word |
|----------|---------------------------|
| 1. weight | a number word |
| 2. hoarse | paddles for rowing a boat |
| 3. flute | stringed musical instrument |
| 4. globe | lower part of ear |
| 5. drift | a split or break |
| 6. graze | destroy completely |
| 7. hail | be ill |
| 8. invent | an opening |
| 9. brand | outer coat of wheat kernel |
| 10. coupon | brilliant move |
| 11. diner | loud noise |
| 12. kayak | Asian ox |

Note: In the above exercise students are asked to choose only the hidden word that fits the definition. A variation of this exercise would be to give students words and have them find their own hidden words without clues. Students may find more than one word within each larger word.

Teachers might also call attention to hidden words within sentences that happen by chance arrangement of letters. For example, in the sentence "I saw Bob at home," the student can try to find the animal name (*bat*).

Teachers may provide sentences with hidden words for students to find, or groups of words may be given to see if students can hide them within sentences.

1. This is an uncommon key. (*monkey*)
2. They will be arriving soon. (*bear*)
3. Eskimos try to keep igloos warm. (*pig*)

At a slightly higher level, teachers may provide hidden word puzzles, square or rectangular forms in which words are run together horizontally and vertically. The advantage of this technique lies in the ease with which the puzzle can be constructed. Unlike the crossword puzzle, there are no blank spaces or numbers to contend with. Words are laid out in a grid, and spaces in between words can be filled in with letters at random.

In forming a hidden word puzzle, teachers may select a concept (such as "short" and "long," or a category (such as colors, space terms, school subjects, professions, parts of speech, or proper nouns). A list of hidden words may be provided with the puzzle, or students could be challenged to find as many words as possible with no clues.

The example below uses words related to the concept of "small." Students circle each word as illustrated.

**Hidden Word Puzzle**

```
m  e  a  g  e  r  m  i  n  i  a  t  u  r  e
i  o  t  a  l  l  i  e  p  i  t  t  z  e  l
c  j  o  t  i  s  c  a  n  t  d  w  a  r  f
r  s  m  a  l  l  r  m  o  l  e  c  u  l  e
o  u  t  i  n  y  o  p  o  i  b  t  w  r  x
c  n  h  f  m  u  n  c  x  l  u  s  e  u  i
o  d  u  r  c  h  i  n  t  l  t  e  e  n  g
s  e  m  i  c  r  o  b  e  i  e  s  s  t  u
m  r  b  s  w  e  e  m  r  p  y  g  m  y  i
i  s  a  t  d  i  m  i  n  u  t  i  o  n  t
n  i  n  u  u  m  i  n  u  t  e  l  f  o  y
i  z  t  n  m  a  r  u  d  i  m  e  n  t  m
m  e  a  t  p  c  e  t  o  a  t  h  i  n  i
u  a  m  e  y  r  l  i  o  n  f  i  n  e  t
m  l  o  d  e  o  p  a  r  t  i  c  l  e  e
```

**Across**

| | | | |
|---|---|---|---|
| meager | scant | urchin | minute |
| germ | dwarf | microbe | elf |
| miniature | small | wee | thin |
| iota | molecule | pygmy | fine |
| jot | tiny | diminution | particle |

**Down**

| | | | |
|---|---|---|---|
| microcosm | Tom Thumb | minutia | runt |
| minimum | bantam | Lilliputian | elf |
| undersize | stunted | ant | mite |
| atom | micron | wee | |

## Anagrams

The teacher may use anagrams (words made by transposing letters of one word to form another) to give students practice in word formation and spelling. The word *anagram* comes from Greek *ana-*, back, + *gramma*, letter. Anagrams may be used to build students' interest in words, offering them the opportunity to concentrate on the manipulation of letters to form words.

The teacher may have students interchange the letters of a key word and write in the blank another word appropriate to each definition.

Shorter words may be made by omitting some letters of the key word and transposing the rest. For example:

1. Key word: rail
   Definition: a lion's den
   New word: lair

2. Key word: rail
   Definition: one who lies
   New word: liar

3. Key word: rail
   Definition: what you breathe
   New word: air

4. Key word: bear
   Definition: uncovered
   New word: bare

5. Key word: bear
   Definition: what you hear with
   New word: ear

6. Key word: bear
   Definition: plural of "is"
   New word: are

A favorite variation of this that is easily adaptable to any ability and age is having students see how many words they can form from key words.

| Key word | Words formed from key word |
| --- | --- |
| 1. turn | urn, nut, run, rut, tun . . . |
| 2. mean | man, men, am, name, me, an . . . |
| 3. cheat | heat, eat, hat, cat, tea, hate . . . |
| 4. course | sour, our, rose, core, us, sore, use . . . |
| 5. listen | tinsel, enlist, list, ten, tin, tile, let, lint . . . |
| 6. fortune | fort, forte, tune, turn, turf, route, tone . . . |

Another approach is to present the anagrams in context. For example, the student rearranges the letters in each italicized word below and writes the appropriate anagram.

Example: *Untied* we stand, divided we fall.    united

| | |
| --- | --- |
| untied | 1. His shoelace is *united*. |
| sword | 2. The guard drew a *words*. |
| ambled | 3. The old man *blamed* around the park. |
| tinsel | 4. They decorated the tree with *silent*. |
| luster | 5. The paint on the new car had an attractive *rustle*. |
| heart | 6. To reach the mind we first must touch the *earth*. |
| care | 7. He didn't seem to *race* whether he won or not. |
| evil | 8. Love of money is the root of all *vile*. |
| ample | 9. There is *maple* room for dancing. |
| tastes | 10. There is no disputing about *states*. |

Students may be given anagram exercises focusing on a specific category, such as the names of the days and months.

| Column A | Column B |
| --- | --- |
| 1. yam | May |
| 2. ah sturdy | Thursday |
| 3. bear fury | February |
| 4. say duet | Tuesday |
| 5. do many | Monday |

|       |             |           |
|-------|-------------|-----------|
| 6.    | cede berm   | December  |
| 7.    | den say dew | Wednesday |
| 8.    | me on verb  | November  |
| 9.    | a sturdy a  | Saturday  |
| 10.   | charm       | March     |

Students may be asked to find the colors hidden in the clues below.

|     |              |            |
|-----|--------------|------------|
| 1.  | gore an      | orange     |
| 2.  | lube         | blue       |
| 3.  | we hit       | white      |
| 4.  | genre        | green      |
| 5.  | rule pp.     | purple     |
| 6.  | low lye      | yellow     |
| 7.  | in k.p.      | pink       |
| 8.  | quit rouse   | turquoise  |
| 9.  | a man a quire| aquamarine |

Another variation of this exercise is school subjects:

|     |              |            |
|-----|--------------|------------|
| 1.  | tar          | art        |
| 2.  | shingle      | English    |
| 3.  | chair met it | arithmetic |
| 4.  | pen gills    | spelling   |
| 5.  | ring wit     | writing    |
| 6.  | egg ray hop  | geography  |

## Palindromes

Words, phrases, and sentences that read the same forwards and backwards are called *palindromes,* from the Greek *palindromos,* meaning "running back again," from *dromos,* "running; course." (Note the related words *dromedary* and *hippodrome.*) The teacher might present a palindromic word and phrase and ask students what they notice about them:

> sees
> Walsh's law

Some other examples of palindromes are as follows:
> Hannah    Otto    rotor    level
> stops spots    gold log
> Name no one man.
> Red root put up to order.
> A man, a plan, a canal—Panama.

After he lost his power and was exiled to the island of Elba, Napoleon might have said:
> Able was I ere I saw Elba.

The teacher can provide clues and have students write palindromes.

1. A female sheep.   _____ (ewe)
2. Paper showing ownership of land.   _____ (deed)
3. A baby wears one.   _____ (bib)
4. A method for detecting distant objects in the air.   _____ (radar)
5. Another way to say hang as in "hang the curtain."   _____ (put up)
6. You see with it.   _____ (eye)
7. Eskimo boat.   _____ (kayak)
8. A joke.   _____ (gag)

Students might enjoy keeping their own lists of palindromes. Perhaps the class could have a contest in which the lists would be judged for both length and originality.

## Consonant-Vowel Substitution

To build students' interest in word formation, teachers can challenge them to make words by manipulating letters within a prescribed form. As we have previously pointed out, interest in words may be heightened by various kinds of word games. The following game requires close attention to letter discrimination and can be a means of providing practice in concentration on words and spelling. Many of the key words used are antonyms.

In this exercise the student must change only one letter at a time to form a new word; for example, moving from *like* to *hate* in three steps or from *well* to *sick* in four steps:

| | |
|---|---|
| like | well |
| lake | will |
| late | sill |
| hate | silk |
| | sick |

The teacher will note that most of the beginning items in the examples below are words likely to be known by younger students. Some of the later material that involves more steps or more difficult words is suitable for the higher grade levels. The number of steps used is not important. One student may take more or fewer steps than another, but all students must change only one letter at a time. And the words used to go from one key word to another may differ. For example, the student may move from *dog* to *cat* in at least two ways:

| | |
|---|---|
| dog | dog |
| cog | dot |
| cot | cot |
| cat | cat |

1. calf
   <u>c</u> a <u>l l</u>
   <u>b</u> a <u>l l</u>
   bull

2. pig
   b <u>i</u> g
   b <u>a</u> g
   s <u>a</u> g
   s <u>a</u> <u>y</u>
   sty

3. give
   <u>g</u> <u>a</u> <u>v e</u>
   <u>c</u> <u>a</u> <u>v e</u>
   <u>c</u> <u>a</u> <u>k e</u>
   take

4. wet
   <u>b</u> <u>e</u> t
   <u>b</u> <u>a</u> t
   <u>b</u> <u>a</u> <u>y</u>
   <u>d</u> <u>a</u> <u>y</u>
   dry

5. cool
   <u>w</u> <u>o</u> <u>o</u> l
   <u>w</u> <u>o</u> <u>o</u> <u>d</u>
   <u>w</u> <u>o</u> <u>r</u> <u>d</u>
   <u>w</u> <u>a</u> <u>r</u> <u>d</u>
   warm

6. find
   <u>f i n</u> e
   <u>l i n</u> e
   <u>l o</u> <u>n</u> e
   lose

7. work
   <u>p</u> <u>o</u> <u>r</u> k
   <u>p</u> <u>o</u> <u>r</u> t
   <u>p</u> <u>o</u> <u>s t</u>
   <u>p</u> <u>e</u> <u>s t</u>
   rest

8. hard
   <u>h</u> <u>a</u> <u>r e</u>
   <u>b</u> <u>a</u> <u>r e</u>
   <u>b</u> <u>o</u> <u>r e</u>
   <u>s</u> <u>o</u> <u>r e</u>
   <u>s</u> <u>o</u> <u>r t</u>
   soft

## Adding Letters To Form New Words

Students can also play with word formation by taking given words and adding and transposing letters to form new words. This exercise can be structured to form pyramids made of words of increasing length. Each step requires that all the letters in the previous word be used, in addition to one or two new letters:

```
a b l e          i c e
t a b l e        l i c e
t a b l e t      s l i c e
                 s p l i c e
```

To make this word game a whole class activity, the teacher can divide the class into two or more teams. Members of each team take turns adding one or two letters to make new words. The degree of difficulty can be varied by setting the number of words needed in a pyramid—four, five, or six are suggested. Or the goal may be to form as big a pyramid (as many words) as possible.

On the whole, words to which mere inflectional endings are added, such as *run, runner, running,* should not be counted as new words, although a teacher in the lower grades might try this approach to provide practice in using endings. Likewise, the teacher might decide to accept the addition of prefixes to form new words: *migrate, emigrate, immigrate.*

A few word groups suitable for various levels are included below. The teacher might write the first word of a group on the chalkboard and have the teams proceed on their own.

| 1. | 2. | 3. | 4. |
|---|---|---|---|
| I | ad | or | nor |
| it | cad | for | corn |
| fit | card | fort | acorn |
| fist | cared | forte | carton |
| first | carted | forest | cartoon |

| 5. | or | 6. | in | 7. | had | 8. | to |
|---|---|---|---|---|---|---|---|
| | ore | | fin | | hard | | top |
| | wore | | fine | | heard | | stop |
| | worse | | define | | thread | | pouts |
| | lowers | | refined | | thrashed | | spouts |
| | flowers | | | | | | sprouts |

## Suggested List of Word Games

The teacher can get many ideas for word game exercises from commercial word games. The list below is a sampling of games available through stores and school supply companies. Not included in this list are computer games. While there are many excellent software programs available, it is recommended that teachers refer to specific computer catalogs and recent reviews of new games to find ones that will match their system and needs.

*Alphadeck.* Twenty-one letter-card games in alphabetizing, phonics, spelling. One player to whole class. Educator's Publishing Service, Inc., Cambridge, Massachusetts 02238.

*Board Talk.* Players move around board, collecting letters and building words; first player with longest word wins. Up to four players. New England School Supply, Agawam, Massachusetts 01001.

*Boggle* and *Big Boggle.* Players find hidden words in adjacent letters from grid of 4 x 4 letters or 5 x 5 letters. Up to four players. Parker Brothers, available through New England School Supply, Agawam, Massachusetts 01001.

*Can Do! Structural Analysis.* Card games on plurals, syllables, contractions, compounds, prefixes, suffixes. Ideal School Supply, Oak Lawn, Illinois 60453.

*Can Do! Vocabulary.* Card games on six vocabulary skills, including synonyms, antonyms, homonyms, verbs, nouns. Ideal School Supply, Oak Lawn, Illinois 60453.

*CHIPS.* Bingo-type game provides practice on short vowel words with consonant-vowel-consonant, initial consonant blends, final consonant blends, initial-final consonant blends. Up to four players. Educator's Publishing Service, Inc., Cambridge, Massachusetts 02238.

*Consonant Lotto* and *Vowel Lotto.* Provides practice in hearing and learning initial consonants and blends, medial vowels and vowel combinations. Garrard Publishing Co., Champaign, Illinois 61820.

*Double Talk.* Players use letter cards to create two complete words before anyone else; throws of the dice allow players to rearrange and replace cards. Up to four players. New England School Supply, Agawam, Massachusetts 01001.

*Educational Password.* Revised version of Password for elementary students. From two players to whole class. Milton Bradley, available through New England School Supply, Agawam, Massachusetts 01001.

*Game Drawer Series.* Tic-tac-toe, track games, puzzles, card games, lotto, bingo, game variations focus on decoding skills. Drawer 7 (Grades 2-3): blends, digraphs, short vowels, plurals, words in context. Drawer 8 (Grades 3-4): silent consonants, long vowels, verb forms, compounds, words in context. Drawer 9 (Grades 4-5): vowels modified by *r* and *l,* vowel diphthongs, root words and comparison suffixes, prefixes, words in context. Drawer 10 (Grades 5-6): consonant and vowel clusters, compounds, prefixes, suffixes, roots, words in context. Ideal School Supply, Oak Lawn, Illinois 60453.

*Junior Worbage.* Word building game develops encoding, spelling, vocabulary. Two to four players or two teams. Ideal School Supply, Oak Lawn, Illinois 60453.

*Last Word.* Players form words on field on letter tiles and pick up tiles for points. Two to four players. Milton Bradley, available through New England School Supply, Agawam, Massachusetts 01001.

*Megamix.* Players twist rings to form words. One or more players. Selchow & Righter Co., New York, New York 10010.

*Password.* Word association game. Three or four players. Milton Bradley, Springfield, Massachusetts 01101.

*Phonic Rummy.* Provides practice on basic sight vocabulary, reinforcement of vowel sounds, blends, digraphs. Six different levels from readiness to intermediate. Kenworthy Educational Service, Buffalo, New York 14205.

*Pronto.* Players roll letter cubes and use them at once to form words or save on pads for potentially more points. One or two players. Selchow & Righter Co., New York, New York 10010.

*Qwink.* Players make words on own boards using same letters as they are called out. Two players. Selchow & Righter Co., New York, New York 10010.

*Reader's Digest Q & A.* Self-contained electronic package with small computer to display right or wrong, keep score. Comes with two booklets: Word Power (based on *Reader's Digest* feature) and Brain Power (variety of subjects). Other booklets include Word Power II, Junior Word Power I and II, Science, History, Sports, others. One or two players or teams. Selchow & Righter Co., New York, New York 10010.

*Scrabble.* Original crossword game. Two to four players. Selchow & Righter Co., New York, New York 10010.

*Scrabble Duplicate Edition.* Players all play same letters each turn, forming words on Scrabble scoring sheets. For any number of players. Selchow & Righter Co., New York, New York 10010.

*Scrabble for Juniors.* Edition for ages 6-10. Selchow & Righter Co.

*Scrabble Sentence Game for Juniors.* Players ages 6-12 create sentences. Two to four players. Selchow & Righter Co., New York, New York 10010.

*Sea of Vowels.* Two game possibilities focusing on long and short vowels, vocabulary enrichment. Two to six players or two or three teams. Ideal School Supply, Oak Lawn, Illinois 60453.

*Sentence Builder.* Includes basic word cards, upper and lower-case letters, punctuation marks. Various games possible. Milton Bradley, available through New England School Supply, Agawam, Massachusetts 01001.

*Silly Sounds.* Players learn consonants, form word combinations (adjective-noun, noun-verb, verb-adverb), build vocabulary. Two to six players. Ideal School Supply, Oak Lawn, Illinois 60453.

*Space Flight.* Players work on initial blends and vocabulary to complete journey to a planet. Two to six players. Ideal School Supply, Oak Lawn, Illinois, 60453.

*Spar.* Companion to *Spello,* reinforces advanced spelling and language skills. Two to four players. Ideal School Supply, Oak Lawn, Illinois, 60453.

*Spello.* Provides practice in spelling, increases vocabulary, six degrees of difficulty. Two to six players. Ideal School Supply, Oak Lawn, Illinois 60453.

*Start Your Engines.* Provides practice on word families and initial consonants. Two to four players. Ideal School Supply, Oak Lawn, Illinois 60453.

*Syllable Game.* Provides practice in word attack, familiarity with common syllables. One or two players. Garrard Publishing Co., Champaign, Illinois 61820.

*Syllable Plus.* Provides practice in identifying syllable types in mono- and polysyllabic words. One to five players. Educator's Publishing Service, Cambridge, Massachusetts 02238.

*Upwords.* Players build words with tiles, form new words by changing one or more letters of existing words, adding layers and scores. Two to four players. Milton Bradley, available through New England School Supply, Agawam, Massachusetts 01001.

*Vocabulary Building Game.* Players blast off on mission through space.

Includes dictionary skills as well as vocabulary. Up to six players. New England School Supply, Agawam, Massachusetts 01001.

*Vocabulary Quizmo.* Lotto game on synonyms and antonyms. Up to whole class. Milton Bradley, available through New England School Supply, Agawam, Massachusetts 01001.

*Wingo-Wordo.* Bingo-type game provides practice on consonant and short vowel sounds and letters. Up to six players. Educator's Publishing Service, Cambridge, Massachusetts 02238.

*Word Challenge.* Game set with sixteen word games, letter cards, and chips. Ideal School Supply, Oak Lawn, Illinois 60453.

*Word Demons.* Provides practice in non-phonetic words, grades 2 and above. Educator's Publishing Service, Cambridge, Massachusetts 02238.

*Word War.* Players build words on re-usable crossword-type boards. Up to nine players. New England School Supply, Agawam, Massachusetts 01001.

# Chapter Thirteen

# Testing as Teaching

Testing is a highly useful part of vocabulary instruction because (1) students must pay close attention to complete the exercise correctly; (2) answers to the questions are clear-cut; (3) students are actively involved; (4) students' ability is being measured; therefore they sense the importance of the exercise; (5) the questions are generally brief; and (6) teachers have a quick measurement of student progress.

But in the area of vocabulary, testing can be much more than an assessment tool. In the process approach to vocabulary, testing is an important instructional technique as well. Brief tests followed by self-correction and class discussion can be viewed very positively by students.

Many people who love language enjoy testing themselves informally. *Reader's Digest* recognizes that fact and includes a vocabulary test in each issue with words from articles and multiple-choice definitions. Also popular is a game called "Dictionary," in which players make up definitions for an unknown word. The real definition is slipped in among the rest, all the definitions are read aloud, and players vote for the one they think is real.

By showing how vocabulary testing can be both fun and challenging, teachers can give their students a more positive outlook on language acquisition. Students look forward to the informal testing and make self-evaluation part of their own study habits.

## Testing and Modality Strengths

It is within the testing situation that a student's learning strength, or modality strength, may be most apparent. As a test becomes more difficult, students rely more on their dominant modality, and they exhibit characteristic behaviors. Visual children tend to close their eyes, stare into space, or stare at a blank wall in an effort to "see" the answer. Auditory children talk to themselves, trying out different words subvocally or debating the different options to see what "sounds" right. Kinesthetic children squirm and fidget in their seats. They may fiddle with their pencils or pens. They often write an answer just to get something on paper, only to erase it when they think it doesn't "feel" right.

In many testing situations, visual children are favored slightly because tests are primarily visual tasks. It is possible that visual children do better than children with other strengths since even a slight recognition of words will help them. As they look at each word or item, familiar configuration patterns may lead them to the right answer even if they are not quite sure why. They sometimes just know when something looks wrong.

Auditory children may test at a slower rate than their ability would indicate. The subvocalizing they do sometimes interferes with the speed at which they can complete the items. Their saying words, definitions, or sentences to themselves is a slow process; when the pressure is great, they may not get past the first few items. Given the opportunity to respond orally, auditory children may improve their scores substantially.

For kinesthetic children, the physical action of filling in test answers is the task to be completed. They tend to lose sight of getting the right answers in favor of just getting through all the items. On standardized test formats, kinesthetic children may impulsively fill in circles according to some pattern, or just because "I haven't filled in an **a** or **b** yet." If the teacher announces the approach of the end of the time limit, kinesthetic children will quickly mark any answers so that they will have completed the test when they hand it in.

## Vocabulary and Modality Strengths

Teachers should also note children's use of language during vocabulary lessons and throughout the day. The words each child uses when writing and speaking will be another clue to his or her dominant modality.

Visual children tend to have separate reading and speaking vocabularies. They are able to recognize words in print that they do not use when speaking. They do not remember new words they have heard until they can also see them written down or until they can write the words themselves. It appears as though visual learners use more descriptive adjectives when writing and speaking. They are more aware of nuances of color, size, and shape.

Auditory learners have the broadest speaking vocabularies. The more auditory learners read, the more they increase their speaking vocabularies, since they subvocalize what they read. Also, they are more likely to pick up words they hear only once and use them in their own speech. They may or may not use them correctly; they like the sound of the words. Auditory learners are more likely to perceive differences in inflection and accent but also may have a harder time discriminating between words that sound alike.

The vocabulary of kinesthetic learners is brief and direct. They may have an inexhaustible supply of verbs—they will be able to demonstrate every possible variation of the verb "to move," from *limp, float,* and *stagger* to *strut, swoop,* and *dash.* But they neither use qualifiers nor react to qualifiers when others use them. They are impulsive, and when they hear a verb as the teacher gives directions or reads a story, they frequently do exactly what they hear. One teacher relates the story of the time she announced, "In fifteen minutes it will be time to go to lunch." One of her students promptly got up and went to the door. He had heard nothing more than "go to lunch" and had reacted accordingly.

# Vocabulary Testing Methods

There are four main ways to test vocabulary: (1) *Checking*—the students check the words they know or don't know. They may also be required to write a definition for each word they know. (2) *Identification*—the students identify a word according to its definition or use by responding orally or in writing. For example, a word may be identified as a synonym of another word. (3) *Multiple-choice*—the students select the correct answer from three or four options. This may be structured to test words and definitions or to test distinctions between words, where the students select the best word to complete a sentence. (4) *Matching*—the words being tested are presented in one column, and the matching definitions are presented out of order in another column. This is another form of multiple-choice test.

## Self-Inventory Checklist

In using a self-inventory checklist, students merely check the words they know (or don't know), thus determining for themselves, to an extent, their word knowledge. They may be asked to define several of the words they know. Later they may consult a dictionary to see how accurate their answers were. The purpose is to alert students to the state of their word knowledge, to show them their strengths and weaknesses.

Various lists may be constructed, preferably having some relationship to the students' areas of study or interests. For example, the teacher may present a list of geography terms such as the following, for students to check:

| | | |
|---|---|---|
| glacier | oasis | peninsula |
| swamp | tundra | arctic |
| crater | isthmus | ravine |
| canyon | savanna | prairie |
| reef | strait | timberline |
| delta | tributary | atoll |

One variation of the self-inventory uses the symbols +,✓ , -, O. Students indicate on a chosen list of words how well they know each word.

+ means "I know it well; I use it."
✓ means "I know it somewhat."
- means "I've seen it or heard of it."
O means "I've never heard of it."

The teacher may list words related to a subject to be studied, such as health:

| | | |
|---|---|---|
| muscle | protein | calcium |
| diet | carbohydrate | cholesterol |
| energy | calories | thiamine |
| vitamin | nutrition | strength |

The same technique may be used diagnostically by an English teacher, for example, to measure knowledge of literary terms. Words might include the following:

| | | |
|---|---|---|
| drama | lyric | metaphor |
| dialogue | essay | metonymy |
| couplet | simile | irony |
| sonnet | personification | soliloquy |

## Identification

The teacher may structure identification exercises in several ways. Students can be given a list of words and asked to provide a synonym or antonym for each, or they can be given definitions and asked to provide the corresponding words.

Students write an antonym for each word.
1. expensive
2. clumsy
3. wide
4. shallow
5. weak
6. wet

Students write a word to match each definition.
1. a small woodland animal with gray fur, having black face markings and a bushy ringed tail
2. a one-wheeled cart used for carrying loads
3. a large reptile that lived millions of years ago
4. a special aircraft with blades that spin above the craft
5. a white or gray mass of tiny drops of water or ice in the sky

## Multiple-Choice Testing

This format can be used to test knowledge of definitions, word origins, or other concepts. In the first example, students circle the meaning of the underlined word.
1. The molten lava flowed down the mountainside in a glowing stream.
   melted    icy
2. A lethargic dog was dozing on the porch in the summer sunshine.
   ambitious    drowsy
3. Without meaning to, Jerry made an involuntary gesture of sympathy towards Sam.
   unintentional    irritated

Students mark **a, b,** or **c** to complete each sentence.
1. The Roman god of fire was Vulcan. A mountain that throws out fiery lava and gases is a __?__ .
   a. lava    b. volcano    c. fire
2. The Titans were very large creatures in Greek mythology. The __?__ is a large and powerful rocket.
   a. Astronaut    b. Space    c. Titan
3. Helios was the Greek god of the sun. An element once thought to be made from the sun is __?__ .
   a. helium    b. iron    c. sunshine

The multiple-choice technique may also be used to point up the distinctions between word meanings. For example, the high school student may be asked to check the best word to complete sentences such as the following:

1. It was a hot day with a great deal of moisture in the air. The day was ( ) parching, ( ) stifling, ( ) balmy.
2. While washing dishes, Mary broke a plate. "You're a big help," her mother said. Mary's mother was being ( ) ironic, ( ) sarcastic, ( ) satirical.
3. Judging from the number of burned trees on the hill, the forest ranger ( ) implied, ( ) inferred that soil erosion would soon be a problem.

Reasons for choices should be discussed after the exercise has been completed.

The teacher may let students correct the exercises by including the answers at the bottom or the left side of the paper (to be covered and disclosed after students complete the test).

A. Matching words with definitions.
1. ____ mobile       a. cut in two            e. ten-sided figure
2. ____ bisect       b. movable               f. yearly
3. ____ octagon      c. one hundred years     g. ten years
4. ____ century      d. eight-angled figure
5. ____ decade

B. Matching roots with definitions.
1. ____ aud      a. look      e. side
2. ____ graph    b. hear      f. sound
3. ____ spect    c. write     g. call
4. ____ phon     d. angle
5. ____ gon

C. Matching prefixes with definitions.
1. ____ penta-   a. one    e. four
2. ____ di-      b. five   f. three
3. ____ mono-    c. six    g. nine
4. ____ quad-    d. two
5. ____ tri-

D. Matching words with related phrases.
Students can be tested on their knowledge of the general meanings of given words by matching these words with other words or phrases (not definitions) that refer to them. The student draws a line from the word to the word or phrase that is generally associated with it.

a. owl       flies high       c. Chihuahua    large
   eagle     called wise         St. Bernard   small

b. carat     diamond          d. dogs         gaggle
   caret     editing             geese         kennel

163

| e. canine | puppy |
|---|---|
| feline | kitten |

| f. spider | web |
|---|---|
| bee | honey |

| g. lions | covey |
|---|---|
| quail | pride |

| h. elephant | memory |
|---|---|
| snake | fangs |

## General List of Vocabulary Testing Methods

(Methods previously described are marked with an asterisk.)

*1. Have students check known words from a list of words.

*2. Have students identify
   a. synonyms for words.
   b. antonyms for words.
   c. words from definitions.

3. Have students write out definition(s) for words. Students can provide their own definitions, or they can use a dictionary. (Use sparingly. It is easy to overdo this approach.)

*4. Have students match words, roots, prefixes, or suffixes with definitions.

5. Have students define roots, prefixes, or suffixes in given words.

6. Present words for division into prefixes, roots, suffixes.

7. Provide roots, prefixes, and suffixes for students to use to form words.
   a. Students write as many words as possible from a given root before consulting a dictionary. Then students use the dictionary to add to the list those words they know but did not recall the first time.
   b. Students use one root in three positions:

| graphite | geographic | telegraph |
|---|---|---|
| (beginning position) | (root position) | (ending position) |

   c. Students combine key roots from a list to form words.

| Word Parts | | Words |
|---|---|---|
| alti | phon(o) | altimeter |
| auto | meter | autograph |
| demos | thermo | thermometer |
| graph(y) | crat | democrat |
| | | phonograph |
| | | demography |
| | | thermography |

   d. Roots and prefixes are laid out in a grid form, with prefixes running vertically and roots running horizontally. Students mark the places within the grid where the prefixes and roots can be combined to form words and then write the words out at the bottom.

|        | duc(t) (lead) | tract (draw) | cycle (wheel) | pel (push) | claim (call) |
|--------|:---:|:---:|:---:|:---:|:---:|
| tri-   |   |   | ✕ |   |   |
| pro-   | ✕ | ✕ |   | ✕ | ✕ |
| ex-    |   | ✕ |   | ✕ | ✕ |
| re-    | ✕ | ✕ | ✕ | ✕ | ✕ |

| tricycle | product | extract | reduce |
|---|---|---|---|
|  | protract | expel | retract |
|  | propel | exclaim | recycle |
|  | proclaim |  | repel |
|  |  |  | reclaim |

8. Have students derive the meanings of words from *internal* context clues (from the meanings of component parts):

*Incapable* means _____ . *Inaccurate* means _____ . Then reverse the procedure: A word meaning *not capable* is _____ .

9. Present a paragraph with some words underlined. Ask students to infer the meanings of the words. Discuss the use of internal and external context clues.

10. Have students derive the meanings of words from *external* context clues (from the relationship to other words in the sentence):

They had lemons, oranges, *pomegranates,* and other kinds of fruit.

11. Have students complete comparisons or analogies:

Black is to white as hot is to _____ .
Zenith is to nadir as apogee is to _____ .

12. Have students cross out the word that doesn't belong (classification tests):

| 1. centurion | senate | Caesar | Mikado |
|---|---|---|---|
| 2. agora | Shinto | acropolis | amphitheater |
| 3. cuneiform | sphinx | Cicero | pharaoh |

13. Have students classify words under given topics.

14. Test students' knowledge of names of countries, rivers, towns, key products, and so on through a multiple-choice or matching format.

1. Tokyo          a. Illinois
2. Chicago          b. New York
3. United Nations          c. Japan

15. Have students name the document, speech, or literary or historical character from several key words in a quotation:

(Students write source.)

countrymen, lend, bury, praise _____
allegiance, republic, indivisible _____
course, events, dissolve, bands _____

16. Test the meanings of words in famous quotations:
    1. pledge, allegiance, republic, indivisible
    2. fourscore, conceived, proposition
    3. events, dissolve, assume, self-evident
    4. preamble, insure, domestic, tranquility
This may be done by multiple-choice or matching tests.

17. Have students substitute the correct word for underlined "boners":
    1. He's not legible for the army. (eligible)
    2. The speaker suffered from allusions of grandeur. (delusions)
    3. My tire is punctuated. (punctured)
    4. My sister had romantic fever. (rheumatic)

18. Test inflectional variations in words to find out if students see the relationship between words of the same root. A list of words is presented in one column, and the student is asked to provide a base word from which each is derived. (If the teacher wishes, students may check themselves by using an answer key like the one on the right.)

|    |                 |             | **Answers** |
|----|-----------------|-------------|-------------|
| 1. | palatial        | _____ | palace      |
| 2. | signify         | _____ | sign        |
| 3. | personification | _____ | person      |
| 4. | wholly          | _____ | whole       |
| 5. | wearisome       | _____ | weary       |
| 6. | wastrel         | _____ | waste       |

Words selected will depend on students' level of attainment. Other words that might be included are as follows:

| | |
|---|---|
| absentee, absent | erasure, erase |
| authenticity, authentic | erroneous, error |
| collegiate, college | partition, part |
| demolition, demolish | persuasive, persuade |
| denunciation, denounce | pilgrimage, pilgrim |
| domesticity, domestic | plurality, plural |
| habitual, habit | pollinate, pollen |
| humanitarian, human or humanity | pretense, pretend |
| indicative, indicate | quietude, quiet |
| exemplify, example | rarity, rare |
| pervasive, pervade | reality, real |
| evasive, evade | remedial, remedy |
| competitive, compete | responsive, response |
| debutante, debut | simplify, simple |
| decisive, decide | sobriety, sober |
| deprivation, deprive | truism, true |
| elephantine, elephant | typical, type |

# Appendices

# Appendix A

## List of Common Prefixes and Derived Words

| Prefix | Meaning | Example Words |
|--------|---------|---------------|
| a- | on | ashore, aboard, afire, atop, afoot |
| a- (ad-)* | to | amuse, amass, ameliorate |
| a-, an- | not, without | atom, anemia, aseptic, apathy, atheism |
| ab- | from | absent, abduct, abdicate, abnormal, abstain |
| ac- (ad-) | to | accident, acquire, accept, accessory, accommodate |
| acro- | height, extremity | acrobat, acronym, acrophobia, acropolis |
| ad- | to | admit, adhere, adverb, adjacent, adjunct |
| af- (ad-) | to | affair, affirm, affect, afferent, affix |
| ag- (ad-) | to | aggression, aggravate, aggregate, agglutinate, agglomeration |
| ambi- | both, around | ambidextrous, ambiguous, ambivalent |
| amphi- | both, around | amphibious, amphibian, amphitheater, amphibiology, amphipod |
| an- (ad-) | to | annotate, announce, annul, annihilate, annex |
| ana- | back, again, up, according to | anachronism, analysis, anaphora, Anabaptist, anabasis, analogy |
| ante- | before | antedate, anteroom, antebellum, antecedent |
| anti- | against | antifreeze, antisocial, antidote, antislavery, antiseptic |
| apo- | away from, from | apogee, apostle, apocryphal, apotheosis, apostasy |
| as- (ad-) | to | ascribe, assist, aspersion, aspect, assault |
| auto- | self | autograph, automobile, automatic, autobiography |
| be- | thoroughly, all around, to make | bewilder, beloved, betray, besiege, befriend, belittle, becalm, besmirch |
| bene- | well, good | benefit, benediction, benefactor, benevolent |
| bi-, bin-, bis- | two, twice | bicycle, bimonthly, bisect, biceps, binocular, biscuit |
| by- | near, aside, from | bystander, bypass, byplay, byroad |
| cata- | down, against, back | catalog, catapult, cataract, catacomb, catastrophe |
| cent- | hundred | century, centenary, centipede, centimeter |
| circu-, circum- | around | circuit, circumnavigate, circumference, circumlocution |
| co- (com-) | together, with | coworker, cooperate, coexist, coalition |
| col- (com-) | together, with | collect, collaborate, college, colloquial |
| com- | together, with | combine, companion, compact, compose |
| con- (com-) | together, with | connect, concentrate, conference, congress |
| contra-, contro- | against | contrast, contradict, contrary, contraband, contravene, controversy, incontrovertible |

*Throughout this Appendix original forms for assimilated prefixes are given in parentheses.

169

| Prefix | Meaning | Examples |
|---|---|---|
| counter- | against, in return | counterclockwise, counterattack, counterbalance, counteract, counterrevolution |
| de- | down, away, reversal, completely | descend, depress, detract, deter, decode, decrease, declare, devote |
| dec- | ten | decade, decimal, December, decathlon |
| deci- | tenth | decimal, decimate, decimeter, decibel |
| demi- | half, partly | demigod, demimonde, demitasse |
| di- | two | diphthong, dioxide, divalent, dilemma |
| dia- | through, across, between, apart | diameter, diagonal, dialogue, diaphragm, diagnosis |
| dis-, di-, dif- | not, apart from, reversal | dishonest, disable, diffident, dismiss, discard, differ, divulge, discomfort, disconnect |
| du- | two | dual, duet, duplex, duplicate, duplicity |
| dys- | bad | dyspepsia, dysfunction, dysentery |
| e- (ex-) | out | eject, emit, erupt, elicit, elevate |
| ec- (ex-) | out | ecstasy, eccentric, eclipse, eclectic, ecdysis |
| ecto- | outside | ectoplasm, ectoderm, ectoblast, ectopia |
| ef- (ex-) | out | effect, efferent, effulgent, effort, efficient |
| em- (en-) | in | empathy, empiric, embrace, embark |
| en- | in | encircle, enfold, encase, enclave |
| endo- | inside | endoderm, endoskeleton, endocrine |
| enter- (inter-) | among, between | entertain, entertainer, enterprise |
| epi- | upon, in addition | epilogue, epidermis, epitaph, epidemic |
| equi- | equal | equilateral, equilibrium, equinox, equivalent |
| eu- | well, good | eulogy, euphemism, euphonious, eugenics |
| ex- | out | exit, extract, exclude, excerpt, exaggerate |
| exo- | outside of | exoderm, exoskeleton, exocentric |
| extra- | outside, beyond | extravagant, extracurricular, extradite |
| for- | prohibit, omit | forfend, forgo, forlorn, forswear |
| fore-, for- | before, in front | foresee, foretell, foreground, forward |
| forth- | forward, onward | forthcoming, forthright, forthwith |
| hemi- | half | hemisphere, hemiplegia, Hemiptera |
| hept- | seven | heptagon, heptangular, heptarchy |
| hetero- | different | heteronym, heterogeneous, heterodox, heterosexual |
| hex- | six | hexagon, hexameter, hexahedral |
| holo-, hol- | whole | holocaust, holography, holistic |
| homo- | same | homogenized, homonym, homogeneous |
| hyper- | over, beyond | hypersensitive, hyperacidity, hyperbole |
| hypo- | under, too little | hypodermic, hypotenuse, hypochondriac |
| il- (in-) | not | illegal, illogical, illegible, illiterate |
| im- (in-) | into | immerse, immigrate, implant, impale |
| im- (in-) | not | immaterial, impartial, immaculate |
| in- | into | include, incorporate, incentive |
| in- | not | inactive, informal, incorrigible |
| infra- | below | infrared, infraglacial, infrastructure |
| inter- | between, among | international, intermission, intercede |
| intro-, intra- | into, within | introduce, introvert, introspective, intramural, intravenous |
| ir- (in-) | not | irregular, irresistible, irreverent, irrational |
| iso- | equal, same | isobar, isometric, isosceles, isotope |
| kilo- | 1,000 | kilocycle, kilogram, kilometer, kilowatt |
| macro- | large, long | macron, macroscopic, macrometer |
| mega- | large | megalomania, megaphone, megalith |
| meso- | middle | mesoderm, Mesozoic, mesosphere |

| | | |
|---|---|---|
| meta- | change, beyond | metaphor, metamorphosis, metabolism, metaphysics |
| micro- | small | microscopic, microphone, micrometer |
| mid- | middle | midday, midnight, midship, midwestern |
| milli- | 1/1,000 | millimeter, milligram, millisecond |
| mis- | wrong | misspell, misdeed, misinterpret |
| mono- | one | monarch, monocle, monoplane, monorail |
| multi- | many | multitude, multimillionaire, multicolored |
| myria- | countless, 10,000 | myriad, myriapod, myrialiter, myriameter |
| ne-, neg- | not | never, nefarious, neuter, neglect |
| neo- | new, modern | neon, neologism, neophyte, Neolithic |
| non- | not | nonstop, nonsense, nonentity |
| nona-, novem- | nine | nones, nonagon, November, novena |
| o- (ob-) | away, against, to, toward | omit, omission |
| ob- | away, against, to, toward | obey, object, obstacle, obdurate |
| oc- (ob-) | away, against, to, toward | occasion, occlude, occupy |
| oct- | eight | octopus, October, octagon, octave |
| of- (ob-) | away, against, to, toward | offer, offend, offensive |
| off- | from | offshore, offshoot, offspring, offset |
| olig- | few | oligarchy, oligopoly, Oligocene |
| omni- | all | omnipotent, omnivorous, omniscient, omnibus |
| on- | on | ongoing, onshore, onside, onslaught |
| op- (ob-) | away, against, to, toward | oppose, opportune, oppressive, opprobrium |
| ortho- | straight, right | orthodontia, orthodox, orthography, orthopedics |
| out- | surpassing, outside of | outreach, outrun, outstanding, outskirts, outlying, outfield, outsider, outcast |
| over- | above, beyond | overhead, overwhelm, overdone, overshoot |
| pan- | all | pandemonium, panorama, panacea, pan-American |
| para- | beside, beyond | paragraph, parallel, parasite, paradox, parable |
| pen-, pene- | almost | peneplain, peninsula, penultimate |
| penta- | five | pentagon, Pentecost, pentameter, pentathlon |
| per- | through, thoroughly | pervade, perpetual, permanent, permit, perceive, perfect |
| peri- | around, near, about | periscope, perimeter, periphery, peripatetic, perigee |
| poly- | many, more than one | polygon, polysyllable, polygamy, polytheism, polygyny |
| post- | after | postscript, postpone, postdate, posterity, post-bellum |
| pre- | before, in front | predict, presume, precede, predecessor, precocious, precipitate |
| preter- | beyond | preternatural, pretermit, preterition, preterit |
| pro- | before, in front, in place, in favor of | prognosis, program, promise, profuse, pronoun, proponent, pro-liberal |
| pros- | toward, to | proselyte, prosody, prosthesis |
| proto- | first, earliest | protozoa, prototype, protoplasm, protocol |
| pseudo- | false | pseudonym, pseudoscience, pseudomorph |
| quadr-, quatr-, quart- | four | quadruplet, quadruped, quadrilateral, quatrain, quarter, quartet |

PREFIXES

| | | |
|---|---|---|
| quasi- | almost, seemingly | quasi-humorous, quasi-historical, quasi-judicial, quasi-legislative |
| quinque- | five | quinquegenarian, quinquennial, Quinquegesima |
| quint- | fifth | quintet, quintuplet, quintessence |
| re- | back, again, against | refund, retract, remit, relax, reread, rearrange, reluctant, repel |
| retro- | back, backward | retrorocket, retroactive, retrograde |
| se- | aside, apart | secede, seduce, seclude, segregate, secret, select |
| semi- | half, partly | semicircle, semiannual, semifinal, semiconscious, semiformal |
| sept- | seven | September, septenary, septilateral |
| sesqui- | one and a half | sesquicentennial, sesquipedalian |
| sex- | six | sexagenarian, sexennial, sextet, sexagonal |
| sext- | sixth | sextant, sextuple |
| sub- | under, beneath, from below | submarine, subsoil, submerge |
| suc- (sub-) | under, beneath, from below | succeed, succinct, succor, succumb |
| suf- (sub-) | under, beneath, from below | suffix, suffice, suffocate |
| sup- (sub-) | under, beneath, from below | suppose, supplement, suppress, supplant |
| super-, supra- | over, above | supersede, supernatural, superfluous, supersonic, supraliminal |
| sur- (sub-) | under, up from below | surreptitious, surrogate |
| sur- (super-) | over, above | survey, surface, surcharge, surpass, surround, surfeit |
| sus- (sub-) | under, up from below | suspense, suspect, sustain |
| syl- (syn-) | together, with | syllable, syllepsis, syllogism |
| sym- (syn-) | together, with | symbol, sympathy, symphony, symmetry, symbiosis |
| syn- | together, with, same | synthesis, synopsis, synchronous, synapse, synonym, synagogue |
| ter- | three, third | tercentenary, ternary, tertiary |
| tetra- | four | tetragon, tetrarch, tetracycline |
| trans- | across, over, through | transfer, transit, transcontinental, translate, transparent |
| tri- | three | triangle, tricycle, trigonometry, trivial, trilogy, tripod |
| twi- | two, half | twice, twilight, twin, twine |
| ultra- | beyond | ultrasonic, ultraviolet, ultramarine, ultrahigh (frequency) |
| un- | not | unsafe, uncomfortable, unsure, unreliable |
| un- | reverse, remove | untie, unearth, uncover, unpack |
| under- | below | underline, underrate, underbrush, understatement, undertake |
| uni- | one | unit, unicorn, universe, unique, unify, unanimous |
| up- | up | upset, upkeep, upstart, uproar |
| vice- | in place of | vice-president, vice-principal, viceroy |
| with- | back, away, against, with | withdraw, withhold, withstand, within, without |

172

# Appendix B

## List of Common Suffixes and Derived Words

| Suffix | Meaning | Example Words |
|---|---|---|
| -able, -ible | can be, worthy of, inclined to | readable, credible, lovable, peaceable, perishable, terrible, durable |
| -ac | descriptive of | maniac, demoniac, hypochondriac, elegiac |
| -aceous | pertaining to, resembling | cretaceous, crustaceous, herbaceous |
| -acious | tends to be | vivacious, loquacious, pugnacious, fallacious |
| -acity | quality of, state of | tenacity, perspicacity |
| -ad | aggregate | myriad, monad, dyad, triad, pentad |
| -ade | process, action, product of | blockade, escapade, promenade, lemonade, marmalade |
| -age | place of | orphanage, parsonage, anchorage |
| -age | collective | percentage, average, mileage, peerage, baggage |
| -age | act of, result of, condition of | ravage, pillage, marriage, carnage, pilgrimage, damage, shrinkage, coinage |
| -al | relating to | filial, natural, ornamental, royal, critical, comical, political |
| -al | act, process of | denial, referral, betrayal, renewal |
| -an, -n | relating, belonging, believing | veteran, Korean, sylvan, European |
| -ana, -iana | collection of | Americana, Shakespeariana, Johnsoniana |
| -ance, -ancy | quality, state of | variance, resistance, annoyance, importance, vacancy, truancy, occupancy, ascendancy |
| -ant (adj.) | quality, condition of, showing, feeling | variant, defiant, radiant, vacant, buoyant |
| -ant, -ent (noun) | person who | immigrant, resident, student, emigrant, assistant, regent |
| -ar | characterized by, relating to | popular, muscular, linear, polar |
| -arch | ruler | matriarch, patriarch |
| -archy | government, rule | monarchy, oligarchy |
| -ard, -art | person who | drunkard, braggart, coward, wizard |
| -arian | person who believes | humanitarian, libertarian, Unitarian, vegetarian |
| -arium, orium | place, thing used for | planetarium, terrarium, auditorium, emporium |
| -ary | person who, place where, thing which | secretary, sanctuary, dictionary, infirmary |
| -ary | of, relating to | literary, military, reactionary, exemplary, customary |
| -ate (verb) | to make, cause to be | annihilate, liberate, radiate, aerate, motivate, nominate |
| -ate (adj.) | state of, quality of, condition of | fortunate, desperate, passionate, collegiate |
| -ate (noun) | function, office, person who | magistrate, advocate, potentate, associate |

| Suffix | Meaning | Examples |
|---|---|---|
| -ation | action, state of, quality of, result of | continuation, computation, alteration, occupation, moderation, decoration, exhilaration |
| -ative | tendency, nature | preventative, formative, illustrative |
| -ator, -itor | person who, thing which | commentator, aviator, refrigerator, incubator, visitor |
| -cide | killer, killing | insecticide, homocide, genocide |
| -cle | small | particle, article, canticle, cubicle |
| -cracy | government, rule | democracy, autocracy |
| -crat | member, supporter of | plutocrat, aristocrat |
| -cule | small | minuscule, molecule |
| -cy | state of, condition of, process, action | accuracy, diplomacy, lunacy, bankruptcy, piracy, idiocy, vagrancy, truancy |
| -dom | condition, position, domain | freedom, boredom, martyrdom, serfdom, wisdom, kingdom, dukedom, Christendom |
| -ed | to form past tense | painted, moved, hoped |
| -ed | to form adjective | forked, peaked, white-haired |
| -en | made, consisting of, resembling | earthen, ashen, golden, wooden |
| -en | to render or induce | lengthen, shorten, blacken, weaken, frighten |
| -ence, -ency | quality of, state of | dependence, confidence, competence, absence, potency, clemency, frequency |
| -ent | quality of being, that which acts as | different, persistent, reverent, referent, expedient, agent |
| -eous | composed of, nature of | aqueous, igneous, vitreous, nauseous, hideous, beauteous |
| -er, -est | comparative, superlative degree | faster, lighter, clearer, prettiest, tightest |
| -er | person who, thing which, person connected with | carpenter, grocer, officer, blender, plunger, islander, westerner |
| -ern | direction | eastern, western, northern, southern |
| -ery, -ry | place, product, collection | laundry, bakery, bindery, pottery, poetry, tapestry |
| -ery, -ry | characterized by, act, trade | bravery, angry, snobbery, imagery, archery, robbery, masonry |
| -escence | state of | luminescence, opalescence |
| -escent | exhibiting | phosphorescent, iridescent |
| -ese | native, language | Japanese, Maltese, Chinese, Cantonese |
| -esque | in the manner or style of | picturesque, arabesque, burlesque, Romanesque, statuesque |
| -ess | feminine ending | songstress, actress, countess, lioness |
| -et, -ette | little, small | piglet, islet, cigarette, kitchenette, statuette, Jeannette, Harriet |
| -eur | state or quality | grandeur, hauteur |
| -eur | agent, one who | amateur, entrepreneur, chauffeur, masseur, raconteur, saboteur, connoisseur |
| -fer | bearing, carrying | conifer, Lucifer, crucifer |
| -ferous | bearing, producing | coniferous, auriferous, odoriferous |
| -fic | making, causing | scientific, soporific, honorific, calcific |
| -fold | division into, multiplication by | threefold, manifold, thousandfold |
| -form | in the shape of | cuneiform, oviform |
| -ful | characterized by, full of, enough to fill | beautiful, successful, skillful, thankful, cupful, spoonful, mouthful, handful, armful |
| -fy | make or form into | satisfy, amplify, deify, qualify |
| -gram | metric unit | kilogram, milligram |
| -gram | something written | telegram, chronogram, diagram, cablegram |

| | | |
|---|---|---|
| -graph, -graphy | writing, method for writing or recording | telegraph, phonograph, photography, cryptograph, monograph |
| -graphy | area of study | geography, oceanography |
| -hood | state of, quality of, condition of | knighthood, manhood, childhood, likelihood, falsehood, brotherhood |
| -ial | characterized by, related to | commercial, remedial, connubial, fluvial |
| -ian | resembling, follower of, specialist in | Jeffersonian, Parisian, barbarian, Christian, physician |
| -ic, -tic | of, characteristic of | angelic, iambic, apostolic, volcanic, quixotic, genetic, energetic, sympathetic |
| -ician | specialist in | beautician, mortician, technician |
| -ics | scientific, artistic, social practices | acoustics, dramatics, athletics, gymnastics, politics |
| -ier, -yer | person who, place where, thing which | cashier, financier, clothier, chiffonier, brazier, lawyer, sawyer |
| -ile | capable of, suitable for, pertaining to | docile, mobile, virile, versatile, juvenile |
| -ine | like, pertaining to, belonging to | canine, feline, bovine, Florentine, Sistine |
| -ine, -ina | feminine suffix | heroine, Josephine, Czarina, Regina |
| -ing | present participle | sleeping, walking, writing, acting, playing |
| -ing, -ings | materials, actions, products associated with verb form | roofing, bedding, quilting, drawing, painting, sweepings, earnings, shavings, furnishings, filings |
| -ion | act, process, outcome, state of | construction, rebellion, revolution, ambition, dominion, subjection, suspicion |
| -ious | characterized by, tending to be | gracious, ambitious, invidious, various, spacious, infectious, loquacious, pugnacious |
| -ish | nationality, character of, somewhat | Scottish, Turkish, clownish, selfish, ticklish, whitish, bluish |
| -ism | action, process, state of, condition of, doctrine, system | baptism, ostracism, plagiarism, heroism, hypnotism, mysticism, pacifism, stoicism, realism |
| -ist | person who | biologist, theorist, botanist, socialist, impressionist |
| -ity | state of | calamity, felicity, necessity, acidity |
| -ium | element or chemical | uranium, sodium, helium, ammonium |
| -ive | having the nature or quality of, tending to | affirmative, active, passive, conclusive, corrective |
| -ize, -ise | subject to, make into, affect | baptize, sterilize, civilize, temporize, magnetize, Anglicize, advertise |
| -kin | small | manikin, lambkin, napkin, pumpkin |
| -le | repeated action | hobble, crackle, twinkle, mumble, prattle |
| -less | without, free of | witless, childless, doubtless, careless, dauntless, tireless, ageless, ceaseless |
| -let | small | streamlet, ringlet, leaflet, armlet, bracelet |
| -like | resembling | homelike, lifelike, apelike, tigerlike, ghostlike |
| -ling | small, one who is | duckling, gosling, nestling, hireling, underling |
| -logy | study of, speaking | anthropology, biology, zoology, geology, eulogy, tautology, doxology |
| -long | direction, duration | headlong, endlong, sidelong, lifelong |
| -ly | characteristic of, in the manner of | naturally, slightly, personally, sleepily |
| -ment | product, action, state | pavement, increment, development, government, amazement, refinement |
| -meter | measuring device | thermometer, speedometer, audiometer |
| -metry | measurement | telemetry, optometry, symmetry |
| -most | superlative ending | utmost, hindmost, topmost, innermost |

175

| | | |
|---|---|---|
| -ness | state of, quality of, condition of | goodness, greatness, sickness, kindness, wilderness, dimness |
| -nomy | field of study | astronomy, taxonomy |
| -oid | like, resembling | asteroid, spheroid, planetoid, anthropoid |
| -onym | word, name | acronym, pseudonym, synonym |
| -or | state, quality, person who, thing which | error, fervor, pallor, candor, rigor, behavior, auditor, donor, creditor, executor, elevator, reactor, radiator |
| -ory | place where | laboratory, conservatory, observatory |
| -ose | state of, quality of, similar to | verbose, comatose, bellicose, jocose |
| -ose | chemical suffix | cellulose, fructose, dextrose, glucose |
| -osis | state, process, abnormal condition | hypnosis, osmosis, psychosis, neurosis |
| -ous | possessing, full of | poisonous, riotous, joyous, bulbous |
| -phile | one who loves or prefers | audiophile, Anglophile |
| -phone, -phony | sound device, sound | telephone, radiophone, cacophony, antiphony |
| -s, -es | plural ending | theaters, streets, bunches, classes |
| -scope | instrument for seeing | microscope, telescope, kaleidoscope |
| -ship | state of, quality of, office of, art, skill | hardship, friendship, censorship, authorship, partnership, horsemanship, penmanship |
| -some | like, tending to be, a group of | awesome, bothersome, cumbersome, wholesome, twosome, threesome |
| -some | body | chromosome, chondriosome |
| -ster | one who is or does | youngster, mobster, gangster, trickster |
| -th, -eth | ordinal numbers | tenth, millionth, twentieth, thirtieth |
| -tion | action, process | fraction, addition, introduction, composition, assumption, absorption |
| -tude | state of, condition | amplitude, platitude, gratitude, altitude, fortitude |
| -ular | characterized by | circular, cellular, granular, tubular |
| -ule | little, small | capsule, tubule |
| -ulent | abounding in | corpulent, fraudulent, truculent, succulent |
| -uous | of the nature of | contemptuous, tempestuous |
| -ure | act, process, office, function | censure, exposure, enclosure, failure, judicature, prefecture, legislature |
| -ward, -wards | course, direction | toward, backwards, homeward, forward, westward |
| -ways | manner, direction | sideways, always, crossways, longways |
| -wise | way, manner | clockwise, lengthwise, slantwise |
| -y | characterized by, resembling, condition or state of | dreamy, chilly, lumpy, sleepy, windy, jealousy, inquiry, monarchy, recovery, victory |
| -y, -ey, -ie | diminutive suffix | doggy, birdie, daddy, Jeanie |

# Appendix C

## List of Common Roots and Derived Words

| Root | Meaning | Derived Words |
|------|---------|---------------|
| ācer, ācr | sharp, bitter | acrid, acrimony, acerbity, exacerbate, eager |
| acus | a point, needle | acute, acuity, acumen, cute |
| aequus | equal | equality, equator, equity, equation, equivocal |
| aēr | air | aerial, aerate, aerosol |
| aestheticus | sensation | aesthetic, esthete, esthetics, anesthesia |
| ager, agros | field, land | agriculture, agrarian, agronomy |
| agere, āctus | do, move | agenda, agile, agitate, agility, actor, activate, react, exact |
| agōn | a contest | agony, antagonist, protagonist |
| Akadēmia | plot of ground in Athens | academy, academic, academe |
| albus | white | albumen, albino, alb |
| algos | pain | nostalgia, analgesic, neuralgia |
| alius | other | alias, alien, unalienable, alienate |
| alpha | beginning | alphabet, alphabetize, alpha particle |
| alter | other | alteration, alternate, altercation, subaltern |
| altus | tall, high | altitude, alto, altimeter, exalted |
| amāre | love | amateur, amiable, amity, amorous |
| ambīre | go around | ambient, ambition, ambiguous |
| ambulāre | walk | amble, ambulance, somnambulist, perambulator |
| angulus | corner | angle, rectangle, angular, quadrangle |
| anima | life, spirit | animal, animate, animator, inanimate |
| animus | soul, mind | animosity, unanimous, equanimity, animadversion |
| annus | year | anniversary, annual, biannual, annuity, biennium, perennial |
| aptus | fit | apt, adapt, aptitude, inept, attitude |
| aqua | water | aquarium, aquatic, aqueduct, aqueous |
| arbiter | judge | arbiter, arbitrary, arbitrate |
| arbor | tree | arboreal, arboreous, arboriculture |
| arcus | bow, arc | arc, arch, archery, arcade |
| arch, arkhos | chief, ruler | architect, monarch, archbishop |
| arch, arkhaios | ancient, beginning | archaic, archaeology, archives, archetype |
| arithmos | number | arithmetic, logarithm |
| arma | weapons | arms, armor, armory, armistice |
| ars, art− | skill, art | artist, artificial, artful, artifact |
| astēr, astro | star | asterisk, astronomy, astronaut, disaster |
| athlon, athl | prize, contest | athlete, athletic, decathlon, pentathlon |
| atmos | vapor | atmosphere, atmospheric, atmometer |
| audīre | hear | auditorium, audience, audible, audition, obey |
| augēre, auctus, auctor | increase, create | augment, auction, author, authority |

| aurum | gold | aureole, aureate, auriferous, oriole |
|---|---|---|
| avis | bird | avian, aviator, aviary, aviculture |
| bellum | war | belligerent, bellicose, antebellum, rebellion |
| bene | well, good | benediction, benefit, beneficial, benevolent |
| biblio | book | Bible, bibliography, bibliophile |
| bio | life | biology, biography, biopsy, symbiotic |
| bonus | good | bonus, bonanza, bona fide |
| brachi | arm | brace, embrace, brachiopod, bracelet |
| brevis | short | brief, brevity, abbreviate, breve |
| cadere | to fall | cadence, cascade, chance, accident, occasion |
| caedere, cisus | cut | decide, concise, incision, incisive, scissors |
| calor, calidus | heat, warm | calorie, caldron, scald |
| calx, khalix | lime, stone | calcium, calculate, incalculable, calculus, chalk |
| camera, kamara | room, vault | camera, bicameral, chamber, chamberlain |
| campus | field | camp, campus, campaign, encamp |
| candēre | glow, white | candle, candid, candidate, incandescent |
| cantāre | sing | cantata, incantation, chant, recant, incentive |
| caper | goat | caper, caprice, capricious, Capricorn |
| capere | take, hold | capable, capacity, captive, capture, chase, accept, receive, participate, occupy |
| caput | head | captain, cape (headland), capital, decapitate, capitulate, chapter |
| cāro, carn | flesh | carnal, incarnation, carnivorous, carnival |
| causa | reason | cause, causation, accuse, excuse |
| cavus | hollow | cave, cavern, cavity, excavate |
| cēdere | go, yield | cede, precede, recede, proceed, process, cease, cessation |
| cella | small room | cell, cellar, cellular, cellulose |
| cēnsēre | judge, assess | censor, censorship, census, censure |
| centrum | center | central, eccentric, centrifugal, egocentric |
| centum | hundred | cent, centennial, century, percentage |
| certus, cernere | determine | certain, certify, certificate, ascertain, discern, decree |
| charta | leaf of paper | card, chart, charter, carton, cartoon |
| ciere, citāre | move | cite, citation, excitement, incite, recite |
| cine, kine | ring | cinema, cinematography, kinetic, kinesthesia |
| circus | rouse, call forth | circle, circus, circular, circuitous |
| cīvis | citizen | civil, civic, civilian, civilization |
| clāmāre | call, shout | claim, clamor, exclaim, proclamation |
| clarus | class, group | clarity, declare, clarify |
| classis | clear | classify, classical, classics |
| claudere, clausus | shut, close | close, closet, cloister, claustrophobia, include, conclude, exclusive, seclusion |
| clīnāre | lean | decline, recline, incline, declension |
| cognoscere, cognitus | know, learn | recognize, cognitive, incognito |
| colere, cultus | cultivate | culture, cultivate, agriculture, cult |
| color | color | discolor, colorful, Colorado, coloration |
| commūnis | common | community, communism, communion, communicate |
| cor, cord | heart | cordial, accord, discord, concord |
| cornū | horn | unicorn, cornucopia, corner, cornet |
| corōna | wreath, crown | corona, coronation, coronary, coroner |
| corpus | body | corps, corpuscle, corpse, corporal, corporation |

| | | |
|---|---|---|
| creare | make, create | recreation, creature, creator, creativity |
| crēdere | believe | credit, incredible, credulous, credence |
| crēscere | grow | crescent, decrease, increment, crescendo |
| crīmen | judge, accuse | crime, criminal, incriminate, discriminate |
| criticus, kritikos, krinein | critical; separate, choose | critic, criticize, critical, criterion |
| cruc, crux | cross | crucify, crux, crucial, excruciating |
| culpa | fault, blame | culpable, culprit, exculpate, mea culpa |
| cumbere | lie, recline | incumbent, succumb, recumbent |
| cumulus | pile, heap | accumulate, cumulative, cumulus |
| cūra | care | cure, manicure, accurate, curator, secure |
| currere | run | current, currency, curriculum, occur, incur, excursion, cursive |
| cyclus | circle | cycle, cyclone, cyclist, cyclorama, encyclopedia |
| damnum | harm, loss | damage, condemn, indemnity |
| datus, dare | give | date, data, antedate, edition |
| decor | proper, fitting | decoration, decor, decorum, decorous |
| dēfendere | ward off | defend, defense, fender, fence |
| dēmos | people | democracy, epidemic, demography, endemic |
| dēnsus | thick | dense, density, condensation |
| dent | tooth | dentist, dental, trident, indent |
| derma | skin | dermatology, hypodermic, epidermis, pachyderm |
| dīcere | say | dictate, diction, predict, abdicate, verdict, contradict |
| digitus | finger | digit, digital, digitate, prestidigitation |
| dignus | worthy | dignity, dignitary, indignant, dignify |
| dividere | separate | divide, division, divisor, dividend |
| docēre | teach | doctor, doctrine, indoctrinate, documentary, docent |
| dominus | master | dominate, dominant, domain, dominion, domineering |
| donāre, dōnum | give, gift | donate, donor, pardon |
| dormīre | sleep | dormant, dormitory, dormer |
| drama | deed, play | drama, dramatize, dramatic, melodrama |
| dromos | running course | airdrome, syndrome, palindrome |
| dubitare | doubt, waver | dubious, doubt, indubitable |
| ducere | lead | duct, conduct, educate, deduce, aqueduct |
| duplex, duplic- | double, twofold | double, duplicate, duplicity, duplex |
| dūrus, dūrāre | hard, to last | durable, endure, duress, duration, during |
| dynamis | power | dynamite, dynamic, dynasty, dynamo |
| ēlektron | amber | electric, electrocute, electrode, electron |
| emere | buy, obtain | exempt, redeem, redemption, example, preempt, caveat emptor |
| equus (cf. aequus) | horse | equine, equitation, equestrian |
| ergon | work | energy, erg, ergometer, synergism |
| errāre | wander | err, error, erratic, erroneous, aberration |
| esse | be, exist | essential, essence, quintessence, interest |
| ethnos | nation | ethnic, ethnocentric, ethnology |
| ēthos | custom | ethic, ethical, ethos, ethology |
| facere | do, make | fact, factory, manufacture, benefactor, facsimile, effect, efficient, defect, feasible, suffice |
| facilis | easy | facility, facilitate, facile, difficult |
| fallere | deceive | false, fallacy, infallible, fallacious |
| favere | favor | favorite, unfavorable, favoritism, disfavor |

| | | |
|---|---|---|
| fēmina | woman | female, feminine, effeminate |
| ferre | carry, bear | transfer, refer, infer, differ, offer, circumference, suffer |
| fervēre | be hot, boil | fervent, fervid, fervor, effervesce |
| fidēs, fidere | faith, trust | confide, fidelity, infidel, diffident |
| figūra | form | figure, disfigure, figurative |
| fīlius | son | filial, affiliate, affiliation |
| fingere, fictus | form, mold | figment, fiction, fictitious, effigy |
| finis | end | final, finish, finite, infinite |
| firmus | steady | firm, confirm, infirm, affirm, firmament |
| fixus, figere | fasten | fix, fixation, fixture, suffix, prefix |
| flagrāre | blaze | flagrant, conflagration |
| flamma | flame | flame, flammable, flamboyant |
| flectere, flexus | bend | flex, flexible, reflect, reflector, deflect, inflection, reflex |
| fluere | flow | fluid, fluent, influx, affluent |
| folium | leaf | foliage, folio, portfolio, bifoliate |
| fōrma | shape | formation, uniform, reform, transform |
| fortis | strong | fort, fortify, fortitude, effort |
| fortūna | chance, fate | fortune, fortunately, fortuitous, fortuity |
| frangere, fractus | break | fraction, fracture, infraction, fragile, fragment |
| front | front | frontal, frontier, confront, affront, effrontery |
| fugere | flee | fugitive, refuge, refugee, centrifugal |
| fūmus | smoke | fume, fumigate, perfume, fumitory |
| functiō | performance | function, malfunction, functional |
| fundus | bottom | fund, fundamental, profound, profundity, foundation, founder |
| fūsus, fundere | pour, melt | fuse, transfusion, fusion, diffuse, profuse, foundry |
| genus | race, birth | genus, genre, generation, progeny, genocide, miscegenation |
| gentīlis | of the same clan | gentle, genteel, gentlemen, gentry |
| geo | earth | geography, geometry, geode |
| gnosis | knowledge | gnostic, agnostic, diagnosis, prognosticate |
| gradus | step, rank | grade, gradual, graduation, degree, degrade |
| gramma | letter | grammar, monogram, telegram, epigram |
| grandis | great | grandeur, grandiose, grandiloquet, aggrandize |
| graphein | write | graphic, graphology, autograph, paragraph, biography |
| grātus | pleasing, favorable | grace, gracious, grateful, gratitude, congratulate, disgrace, agree |
| gravis | heavy | grave, gravity, gravitate, aggravation |
| gustus | taste | gusto, gustatory, disgust |
| habēre | hold, have | habit, habitual, inhabit, exhibit, able, ability, habilitate |
| haerēre | stick | adhere, adhesive, coherent |
| harmonia | harmony | harmonica, harmony, philharmonic |
| hedra | side, seat | polyhedron, tetrahedron, cathedral |
| hēlios | sun | helium, heliotrope, heliocentric |
| historia | knowing | history, story, prehistoric, historian |
| homō, homin- | man | hominoid, homage, homicide, Homo sapiens |
| homos | same | homogenized, homonym, homograph |
| honōs, honōr- | honor | honor, honest, dishonorable, honorific |
| hōra | hour | hour, horoscope, horologe, horoscopy |
| hospes, hospit- | host | hospital, hospitable, hospice |

| | | |
|---|---|---|
| hūmānus | human | human, humane, humanitarian, inhumanity |
| humus | earth, soil | humus, humble, humiliate, exhume |
| hudor | water | hydrant, hydrogen, hydrophobia, dehydrate |
| idem | same | identity, identical, identify, identification |
| idios | personal, peculiar | idiot, idiom, idiomatic, idiosyncrasy |
| ignis | fire | ignite, ignition, igneous |
| īgnōrāre | not know | ignore, ignorant, ignorance, ignoramus |
| imāgō | image | image, imagination, imaginary, imagery |
| īnsula | island | insulate, insular, peninsula |
| integer | whole | integer, integrity, integrate, integral |
| īra | anger | irate, ire, irascible |
| īre | go | exit, transit, transient, circuit |
| jacere | throw | project, projector, reject, eject, adjacent, objective |
| jūdex, jūdic- | judge | judge, judicial, adjudicate, judicious |
| jungere, junctus | join | junction, juncture, conjunction, adjunct |
| jūs, jūr- | law, right | jury, perjury, jurisdiction, jurisprudence |
| jūstus | just | justice, justify, justification |
| kallos | beauty | kaleidoscope, calligraphy, calisthenics, calliopsis, Calliope |
| khrōma | color | monochrome, chromatic, chromosome |
| khronos | time | chronic, chronicle, chronology, anachronism |
| kosmos | universe, order | cosmos, cosmic, cosmopolitan, microcosm, cosmetic |
| labor | labor | laborious, laboratory, elaborate, collaborate |
| lapsus | slip, error | lapse, elapse, relapse, collapse |
| legāre | send | delegation, delegate, relegate |
| legein, logos | speak, speech | logic, logogram, dialogue, catalogue, prologue |
| legere | gather, choose, read | elect, select, electoral, collection, neglect, legion, legend, legible |
| lever, levis | raise, light | leverage, levy, elevator, levity, alleviate, levitation |
| lēx, lēg | law | legal, legitimate, legislate |
| lexis | word | lexicon, lexicography, dyslexia |
| līber | free | liberty, liberate, liberal, deliver |
| liber | book | library, libretto |
| lībra | scale, pound, balance | deliberate, Libra |
| ligāre | bind | ligature, ligament, obligation, religion |
| līnea | thread | line, linear, lineage, delineate |
| lingua | tongue | lingual, linguistics, linguist, bilingual |
| linquere | leave behind | relinquish, relic, dereliction, delinquent |
| liquēre | to be liquid | liquor, liquefy, liquidate, liquidity |
| lithos | stone | monolith, paleolithic, neolithic, lithograph |
| littera | letter | literature, literary, literal, obliterate |
| locus | place | local, location, dislocate, localize |
| longus | long | longevity, longitude, elongate, prolong |
| loquī, locūtus | speak | locution, loquacious, elocution, eloquence, colloquial, soliloquy |
| lūcēre | shine | lucid, translucent, elucidate |
| lūdus | game, play | interlude, prelude, allude, ludicrous, illusion, delusion, elusive |
| lūmen | light | luminous, luminary, illuminate |
| lūstrāre | make bright | luster, lustrous, illustrious, illustrate |
| magnus | great | magnify, magnitude, magnificent, magnanimous |
| malus | bad | malice, malady, malign, malevolent |

| | | |
|---|---|---|
| mandāre | order | mandate, command, demand, remand |
| manēre | remain, dwell | manor, mansion, permanent, remnant |
| manus | hand | manual, manuscript, manipulate, manage |
| mare | sea | marine, submarine, mariner, maritime |
| māter | mother | maternal, maternity, matron, matrix |
| maximus | greatest | maxim, maximum, maximize |
| medērī | heal | medical, medicine, remedial, remedy |
| medius | middle | medium, mediate, mediocre, medieval |
| memor | mindful | memory, memorial, memorandum, commemorate, remember |
| mergere | plunge, dip | merge, merger, emerge, emergency, submerge, immerse, submersible |
| mētīrī, mēnsus | to measure | mensurable, commensurate, dimension, immense, |
| metron | measure | metric, geometric, metronome, diameter, barometer, perimeter |
| mimos | imitator | mime, mimic, mimeograph, pantomime |
| minuere, minus | lessen, less | minute, minus, minor, minuscule, diminutive, minuet |
| mīrārī | to wonder at | miracle, mirage, admire, admirable |
| miser | wretched | miser, misery, miserable, commiserate |
| mittere, missus | send, allow | mission, dismiss, message, admit, permit, committee |
| mnemon, mnasthai | remember | amnesty, mnemonic, amnesia |
| modus | manner, measure | mode, modal, model, modest, accommodate, commodius |
| mollis | soft | mollusk, emollient, mollify |
| monēre | warn, advise | admonish, monitor, premonition |
| mōns, mont- | mountain | mount, mountain, amount, surmount, tramontane |
| monstrāre | show | demonstrate, demonstrative, remonstrate, monstrance |
| morphē | shape | morphology, metamorphosis, amorphic, anthropomorphic |
| mors, mort- | death | mortal, immortal, mortify, mortgage |
| mōs, mōr- | custom | moral, morality, morale, mores |
| movēre | move | movable, remove, movement, motion, motor, promote, mobile, mobility |
| mūnus | office, gift | municipal, remuneration, munificent |
| mūtāre | change | mutate, mutation, commute, immutable |
| nāscī, nātus | be born | nascent, native, natal, innate, nation |
| nectere | bind | connect, connection, annex, nexus |
| negāre | say no | negate, negative, abnegate, deny, renege, renegade |
| neuter | not either | neuter, neutral, neutrality, neutron |
| nocēre, noxa | do harm, hurt | noxious, obnoxious, innocence, innocuous |
| nōmen | name | nominal, nominate, noun, nomenclature, denomination, ignominious |
| norma | pattern, rule | norm, normal, enormous, abnormality |
| nōscere, nōtus | get acquainted | notion, notice, notify, notorious |
| nota | note, mark | note, notation, notable, annotate |
| novus | new | novel, novelty, novice, innovate |
| nox, noct- | night | nocturnal, nocturne, equinox |
| numerus | number | numeral, numerous, enumerate, supernumerary |
| nuntiāre | announce | announce, pronounce, enunciate |
| ōdā, ōdē | song | ode, melody, parody, rhapsody |
| oikos | house | ecology, economy, ecumenical |

| | | |
|---|---|---|
| optāre | choose | opt, adopt, option, optional |
| opus | work | opus, opera, operate, cooperate |
| ōrāre, ōs | speak, mouth | oral, oracle, oratory, adoration |
| orbis | circle | orb, orbit, suborbital, exorbitant |
| ōrdō, ōrdin− | order | order, ordinance, ordinary, ordinal |
| orīrī | rise | origin, originate, orient, orientation |
| ōvum | egg | ovum, oval, ovary, oviparous |
| paed, paido | child | pedantic, pediatrics, encyclopedia |
| pallēre | be pale | pallid, pale, appalling, pallor |
| pār | equal | parity, compare, comparable, disparity |
| parāre | to ready, prepare | parade, parapet, parry, prepare, repair, imperative, imperial, emperor, empire, apparatus |
| pārēre | show | appear, apparent, apparition, disappear |
| pars, partīre | part, divide | part, partial, bipartisan, partition, particle, particular, compartment |
| pater | father | paternal, patriarch, patriot, patronize |
| pathos | feelings | pathos, pathetic, sympathy, apathy |
| patī, passus | suffer | patient, compatible, passion, compassionate |
| pāx, pāc− | peace | peace, pacific, pacify |
| pellere, pulsus | drive, push, beat | compel, repel, expel, propel, pulse, compulsory, impulse, repulsive |
| pendēre | hang | pending, pendant, pensive, pendulum, suspend, appendage, appendix |
| persōna | mask | person, personality, impersonate, personnel |
| pēs, ped | foot | pedal, pedestrian, pedestal, biped, expedite, pedigree |
| petere | seek | petition, appetite, compete, competent |
| phōnē | sound | phoneme, phonics, symphony, saxophone, xylophone |
| phoros, pherein | carry, bear | euphoria, metaphor, semaphore |
| phōs, phōt | light | photic, photosynthesis, photography, phosphorus |
| physica, phusis | nature | metaphysics, physical, physiology, physique |
| placēre | please | plea, pleasant, placid, placebo, complacent |
| plānus | level, flat | plain, plane, explain |
| plaudere | clap the hands | applaud, plaudit, explode, implode |
| plēnus | full | plenty, plentiful, plenary, replenish |
| plēre, plētus | to fill | complete, complement, compliment, comply, replete, deplete |
| plicāre | fold | pliant, apply, reply, replica, multiplication, duplicate, implicate |
| poena | punishment | penalty, penance, penitentiary, punish, punitive |
| polis | city | politic, police, politician, acropolis, metropolis |
| pōnere, positus | place, put | exponent, component, opponent, postpone, position, positive, deposit, preposition |
| populus | people | popular, populate, populous, people |
| porta | gate | portal, port, portcullis |
| portāre | carry | portable, transport, import, export, portfolio, support |
| posse, potens | be able | possible, potential, potent, possess |
| practicus | practical | practice, practicable, chiropractic |
| prehendere | seize | prehensile, apprehensive, comprehension, surprise, comprise |
| premere, pressus | press, force | pressure, suppress, oppress, compress, expression |
| pretium | price | precious, praise, appraise, appreciate |

183

| | | |
|---|---|---|
| prīmus | first | prime, primal, primary, primate, primitive, primeval |
| prīvus | individual | private, privilege, privacy |
| probāre | test, prove | probe, probable, probate, probation |
| probus | good | probity, approve |
| proprius | one's own | proper, property, appropriate, propriety |
| proximus | nearest | proximity, approximation, proximal |
| punctum | point | punctual, punctuate, punctilious, puncture |
| pūpus, pūpa | boy, girl | pupil, puppet, pupa |
| quaerere | seek | quest, query, question, request, inquire, require, exquisite, acquisitive |
| quantus | how much | quantity, quantify, quantitative, quantum |
| quiēs | quiet | quiet, quietus, quiescent, acquiesce, requiem |
| quotus | how many | quote, quota, quotation, quotient |
| rādere, rāsus | scrape | raze, razor, erase, abrasive |
| radius | ray, spoke of wheel | radius, radial, radium, radiation |
| rādix | root | radix, radical, radish, eradicate |
| rārus | seldom, thin | rare, rarity, rarefy |
| rēctus | straight, right | rectify, rectangle |
| regere | guide, rule | regime, region, regiment, correct, erect |
| ratus, rērī | consider, reason | ratio, ration, rate, reason, irrational, rationale, ratiocination |
| rigēre | stiff | rigid, rigidity, rigor, rigorous |
| rōdere | gnaw | rodent, erode, corrode, corrosive |
| rogāre | ask | interrogate, derogatory, abrogate, subrogate |
| rota | wheel | rotate, rotary, rotation, rotogravure |
| ruptus | to break | rupture, abrupt, erupt, interrupt |
| rūs, rūr | country | rustic, rural, rusticity, rusticate |
| sāl | salt | salary, saline, desalinate |
| salīre | leap | sally, salient, desultory, insult, assail, assault |
| salūs, salūt– | health | salute, salutary, salubrious, salutation |
| sānus | healthy, sound | sane, insane, sanity, sanitary |
| satis | enough | satisfy, satiety, satiate, satisfactory |
| scaena | stage | scene, scenario, scenery, scenic |
| scandere | climb | descend, descendant, ascend, transcend |
| schola | school | school, scholar, scholastic |
| sciēns, scīre | know | science, scientific, conscience, omniscient |
| scrībere | write | script, describe, inscribe, scripture, manuscript, subscribe |
| secāre | cut | section, sector, dissect, insect, intersect |
| sedēre | sit | sediment, sedentary, reside, possess, obsession, assess, subsidy |
| senex | old | senator, senior, seniority, senile |
| sentīre, sensus | feel | sense, sensitive, sentiment, sentence, scent, consent, assent, resent, dissent |
| sequī | follow | sequence, sequel, sect, consequence, subsequent, prosecute |
| serere | join, sow | series, insert, exert, assertive |
| servāre | save, keep | reserve, reservoir, preserve, conserve |
| servīre, servus | serve, slave | serve, service, servant, deserve |
| signum | mark, sign | sign, assign, signet, signify, signal, signature, resign, significant |
| similis | like | similar, simile, simultaneous, simulate |
| sistere | take a position, stand | assist, insist, resistance, persistent |
| socius | sharing, comrade | society, social, sociology, associate |
| sōlus | alone | solo, solitude, desolate, soliloquy |
| solidus | solid | solid, solidarity, solder, solidify |

| | | |
|---|---|---|
| solvere | loosen | solve, solution, soluble, dissolve, resolve, absolve |
| somnus | sleep | somnolent, somnambulist, insomnia |
| sonāre, sonus | to sound, sound | sonic, unison, resonant, sonata, sonorous |
| sophos | wise | sophist, sophisticate, philosopher |
| spatium | space | space, spatial, spacious, expatiate |
| specere | look at | spectrum, speculate, spectator, spectacle, specimen, aspect, expect, inspector, perspective |
| species | appearance, kind | species, special, specific, specious |
| sphera | ball, sphere | sphere, spherical, atmosphere, hemisphere |
| spīrāre | breathe | spirit, inspire, respiration, conspirator |
| spondēre | promise, pledge | sponsor, respond, responsibility |
| stabilis | firm | stable, stability, establish |
| stāre | stand | stance, stanch, stay, circumstance, instant, obstacle |
| statuere | set up | statue, statute, institute |
| status | standing, position | status, state, statistics |
| struere | build | structure, construct, instruct, destruction, obstruct |
| stilus | writing instrument | style, stylish, stylize, stylus |
| studēre | be eager | student, study, studious, studio |
| sūmere | take, take up | assume, consume, resume, subsume, sumptuary, sumptuous |
| summus | total, highest | sum, summary, summit, summation |
| surgere | rise | surge, resurge, resource, resurrection, insurrection, insurgent |
| tabula | board, tablet | table, tablet, tableau, tabulate |
| tangere | touch | tangent, tangible, tactile, tact, attain |
| tekhnē | art, skill | technical, technician, technique, technology |
| tempus | time | tempo, temporary, contemporary, temporal, extemporaneous |
| tendere | tend, stretch | tend, tendency, tendon, tensile, attend, extension, intend, intense |
| tenēre | hold | tenacious, tensure, contain, obtain, detention, retention |
| terminus | end, boundary | term, terminate, exterminate, terminal, interminable |
| terra | earth | terrace, territory, terrain, terrestrial |
| terrēre | frighten | terrify, terror, terrible, terrific |
| thermē | heat | thermal, thermometer, thermostat |
| tonos | tone, stretching | tone, tonic, baritone, monotone, overtone, atonal |
| tortus | twist, turn | tortuous, torture, distort, extort |
| tōtus | whole, entire | total, totalitarian, totality, totalize |
| trahere | pull, draw | tractor, traction, tractable, trait, abstract, detract, extract, distract |
| tremere | shake | tremor, tremble, tremulous, tremendous |
| tubus | tube | tube, tuba, tubing, tubular |
| tūtus, tuērī | watch over | tutor, tuition, intuition, tutelage |
| typus, tupos | type, image | type, typical, typography, prototype |
| ultimus | last | ultimate, ultimatum, penult |
| unda | wave | undulate, undulous, inundate, abundant |
| urbs | city | urban, urbane, suburb, conurbation |
| ūsus, ūtī | to use | use, usual, usage, abuse, utility, utensil, utilize |
| vacāre | be empty | vacate, vacant, vacation, evacuate, vacuum, vacuous |
| vādere | go | invade, evade, pervade, pervasive |

| | | |
|---|---|---|
| vagus | wandering | vague, vagrant, vagabond, vagary, extravagant |
| valēre | be strong | valor, value, valiant, invalid, validity, convalesce, prevail |
| vānus | empty | vanish, vain, vanity, evanescent |
| varius | different | vary, various, variety, variegated |
| vehere | carry | vehicle, convey, vehicular, conveyance |
| velle, vol– | wish, will | volition, voluntary, volunteer, benevolent |
| vēlum | sail, covering | veil, reveal, revelation |
| venīre | come | convene, convention, advent, adventure, avenue, prevent |
| verbum | word | verb, verbal, adverb, proverb, verbatim, verbose |
| vertere | turn | version, versatile, avert, convert, conversation, diversion, inverse, reverse |
| vērus | true | very, verify, verdict, aver, veracity |
| via | way | via, viaduct, trivial, deviate, previous |
| vidēre, vīsus | see, sight | video, vision, visual, review, survey, provide, evidence |
| vigēre | be lively | vigor, invigorate, vigorous |
| vincere | conquer | victor, victory, convict, evict, invincible, convince |
| violāre, vīs | force, power | violate, vim, inviolable |
| vīta | life | vital, vitality, vitamin |
| vīvere | live | vivid, vivacious, survive, revive |
| vōcāre | call | vocal, vocalize, vocation, convocation, provoke, revoke, invoke, evoke |
| volvere | roll, turn | revolve, revolution, involve, evolve |
| vovēre | vow, wish | vow, vote, devote, devout |
| zōion | animal | zoo, zoology, zodiac, protozoa |

# Selected Readings

Anderson, Richard, and Freebody, Peter. "Vocabulary Knowledge." In H. Singer and R. Ruddell (Eds.), *Theoretical Models and Processes of Reading.* Newark, DE: International Reading Association, 1985.

Barbe, Walter, and Swassing, Raymond. *Teaching Through Modality Strengths: Concepts and Practices.* Columbus, OH: Zaner-Bloser, Inc., 1979.

Barnhart, Clarence L., and Barnhart, Robert K. *The World Book Dictionary.* New York: Doubleday & Co., Inc., 1986.

Beck, Isabel, and McKeown, Margaret. "Learning Words Well: A Program to Enhance Vocabulary and Comprehension." *The Reading Teacher,* 36 (March 1983): 622-625.

Berlo, David. *The Process of Communication.* New York: Holt, Rinehart & Winston, 1960.

Dale, Edgar. *Bibliography of Vocabulary Studies.* Columbus, OH: Bureau of Educational Research, The Ohio State University, 1949.

————. *Bibliography of Vocabulary Studies,* revised edition. Columbus, OH: Bureau of Educational Research, The Ohio State University, 1957.

————. "Develop Critical Reading." *Reading Improvement,* 13, 1 (Spring 1976): 30-33.

Dale, Edgar, and O'Rourke, Joseph. "A Guide to Vocabulary Skills." *World Book Student Handbook,* Unit 6. Chicago: World Book-Childcraft International, 1978: 41-179.

————. "A Word Builder Guide." *The World Book Complete Word Power Library,* Volume 3, Part 2. Chicago: World Book-Childcraft International, 1981: 2-152.

————. *The Living Word Vocabulary: The Words We Know.* Libertyville, IL: Dome Publications, 1974.

————. *The Living Word Vocabulary.* Chicago: World Book-Childcraft International, 1981.

————. Vocabulary Measurement: Techniques and Major Findings," *Elementary English,* 42 (December 1965): 895-901.

Dale, Edgar; O'Rourke, Joseph; and Barbe, Walter. *Vocabulary Building: Process, Principles, and Application,* Books 1-8. Columbus, OH: Zaner-Bloser, Inc., 1986.

Dale, Edgar, and Razik, T. *Bibliography of Vocabulary Studies,* second revised edition. Columbus, OH. Bureau of Educational Research and Service, The Ohio State University, 1963.

Duffelmeyer, Frederick A. "Teaching Word Meaning from an Experience Base." *The Reading Teacher,* 39 (October 1985): 6-9.

Hodges, Richard. "Vocabulary." Urbana, IL: ERIC Clearinghouse on Reading and Communication Skills, 1984.

Hodges, Richard. "Improving Spelling and Vocabulary in the Secondary School. Theory and Research into Practice (TRIP)." Urbana, IL: ERIC Clearinghouse on Reading and Communication Skills, 1982.

Hudd, Charles Hubbard. *Reading: Its Nature and Development*. Chicago: The University of Chicago Press, 1918.

Johnson, Dale, and Pearson, David. *Teaching Reading Vocabulary*. New York: Holt, Rinehart, and Winston, 1984.

Lenneberg, Eric. *Biological Foundations of Language*. New York: John Wiley and Sons, Inc., 1967.

McKeown, Margaret. "The Acquisition of Word Meaning from Context by Children of High and Low Ability." *Reading Research Quarterly*, 20 (Summer 1985): 482-494.

McKeown, Margaret; Beck, Isabel; Omanson, Richard C.; and Pople, Martha T. "Some Effects of the Nature and Frequency of Vocabulary Instruction on the Knowledge and Use of Words." *Reading Research Quarterly*, 20 (Fall 1985): 522-534.

Morris, William, and Morris, Mary. *Morris Dictionary of Word and Phrase Origins*. New York: Harper & Row Publishers, Inc., 1977.

Morris, William, ed. *The American Heritage Dictionary*. Boston: Houghton Mifflin Co., 1976.

Nagy, William, and Anderson, Richard. "How Many Words Are There in Printed School English?" *Reading Research Quarterly*, 19 (Spring 1984): 304-330.

Nagy, William; Herman, Patricia; and Anderson, Richard. "Learning Words from Context." *Reading Research Quarterly*, 20 (Winter 1985): 233-253.

Ogden. C.K., *Opposition*. London: Kegan Paul, French, Trubner and Co., Ltd., 1932.

O'Rourke, Joseph. *Toward a Science of Vocabulary Development*. Alantic Highlands, NJ: Mouton, 1974.

——— . "Prefixes, Roots, and Suffixes: Their Testing and Usage," paper presented at the International Reading Association Convention, Atlanta, Georgia, April 25, 1979.

——— . "Spelling and Vocabulary Development." *Spelling Progress Quarterly*, 2, 2 (Spring 1985).

Pearson, David. "Changing the Face of Reading Comprehension Instruction." *The Reading Teacher*, 38 (April 1985): 724-738.

——— . "The Function of Metaphor in Children's Recall of Expository Passages." *Journal of Reading Behavior*, 13 (Fall 1981): 249-261.

Rogers, Wanda. "Teaching for Poetic Thought." *The Reading Teacher*, 39 (December 1985): 296-300.

Swisher, Karen. "Increasing Word Power Through Spelling Activities." *The Reading Teacher*, 37 (April 1984): 706-710.

Templeton, Shane. "Young Children Invent Words: Developing Concepts of Word-ness." *The Reading Teacher*, 33 (January 1980): 454-459.

Tyson, Eleanor, and Mountain, Lee. "A Riddle or Pun Makes Learning Words Fun." *The Reading Teacher*, 36 (November 1982): 170-173.

Zutell, Jerry. *Developmental and Cognitive Aspects of Learning to Spell*. Newark, DE. International Reading Association, 1980.

# Index